Praise for Treating Children with Disruptive Behavior Disorders

"This book is written specifically for clinicians, and that focus empowers the reader to gain valuable insights and tools. The language, acronyms, structure, and examples are all very compelling and laser-focused on assisting clinicians to be effective in working with children and adolescents with disruptive behaviors.

Dr. Whitehead is incredibly generous in sharing the tools that he has found useful in practice. They are useful for the clinician (and for parents, teachers, parole officers, etc.) in learning how to modify their view of these clients and support change. There are so many profoundly positive things about this book, but perhaps the most moving to me as a clinician is illustrated in this quote: 'I hope the interventions outlined in this book will give more providers insight into how to see, hear, understand, and touch these wonderful human beings.' Everything in this book did exactly that for me!"

—**Darren Adamson, PhD, LMFT,** National University

"Dr. Whitehead's work with families with difficult children has given him a strong background to write this book, based on his years of experience as a therapist with individuals and with families, especially families with very difficult children. After 24 years of teaching and supervising PhD and master's level students working with high-risk juvenile adolescents and their families, I found that I had a great deal to learn from Dr. Whitehead's models and from his thinking."

—**Richard S. Wampler, PhD, MSW,** licensed psychologist and marriage and family therapist with 33 years of teaching experience plus 5 years as a supervising psychologist in an institution

"This book is a master class in treating children with defiant behaviors. Michael's expertise and compassion shines through on each page. His thorough research and theories are brilliant. Anyone who treats children and families with defiant behaviors needs to read and study this book. It provides hope for both families and clinicians in cases where hope feels lost. This approach has the potential to serve as a catalyst for completely transforming how clinicians engage with children exhibiting these behaviors."

—**Emma Cherry, LCSW**

TREATING CHILDREN WITH

Disruptive Behavior Disorders

An Integrative Play and Systems Theory Approach to Oppositional, Aggressive, and Antisocial Behavior

MICHAEL R. WHITEHEAD, PhD, LMFT, RPT-S™

TREATING CHILDREN WITH DISRUPTIVE BEHAVIOR DISORDERS
Copyright © 2025 by Michael R. Whitehead

Published by
PESI Publishing, Inc.
3839 White Ave
Eau Claire, WI 54703

Cover and interior design by Emily Dyer
Editing by Jenessa Jackson, PhD

ISBN 9781683738671 (print)
ISBN 9781683738688 (ePUB)
ISBN 9781683738695 (ePDF)

All rights reserved.
Printed in the United States of America.

To the many families I have worked with on my clinical journey:
Thank you for your trust.

To all my many mentors, both formal and informal, who are no longer with us:
Karen Wampler, JP "Chief" Lilly, Justin Ure, and Marcus Whitehead.
Each of you has immeasurably impacted my life, allowing me to help others.
Thank you for sharing your time with me.

To my loving and patient wife, Jessica, and each of my four children,
Samuel, William, Abigail, and Luke: All of this is for you.

Table of Contents

Introduction: "No Hope..." 1

1. **Training Buffaloes** 7
   Why Buffaloes? 8
   What Are Disruptive Behavior Disorders? 11
   Key Takeaway 12

2. **The Research: Being Evidence Informed** 13
   The Research on Disruptive Behavior Disorders 15
   Integrative Systemic Play Therapy 21
   Key Takeaway 21

3. **The Foundation: Key Principles in Understanding Disruptive Behavior Disorders** 23
   Theory of Temperament 24
   Coercion Theory 36
   Integrative Systemic Play Therapy: An Overview 42
   Key Takeaway 46

4. **Assessment: Identifying and Tracking Coercion** 49
   Intake Session 49
   Joining Sessions 56
   Case Example: *Kehlani* 59
   Key Takeaway 72

5. **BISON Phase B: Bio-Emotion Regulation** 73
   Assessing Regulation 74
   Increasing Regulation 81
   Case Example: *Bruce* 84
   Key Takeaway 88

vii

6. **BISON Phase I: Individual Play** 89
   Basic Skills for Individual Play and One-on-One Time 90
   Explaining Individual Play to Parents 92
   Introducing One-on-One Time 93
   Case Example: *Jimmy* 97
   Key Takeaway 103

7. **BISON Phase S: Successful Communication** 105
   Ineffective Commands 106
   Effective Commands 109
   Emotion Coaching 116
   Family Meetings 122
   Case Example: *Carol* 125
   Key Takeaway 128

8. **BISON Phase O: Organized Play** 129
   Introducing Organized Play to Children 130
   Common Reasons to Introduce Organized Play 130
   Introducing Organized Play to Adolescents, Preteens, or Older Children 140
   Case Example: *Isabella* 141
   Key Takeaway 146

9. **BISON Phase N: Nurturing Play** 149
   Filial Play Therapy 150
   Managing Parental Resistance 150
   Potential Roadblocks 152
   Case Example: *Noe* 155
   Key Takeaway 159

10. **Troubleshooting and Maintenance** 163
    Common Troubleshooting During BISON Phases 164
    Entering Graduation and Maintenance 169
    Key Takeaway 170

11. Putting It All Together 171
    My Brother Marcus 171
    My Daughter Abigail 174
    Case Example: *Adam* 176
    Key Takeaway 186

Appendix 187
References 199
Acknowledgments 207
About the Author 209

Introduction: "No Hope..."

Parents Sandra and Tino followed me down the hall of my university clinic to our therapy room. I had already seen their son, Anthony, three times. He was seven years old, and his parents suspected he had attention-deficit/hyperactivity disorder (ADHD). They wanted to try a nonmedication treatment for his "behavior problems." Stopping at the door to our reserved room, I turned toward Anthony's parents. I was surprised to see that Sandra looked on the brink of tears and Tino looked angry. This was one of my first cases as a beginning therapist, and I wondered whether I had done something wrong. I'd had successful cases before, but working with kids this young was new to me. I still hadn't taken a play therapy course, and I was devouring books about child therapy between sessions so I could be prepared each week. At that moment, I was more uncertain than ever about my ability to help them.

When I first met Sandra and Tino, I had recommended that they get Anthony a psychological evaluation to clarify his diagnosis and help guide my treatment approach. Today, we were meeting to go over the results of that evaluation, which I had not yet seen. We entered the room, and almost immediately Sandra broke down in tears. Tino could see that I was confused by this shift in her demeanor from previous conversations, so he helped me understand Sandra's reaction: "ODD! That's what the evaluation found. Oppositional defiant disorder! Sure, he has some mild ADHD, but it says his behaviors are a result of ODD."

"Oh, great," I said. "Now we know how to move forward. This is amazing."

"Amazing? How can you say that?" Sandra replied, still in tears. "The psychologist told us the best we can expect from Anthony is a menial job, like a cashier or mechanic, or criminal behavior! She said we should prepare ourselves to just be glad if he stays out of jail. There is NO HOPE for Anthony!"

My mouth dropped open. I could feel my chest tighten, my muscles tighten, and my face start to flush. I recognized this angry reaction as countertransference and took a deep breath. I went on to explain to Sandra and Tino that I had been doing a lot of reading about ODD, since it is often comorbid with ADHD, and what I was finding in the research literature was completely the opposite of what this psychologist had said to them. There *was* hope, and from what I was reading, lots of it!

Changing the Narrative

Ever since that session with Sandra and Tino, I have had hundreds of similar sessions with other parents of children diagnosed with ODD. Many times, they are exhausted, hopeless, and afraid of what the future will hold for them and for their child. The literature on ODD for the lay population typically reads the same: Children with ODD will not achieve much in their lives, and parents are lucky if they don't end up in jail or prison. I have had to remind my clients *not* to read anything on the internet about ODD and to only read materials I send them. They seem a bit taken aback by these recommendations, but I simply say that the research literature has been offering hope for clinicians and families about ODD since the 1970s, and it is taking forever for publicly available information on the internet to catch up. For those interested, I provide "research spotlights" in the appendix that briefly digest the research in a one-page format.

Unfortunately, I have found that when I collaborate with mental health clinicians, other health providers, or school staff, they tend to hold the same biased view that there is no hope. This book is intended to counter that viewpoint by compiling all the information and techniques I have successfully used in my work with families where ODD (and other disruptive behavior disorders) are present. Inside, you will find a very straightforward and phasic treatment approach known as *integrative systemic play therapy (ISPT)* that you can tailor to your individual clients between the ages of 2 and 17—no matter how "difficult" or "hopeless" they might seem to be. In fact, over the last 15 years of working with children with disruptive behavior disorders (DBDs), I have regularly been shot by Nerf bullets, spit upon, and occasionally gone home with a few bruises—yet none of these kids was beyond hope.

In chapter 1, I start out by identifying and exploring how the American bison (also called the buffalo) is a great representation for children with DBDs. The build, temperament, and potential of the buffalo maps well onto the experience of families with these types of children. In chapter 2, I thoroughly compile and explain the research on DBDs so you can better explain to your clients how and why this treatment approach works. Chapter 3 reviews the founding theories to this approach and the importance of viewing these cases through a theoretical lens.

The next several chapters outline the assessment (chapter 4) and treatment (chapters 5–9) of children with DBDs. In particular, chapters 5 through 9 discuss how the acronym BISON represents the five phases of treatment: (1) bio-emotion regulation, (2) individual play, (3) successful communication, (4) organized play, and (5) nurturing play. These chapters explain in depth the process of each phase with an emphasis on specific interventions you can use to assist these families. Chapter 10 discusses the processes of troubleshooting, graduation, and maintenance. Troubleshooting may occur adjunctively with each phase to ensure continued progress, while graduation is the process of slowly entering maintenance.

Finally, in chapter 11, I discuss a few of the personal reasons that children with DBDs are close to my heart, beginning with a history of one of my younger brothers, whose underlying (and unaddressed) mental health in childhood likely played a part in his interactions with school staff and family members. I then discuss my own experience as a father of a daughter labeled "the most defiant child I have ever worked with" by a preschool teacher. I explain my and my wife's journey in applying the skills in this book, followed by an update on my daughter, who received a very kind letter from her sixth-grade teacher that perfectly epitomizes my hope for (and the immense potential of) all children with DBDs. To conclude, I describe a case from beginning to end, including how I incorporated troubleshooting strategies and where those were implemented with the phases of treatment.

Key Terms and Case Examples

This book introduces a unique perspective on how to view and treat families with children who have DBDs. First and foremost is the shift from an individual counseling and symptom-treatment model to a systemic family therapy perspective. For clinicians unfamiliar with systems thinking or systemic family therapy, the following terms will assist you as you read:

- **Identified patient:** In systemic family therapy, the whole family is typically viewed as the client, but the term *identified patient* refers to the person within the family system who carries the brunt of the symptoms. Typically, this is the person who carries the diagnosis for billing and treatment planning. Using this term allows providers to continue to hold a whole-family systems perspective while recognizing and utilizing the individual psychotherapy language to describe who in the family is the symptom bearer.

- **Microsystem:** A microsystem is the smallest unit in Bronfenbrenner's (1977) ecological systems theory, which looks at a child's development within the context of their environment. A microsystem is the child's most immediate environment, where most of their day-to-day interactions occur. A family system is typically referred to as a microsystem.

- **Mesosystem:** The mesosystem is typically described as the second level of systems organization. A mesosystem is defined as a combination of two or more microsystems, such as families, schools, and churches, including how they interact and impact each other.

- **Macrosystem:** The macrosystem is best described as the overall cultural or national system. This system is made up of customs, societal norms, and legal and political influences that impact an individual and their micro- and mesosystems.

- **Multidirectional partiality:** This term describes the ability of a systems therapist to provide empathy and understanding to each family member while remaining objective and supportive of each individual and the family as a whole. This is an advanced skill in systemic family therapy that requires practice, tact, and supervision to ensure it is accomplished correctly.

- **Second-order change:** Second-order change refers to a more permanent systemic change within a family. It is more than just a behavioral shift or correction of symptoms; it is a deep shift in how the family understands and interacts with each other.

- **Graduation:** While the traditional term used to denote the end of therapy is *termination*, I opt to use the term *graduation*. Much like moving between phases of treatment, graduation denotes getting better and moving forward yet continuing to learn. I find that using termination language worries parents and that they seem to find new problems to address for fear of having to wait months to get back in. Expressing this transition as graduation eases these concerns, especially as I schedule spaced-out follow-up appointments to ensure continued progress.

For additional information on these terms or for a more detailed overview of systems thinking as it applies to family therapy, I recommend reading sources such as *The Handbook of Systemic Family Therapy* (Wampler, 2020), *The Craft of Family Therapy* (Minuchin et al., 2021), or *Marriage and Family Therapy* (Metcalf, 2023).

As you read on, know that many of the details about the case examples I provide (e.g., names, ages, genders, family makeup) are obscured, altered, or combined to protect client confidentiality. Nonetheless, the essence of the examples is true, especially when it comes to the specific behavior the child exhibited, the language I used in my communications, and the way I approached parents, schools, and community organizations. As I typed these examples, I could see in my mind's eye the look on the faces of my clients, their parents, their teachers, and their probation officers. I recalled the feelings of anxiety, trepidation, and excitement I had as I started therapy with them. I also experienced a swelling of care, concern, and joy for each of these families for allowing me to share their journey with them.

It is my hope that you, too, will feel this same sense of care, concern, and joy when you work with families of children who have DBDs. Although these kids are often seen as wild beasts, with no hope for the future, when they are treated with respect, compassion, and understanding, they can overcome even the most seemingly insurmountable challenges. It is up to you to lead the way. ∎

CHAPTER 1

Training Buffaloes

The first time I saw a buffalo in real life, I was 12 years old. My parents had packed the six of us kids into a Buick station wagon for a family vacation to Yellowstone National Park. Within 45 minutes of entering Yellowstone, we had to stop for a herd of buffalo crossing the street.

If you have ever seen a buffalo in person, you can imagine the awe and wonder I felt upon seeing them for the first time. These majestic horned animals, packed with muscle and layered in shaggy brown fur, were close enough to touch if I just rolled down the window or opened the door. My parents were quick to warn us *not* to roll down our windows and to admire these animals from the safety of our car. The word *safety* is relative because these animals are capable of destroying a vehicle and seriously harming everyone inside the car if they see it as an obstacle, challenge, or slight hindrance.

The traffic stalled, and everyone in our car and in the cars surrounding us breathlessly admired these seemingly docile creatures. It was much like the scene in *Jurassic Park* when the main characters first saw the dinosaurs. I felt goose bumps on my arms as we watched this herd demand the respect of everyone around them. It was as if the buffaloes knew they were stronger than the vehicles. Suddenly, two buffaloes rammed each other and butted heads. The thud reverberated in my chest. My parents' and siblings' expressions changed from awe to fear. I wondered whether our vacation would end right there and then. These once docile and seemingly harmless creatures suddenly became a threat. Similarly, sometimes children who seem docile on the outside are filled with hidden strength, determination, and potential.

Why Buffaloes?

The buffalo analogy began with a family therapy session with Frederick, a 10-year-old child who, according to his school and parents, was beyond control. He would yell, curse, throw objects, and kick his father. He struggled to make friends and seemed sullen all the time. His behavior was also erratic and unpredictable. When his parents asked him to do chores, he would stand in front of them, cursing and throwing objects at anyone who would try to move close to him or talk to him. One day, when Frederick's mother was helping him with his homework, he became increasingly agitated, leading him to slam the pencil on the table and scream that all he wanted to do was go back to see his old friends, as his family had recently moved to a new state. He screamed that he wouldn't do anymore schoolwork until she took him back. When Dad heard the screaming, he came in to see whether he could help Frederick calm down. This only aggravated Frederick further, and he stood up from the table, slammed the chair to the ground, kicked his father, and ran off saying he wished he was dead. His parents were at their wits' end. This event is what led to them calling my office and scheduling an appointment.

During the intake appointment (which typically includes only parents—this will be explained more in chapter 4), it became clear that Frederick's parents wanted me to see only Frederick, and they were quite confused and a bit frustrated when I explained that my family-focused play approach included parents as well. They believed that the problem was all Frederick and that if I helped him individually, things would get better. They also insisted that they had tried play therapy before, and it got them nowhere. At the time, I was the only credentialed play therapist in the town, so I was certain that the approach they had tried before didn't work because it was not executed correctly. I shared some of the differences between the approach they had tried previously and my approach, and they agreed to give it a try for a few sessions; if they didn't see improvements, they would go somewhere else. I thanked them for their honesty and dedication to getting Frederick help.

During our first family session together, Frederick, who was smaller than my own 10-year-old at the time, walked into our lobby wearing thin sandals and hanging his head down almost the whole time. It was hard to imagine the destruction his parents had described coming from such a small person. He seemed like a small, frightened animal. At this first session, I suggested that we all play UNO. The idea was for me to get to know how the family interacted, but Frederick was not having it.

"My parents hate me. They think I'm everything that's wrong in our family. That's why we're here!"

I turned to his mom and dad to see what they would say. Dad agreed. In his mind, Frederick was clearly the problem, and there was no use playing a game when Frederick was being so rude.

Mom, on the other hand, showed empathy and validation. "Frederick, we love you. We can see you're hurting. We just want you to feel better."

After about 15 minutes, I asked to meet individually with each parent and Frederick, starting with his mother. After Dad left the room, Frederick and Mom seemed to get along well, and Frederick was even willing to play UNO with her. She smiled at Frederick when he would make a face at her because of some move she made. He looked at her when he was planning to use a power card, after which she would fake disappointment and frustration about having to draw four cards or skip her turn. Mom would ask Frederick casual questions, and he seemed to forget that I was in the room. They also talked about Frederick's biggest frustration: a recent move from out of state. Mom listened as Frederick explained feeling like Dad had made the decision without considering how it would impact the family. Frederick was struggling with his new school, missing his old friends, and feeling like an outcast in a much bigger city than he was used to. Frederick expressed feeling like Dad was always picking on him and making him do more than his siblings. He mentioned thinking that no one in the family loved him, including his mother.

Frederick was a completely different animal when his dad came into the room. As soon as Mom left, Frederick's previously docile face exuded vitriol. It was as if he suddenly recalled that I was in the room, and instead of being a passive observer, I was an ally of Dad's. He didn't even give us a chance to play UNO and quickly yelled, "You are such an idiot for making us move. I hate your guts. You are just a stupid jerk that doesn't know how to keep a job." When he saw me in his periphery, he said, "Can you believe this dumbass thinks he's a good father?"

Dad was getting more aggravated and attempted to calm Frederick by putting his hands on Frederick's back. In response to this touch, Frederick immediately started kicking his dad in the shins. Knowing that I only had a few sessions to convince the parents of my approach—and thinking that Dad wouldn't want to return for more abuse—I leaned over to Frederick and said, "I know you are angry with your dad, and you'd like to kick him. However, in my office, dads are not for kicking. If you need to kick something, you may kick me or the couch. Which would you prefer?" This briefly shocked both Dad and Frederick, but it worked: Frederick stopped kicking his dad and slowly started kicking me. Dad kept a wary eye on me, I'm sure thinking something like *What is this crazy person doing? How is this going to help?*

Frederick spent the rest of the session kicking my shins and telling me how much he hated his dad. Dad was watching with a bewildered look on his face the entire time. While he was mostly just watching, I had to put my hand up to remind him to just give me some flexibility in my approach. With each kick, I would track Frederick's behavior and validate his emotions.

"You are really mad. You need your dad to know that you don't like him. You are using all your strength in your legs to show me just how mad you are. You don't think anyone hears you. You think nobody cares about you. You just want to be heard."

When we had only five minutes left, Frederick broke down in tears. Seeing the tears, I continued to track: "You look sad. Or did you get hurt? It seems like you are still angry, but now you have a lot of sadness coming out."

After about three more kicks from Frederick, he turned to his dad and said, "I'm sorry."

Looking even more bewildered and shocked, his dad also started to cry as he said, "Frederick, I love you."

"Why would you move us? I hate it here. Why did you have to change jobs? I just don't understand why we had to move."

Dad reached out to Frederick and was about to say something, presumably to answer those questions, but I shook my head and gestured to him to hug Frederick and say nothing. Seeing that his dad had reached out instead of shunning him, Frederick turned toward his father and fell into his arms, still sobbing. This was the beginning of a very long road of recovery and repair for Frederick and his family.

When the family left the session, I didn't think Frederick had done any damage to me because for the rest of the day, my shins didn't really hurt. That night, however, my wife asked what had happened to my leg. Faint bruises were forming all over my shins.

A week later, my wife saw an episode of *Odd Animal Couples* about a man named R. C. Bridges and his pet buffalo named Wild Thing. R. C. was trying to "train" the buffalo, who had failed to nurse with his mother, so they could eventually live in harmony with each other. He described an instance when he felt overwhelmed and lost about what he should do because "nothing worked." He decided to go out with Wild Thing and stay out the entire day, no matter how long it took for him to get trained. Throughout that day, Wild Thing headbutted R. C. all up and down his legs, but R. C. kept at it. Eventually, Wild Thing gave up and perceived R. C. as the one in charge.

My wife laughed. "That's what happened to you. You're training buffaloes."

Wild Thing, now a full-grown buffalo, allows R. C. to enter his pen, grab his horns, and brush his hair. (Don't try this at Yellowstone.) When the interviewer asks R. C. whether he is ever afraid of the buffalo, he says, "I don't think he'd hurt me; if he does hurt me, it'd be an accident." Later in the video, Wild Thing very delicately walks in and out of R. C.'s house, disturbing nothing. The buffalo sniffs at trinkets and decorations as he explores. At one point, R. C. casually mentions to the interviewer that Wild Thing will purposefully leave the house to relieve himself. When R. C. is asked how he potty trained the buffalo, he replies, "I don't know that you can potty train a buffalo! But you've got to understand that he knows everything I do is for him. I would never do anything against him. It's always for his protection or for his happiness."

The video sent chills down my spine. It was exactly my approach when I work with children with DBDs. I knew my wife was right: These children often have unmet needs (like Wild Thing's failure to nurse), and they often require a strong sense of commitment from their caregivers (like R. C. spending all day training the buffalo calf). They also need others to recognize that they are strong and loving individuals (like R. C. believing that Wild Thing would never hurt him). Most importantly, they need adults in their lives dedicated to their protection and happiness, just like R. C. was dedicated to Wild Thing.

What Are Disruptive Behavior Disorders?

Children who exhibit challenging, oppositional, defiant, violent, or antisocial behaviors fall within a mental health classification known as disruptive behavior disorders, or DBDs for short (Karnik & Steiner, 2005). The official *DSM-5-TR* diagnoses for the various DBDs include oppositional defiant disorder, conduct disorder, intermittent explosive disorder, and disruptive mood dysregulation disorder (American Psychiatric Association, 2022). While these are distinct disorders, they all share several traits in common, including emotion dysregulation, noncompliance to authority figures, physical or verbal outbursts, socialization difficulties, and strained family or peer relationships.

Social scientists have mixed views on how DBDs develop and whether they are stand-alone mental health disorders or the result of poor environmental factors, such as chaotic or nonsupportive family, harsh or inconsistent parenting, unsafe neighborhoods, or abuse (Karnik & Steiner, 2005; Wampler & Whitehead, 2020). The view I take in this book (and with my ISPT approach) is that "children will do well if they can" (Greene & Ablon, 2005). This means that children may not have developed the skills needed to engage in prosocial interactions, but they are doing the best with what they have. Keeping in mind the systemic interactions and mitigating circumstances that increase the likelihood of a child developing a DBD, this approach recognizes that children, like buffaloes, are amazing and majestic creatures who need respect, love, and careful handling.

Key Takeaway

Many, if not all, of the children I've seen with a DBD are very strong and determined individuals. Like their buffalo counterparts, they can be unpredictable and aggressive. Sometimes they appear unassuming, calm, and mild mannered, and then they all of a sudden have an outburst that shocks everyone. These outbursts can last for hours with no end in sight, unsettling loved ones who often have no idea how it happened or, worse, how to get the calm back. However, as you'll learn in this book, the key to working with these kids is understanding the underlying reasons for their behavior, recognizing how the environments they are in may contribute to these behaviors, acknowledging problematic cycles that reinforce these behaviors, and compassionately intervening to accommodate for, alter, and decrease these various factors to bring back the calm.

In the next chapter, I'll provide an overview of the research regarding DBDs, including their comorbidities, their identified course of development, and the current treatment recommendations. By gaining an understanding of the research behind these disorders, you can better explain to your clients how and why ISPT will work.

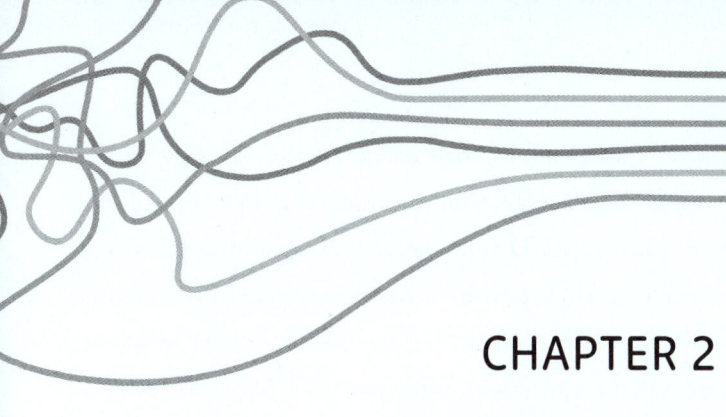

CHAPTER 2

The Research: Being Evidence Informed

Although there are several different types of DBDs, the most familiar diagnoses are oppositional defiant disorder (ODD) and conduct disorder. Kids with an ODD diagnosis exhibit argumentative or defiant behavior toward authority figures as well as angry or irritable mood. They may lose their temper often, refuse to follow rules, or deliberately annoy others. Although it is developmentally appropriate for kids to exhibit some of these behaviors around age two or three, generally around the time of language mastery, kids with ODD exhibit symptoms that are more frequent, persistent, and extreme. In addition, ODD can be mild, moderate, or severe based on how many settings in which the individual exhibits symptoms: mild (only one setting), moderate (at least two), or severe (three or more; American Psychiatric Association, 2022). The symptoms outlined in the *DSM* must be present for at least six months and occur with nonsiblings. Currently, between 3 and 5 percent of the general population is diagnosed with ODD (Hawes et al., 2023).

Conduct disorder is the diagnosis for even more severe cases of ODD. Many times, an individual is first diagnosed with ODD, and as they age and fail to develop prosocial skills, the diagnosis devolves into conduct disorder. In fact, conduct disorder is rarely diagnosed before ODD (Lin et al., 2022). Kids with conduct disorder engage in a variety of rule-breaking and aggressive behaviors that put others at risk, such as being cruel to others and animals, destroying property, stealing, setting fires, and running away from home. These are the kids who will stare you in the eye and kick a puppy as you tell them to stop. Conduct disorder is estimated to be present in a little under 6 percent of the population (Frick & Kemp, 2021).

The other less common DBD diagnoses are intermittent explosive disorder and disruptive mood dysregulation disorder (DMDD). Intermittent explosive disorder has been in the *DSM* for some time, but DMDD is a relatively new condition, with an average onset between ages 6 and 10 and an estimated prevalence rate of between 5 and 10 percent (American Psychiatric Association, 2022; Burke et al., 2024). While both disorders primarily involve disturbances of emotion regulation, DMDD consists of mostly severe and aggressive outbursts intermixed with an overall irritable mood; some consider it a precursor to bipolar disorder (Fristad et al., 2016; Hangül, 2024; Sparks et al., 2014). Symptoms of intermittent explosive disorder, on the other hand, primarily consist of spontaneous angry and aggressive outbursts intermixed with a generally positive or neutral mood. The average onset of intermittent explosive disorder is 17 years old, and it has an estimated maximum prevalence rate of just under 3 percent (Scott et al., 2016).

Finally, while antisocial personality disorder is technically a DBD, this book will not cover it since it cannot be diagnosed before age 18. However, it is important to point out that many parents, media outlets, and some providers falsely believe that antisocial personality disorder is the eventual end diagnosis for those with ODD (Burke et al., 2010; Woodard et al., 2019; Rowe et al., 2010; Salisbury, 2013). This misconception leads many parents to fear that their child will become a psychopath after an ODD diagnosis (De Los Reyes & Lee, 2017; Schroeder, 2016). While the presence of conduct disorder symptoms is required to establish a diagnosis of antisocial personality disorder, this still does not mean those with conduct disorder will eventually become antisocial. The truth is, only about 10 percent of kids with ODD will eventually develop the criminal behavior characteristic of conduct disorder or antisocial personality disorder (American Academy of Child and Adolescent Psychiatry, 2024; Lahey et al., 2005; Wampler & Whitehead, 2020). To put it another way, over 90 percent will *not*.

Regardless of diagnosis, one thing that all individuals with DBDs have in common is emotion regulation difficulties and escalation of aggressive or defiant behaviors, which can lead to reciprocal emotion regulation difficulties and escalation of behavioral responses in those around them (e.g., harsh punishment, relationship withdrawal). This book identifies the underlying common factors and applications of interventions that can positively impact individuals and families with any DBD diagnosis.

The Research on Disruptive Behavior Disorders

My master's program strongly emphasized the scientist-practitioner model, wherein I was trained to consistently evaluate and integrate clinical research (the "scientist" aspect of the model) into my professional practice (the "practitioner" aspect of the model). Given that this training on the intersection between research and practice has helped me provide the most effective interventions for my clients, the remainder of this chapter explores the research literature on DBDs, including their etiology, historical treatments, common comorbidities, and best practices for treatment.

Etiology and Course of Development

DBDs result from a complex mixture of biological and environmental factors. *Biological factors* include abnormalities in certain neurotransmitter systems (Lee & Coccaro, 2001), genetic predisposition for low frustration tolerance (Deater-Deckard et al., 2024), exposure to stressors and stress hormones in utero (López-Morales et al., 2023), physical illness in early childhood (Karnik & Steiner, 2005), and attachment-related difficulties (Bizzi & Pace, 2020; DeKlyen, 1996). Additionally, children who experience DBDs typically struggle with two aspects of regulation: behavior regulation (i.e., the ability to plan for the future or inhibit impulses) and emotion regulation (i.e., the ability to manage distress during frustrating tasks; Perry et al., 2018).

Environmental factors at the family level can include marital discord, parental mental health concerns, financial and residential instability, minimal adult supervision, and exposure to family violence. While these factors could lead to disruptive behavior in almost any child, children who have some of the biological sensitivities mentioned above are more likely to go on to develop DBDs. In addition, environmental factors at the societal level can increase the propensity of DBDs as well. This includes growing up in an environment characterized by oppression, poverty, community violence, school violence, and limited social mobility. For example, children who live in stressful or unsafe urban environments can develop coping skills, like hypervigilance around authority figures or community outsiders, that activate biological and family vulnerabilities.

When both biological and environmental factors are properly assessed, an evidence-informed treatment approach is more likely to be successful. Sometimes, you can't intervene on the societal level, but you can provide support in the form of family, couples, or individual therapy to increase a child's adaptive coping skills and provide the support needed for the family and parents.

Common Comorbidities

DBDs are often diagnosed with a whole host of other mental health concerns, especially ADHD, anxiety, autism, and depression. ADHD is seen most often, with estimates ranging from 50 to 80 percent (Hazell, 2010; Hudec & Mikami, 2018)—although anxiety, autism, and depression aren't that far behind, with estimates ranging from 50 to 60 percent for anxiety and autism and 40 to 50 percent for depression (Lecavalier et al., 2019; Nock et al., 2007). In fact, around 92 percent of children with ODD have another underlying or contributing mental health concern (Nock et al., 2007). The bottom line is that children with DBDs aren't usually dealing with just one problem. Many times, when these underlying problems are addressed, the DBD behaviors may decrease so drastically that treatment is no longer needed. Of course, even without other contributing factors, ISPT can reduce DBD behaviors.

Evidence-Based vs. Evidence-Informed Treatments

While there are many evidence-based treatments for DBDs that have received substantial research support, the financial costs and training timelines associated with these treatments make it extremely difficult for many providers to obtain. For example, parent-child interaction therapy (PCIT) requires an upfront payment of $4,500 and a commitment of one week for training. Supervision and continuation of certification requires additional time and financial commitments. Similarly, the full cost of TheraPlay certification training is between $3,000 and $8,000, depending on how much training you wish to get. For full certification, the price is toward the $8,000 range. Supervision and certification fees are additional to the general training fees. Both certification paths can take anywhere between two and four years, depending on the availability of training opportunities and supervisor availability.

As a result, clinicians tend to either not get the training or not see clients whose presenting problem is a DBD. For this reason, I consider the approach I take in this book to be "evidence informed" rather than "evidence based." *Evidence-based* interventions have a strong and structured protocol, are based on experimental research, and have fidelity measures in place to ensure the providers are using the intervention as developed and examined (American Psychological Association Presidential Task Force on Evidence-Based Practice, 2006; Kazdin, 2017). These interventions are typically referred to as *manualized treatments*. While this is a high bar to meet, evidence-based interventions are extremely important in the clinical field because they allow providers to feel confident that the strategies they are using will lead to actual change in clients, and it is easier to identify success in a research study.*

In contrast, *evidence-informed* interventions take evidence-based interventions, or interventions that have shown relative effectiveness in the research literature, and draw on the therapist's skills and knowledge to decide when to use which intervention for each client (Nevo & Slonim-Nevo, 2011). This approach allows the provider to prioritize the two factors within their control—the therapeutic relationship and therapy expectations—while also using their clinical judgment to identify and tailor the intervention for the client they have in their office. This flexibility is more natural, compassionate, and accessible. It is also consistent with using a "common factors" approach to treatment, which suggests that the quality of the therapeutic alliance as well as the client's hope and expectation for change affect treatment outcomes more than the specific modality used (Karam & Blow, 2023; Wampold, 2001).

Additionally, an evidence-informed approach allows providers to incorporate trauma-informed strategies into treatment, which is key given that families of children with DBDs often experience trauma, either from their child's outbursts or outsiders' judgment and scorn or as a result of generationally transmitted trauma (see chapter 5). The ISPT strategies I describe in this book are based on an evidence-informed approach, and it is my hope that the flexible and integrative nature of ISPT will allow clinicians to better advocate for and utilize it. In the following section, I review the research literature regarding several treatment interventions that underlie the strategies and phases of ISPT.

Individual Therapy (Traditional Child Psychotherapy)

Traditional child psychotherapy originally attempted to replicate traditional adult psychotherapy models in a format that was functional for children. The thought was that what worked for adults should work for children. Unfortunately, today's research says otherwise. In fact, in what was at the time the most extensive research trial on traditional child psychotherapy, Weiss and colleagues (1999) found some devastating results. Child participants were randomly assigned to one of two treatments: therapy or

---

* When I supervise beginning clinicians or consult with others in the field, I am surprised to see that many professionals operate on outdated or incorrect information regarding DBDs. To help combat this, I create one-page summaries anytime a new helpful study is published. Some of these are provided in the appendix of this book.

academic tutoring. Researchers compared outcomes based on self-report, parent report, and teacher report. What they found was that children in the control group (academic tutoring) had better outcomes than those in the experimental group (therapy). As the authors stated, "The simplest explanation for our findings is that traditional child therapy is not effective" (p. 91).

Studies since then have had better outcomes, though not by much. For example, in one of the most extensive meta-analyses to date, Weisz and colleagues (2017) only found evidence of small to moderate effect sizes when using traditional child therapy to treat various conditions, such as behavioral concerns, anxiety, and depression. For reference, most meta-analyses on adult populations find large effect sizes when examining the efficacy of individual psychotherapy.

Simply replicating adult psychotherapy approaches with children is far from the most effective approach to treating children with mental health concerns. Despite this, many clinicians are still trained in this way. While I'm not entirely sure why this is, I would assume there is a negative inclination toward play therapy as an effective treatment approach. Many providers I have worked with who are not formally trained in play therapy assume that the child and the therapist are simply playing and that no real work is being done. This inclination is intensified when therapists attempt to use play therapy without being properly trained in it, leading to subpar and often unsuccessful outcomes. Fortunately, when play therapy is properly implemented by trained play therapists, the outcomes are better, more effective, and longer lasting.

Child-Centered Play Therapy

Recognizing that adult therapy models don't work for children, Virginia Axline (1981) and others decided to develop more child-friendly approaches. Child-centered play therapy (CCPT), typically referred to as *nondirective play therapy*, views play as the child's language and the therapist as a witness to their process. Although such play therapy approaches were criticized early in their development, studies later demonstrated their value and effectiveness. For example, in one of the first meta-analyses on play therapy, Bratton and colleagues (2005) found large posttreatment effect sizes— with CCPT demonstrating an effect size of 0.92. Subsequent studies have replicated these results with similar effect sizes (Lin & Bratton, 2015; Ritzi et al., 2017; Salter et al., 2016), especially for children exhibiting disruptive behaviors (Parker et al., 2021).

Directive Play Therapy

As play therapy became more recognized in therapeutic circles, more treatment approaches developed, including directive play therapy. Directive play therapy differs from CCPT in that the therapist is not merely a witness to the child's play process but a direct interventionist. Some common directive play therapy approaches include cognitive behavioral play therapy, solution-focused play therapy, Adlerian play therapy, and prescriptive play therapy. While there are many other forms, these are the most utilized and well known. Directive play therapy can also include the use of games or specific interventions geared toward reducing select symptoms.

As with child-centered approaches, directive play therapy has also been found to show large effect sizes when it comes to its treatment success, with Adlerian play therapy being particularly effective for children at risk of disruptive behaviors. One particular study found that combining seven weeks of individual Adlerian play therapy followed by seven weeks of Adlerian group play therapy reduced problem behaviors by about 80 percent (Stutey et al., 2017). This suggests that using some form of directive play therapy is an effective intervention for DBDs.

Filial Play Therapy

Another advancement in the field of play therapy occurred when Bernard Guerney (1964) developed filial play therapy, which is a mixture of play therapy and family therapy. This approach incorporates parents as change agents with their children and seeks to facilitate change from a family system's perspective. While filial play therapy can be conducted individually, it most often takes place with groups of parents. Therapists generally teach parents the basic CCPT skills and then role-play those skills until parents are confident enough to use them with their children. Parents then conduct play sessions at home or in the provider's office while the provider supervises the parents' use of CCPT skills. As parents become more confident and adept, the provider encourages them to conduct weekly play sessions with their children.

Landreth and Bratton (2005) later adapted Guerney's (1964) filial play therapy approach into a more truncated 10-session format, which is also highly effective. Given that both approaches have shown success in reducing aggressive and disruptive behaviors in children (e.g., Rezaeianzadeh & Yazdanfar, 2024), it is clear that including parents in the therapy process makes a huge difference.

Biofeedback

While biofeedback isn't a new concept, it is starting to gain more ground with talk therapists, especially for those working with children and families (e.g., Gottman, 2011; Perry, 2017; Porges, 2011; Siegel, 2011). Traditional biofeedback uses physiological sensors to monitor heart rate, skin conductance, respiration, and even brain wave activity while training the client to consciously regulate their bodily responses using relaxation and breathing techniques.

Although traditional biofeedback utilizes these multiple physiological sensors and responses, heart rate variability (HRV) biofeedback only uses specifically designed pulse oximeters to track an individual's heart rate as well as the variation of time between each heartbeat. HRV biofeedback is a newer approach, yet many programs are advertising its success at reducing ADHD and disruptive behavior symptoms. For example, one set of researchers tested whether a biofeedback video game called *Mightier* (previously known as *Regulate and Gain Emotional Control*, or *RAGE-Control*) could reduce anger outbursts in children by tracking their HRV while playing a tablet game. Amazingly, the researchers found that when used correctly, the game was able to reduce anger outbursts by 62 percent (Ducharme et al., 2021). Parents also reported significant reduction in their parenting stress (Mannweiler et al., 2023). This suggests that adding biofeedback, or some other regulatory training program, to the treatment of children with DBDs is an important aspect of successful treatment (Dormal et al., 2021).

Family Systems Therapy

When working with families where DBDs are present, it is important to be systemically oriented, meaning that you consider a child's presenting problem within the context of the micro-, meso-, and macrosystems in which they operate. Remember that disruptive behaviors encapsulate and impact every relationship and environment the child experiences; they do not only exist in the child. It is for this reason that family therapy—which treats parents and children simultaneously—is the most effective at reducing disruptive behaviors (Carr, 2014; Sheidow et al., 2022). In fact, some researchers have argued that clinicians should provide behavioral parent training (a form of family therapy) when treating disruptive child behaviors (Carr, 2019; McCart et al., 2006). While there are several existing forms of family therapy, including structural family therapy, Bowenian family therapy, and experiential family therapy, the ISPT approach in this book is largely based on a mixture of structural family therapy and Bowenian family therapy.

Integrative Systemic Play Therapy

As I incorporated these various treatment styles to develop my approach for working with DBDs, I struggled to find a term to encapsulate the whole process. I originally decided to call the synthesis of these interventions systemic play therapy, but I then discovered that Lewis (1987) had coined this term to describe her approach of working with inner-city youth and families experiencing multiple presenting problems. Her form of systemic play therapy was a problem-focused, one-on-one play therapy approach involving only the child, with as much collateral contact with the family and extrasystemic participants as possible. Other than in Lewis's original article from 1987, I didn't find another use of the term. In order to avoid any confusion about Lewis's model, and to encapsulate the "common factors" approach first promoted by Wampold (2001) and later specifically advocated for in family therapy interventions by Karam and Blow (2023), I decided to call this approach integrative systemic play therapy (ISPT).

ISPT conveys the idea that providers should integrate various evidence-based play therapy models and theories into their work, building upon the providers' therapeutic skills and allowing flexibility to treat the most urgent symptoms first. In addition to integrating multiple play therapy models, ISPT is systemic in that it requires the provider to keep sight of the many interactions and processes occurring in the family. Lastly, it incorporates the idea that the provider will regularly interact with and become involved in the micro-, meso-, and macrosystems of a client's life. This systemic involvement increases second-order change and solidifies progress.

Key Takeaway

Research and practice outcomes have found that individual child psychotherapy is less effective than either play therapy or family therapy. In addition, play therapy research continues to demonstrate the effectiveness of this approach when conducted by trained providers. Recognizing the importance of family systems approaches when intervening for disruptive behaviors, ISPT draws from various evidence-based interventions and integrates them into a cohesive treatment format. This is more accessible to providers and families and maintains an evidence-informed approach. In the next chapter, I explore the underlying theoretical approaches drawn from in ISPT and clarify why you need a sound theoretical base when addressing child behavior problems and complex family interactions. With these building blocks laid, you will be better equipped at encouraging a systems approach when treating families of children with DBDs.

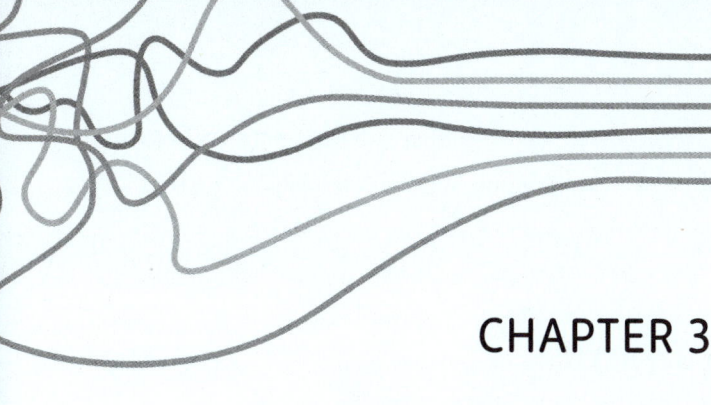

CHAPTER 3

The Foundation: Key Principles in Understanding Disruptive Behavior Disorders

This chapter will outline three theoretical frameworks that explain the origins of disruptive behavior and describe the processes for reducing and eliminating it. First, I explore the theory of temperament as defined by Chess and Thomas (1977) and outline how understanding a child's basic temperament and where they fall within the nine temperament traits plays a big role in the development and treatment of DBDs. Next, I give a brief overview of three important concepts within family systems theory that, when understood, keep disruptive behaviors from spiraling out of control. Finally, I describe how coercion theory has revolutionized treatment approaches for children and families where DBDs are present.

Many clinicians get uncomfortable discussing theories. Theories can be like ideologies, and clinicians their disciples. However, when I thoroughly understand a theory and apply it appropriately with clients, I spend less time on inconsequential content and instead focus on addressing the processes that need adjusting. Those clients get better more quickly. Indeed, as Harvard professor Clayton Christensen (2012) emphasizes in his book *How Will You Measure Your Life?*, if we examine our own lives through the lens of specific theories, we will be better equipped to determine desirable outcomes. As he says, "A robust theory is able to explain what has and what will occur" (p. 5). Theories make it easier to understand complex interactions and concepts.

Viewing DBDs from theoretical lenses allows us to predict how an intervention will impact a child and their family. It also helps the family and those involved see how to use these theories to intervene.

Theory of Temperament

In the late 1950s, amid intense behaviorist philosophy and theories, many schools of psychological thought attributed childhood outcomes to environment and parenting. In response, Chess and Thomas (1977) launched the landmark New York Longitudinal Study (NYLS), born out of a concern that too much was being blamed on parents, specifically mothers. If a child succeeded or was kind, it was all due to the "angel mother." Alternatively, if the child exhibited any mental health defects, was oppositional, or misbehaved in any way, it was because of the "refrigerator mother." As clinicians witnessed an increase in parental anxiety and started to question the validity of these behaviorist theories, Chess and Thomas sought to identify how biology contributes to children's positive or negative trajectories. Their 30-year NYLS study followed 133 children from birth as well as their families. Much of today's understanding about the interplay between personality and environment on child development came from this study or other similar, replicated studies.

One of the main questions Chess and Thomas (1977) tried to answer was to what extent childhood and adult outcomes were the result of external forces (e.g., parenting, neighborhood, school environment), internal forces (e.g., biology, heritability, neurology), or a combination of both. In doing so, they identified nine common personality traits in their sample, which they called *temperament*. Temperament is described as the *how* and *why* of behavior. Another way to explain temperament is like the ingredients in bread. When certain ingredients are mixed together, different textures, shapes, sizes, and tastes of bread emerge. However, the environment plays a big part in *how* the bread comes out. If the environment (room temperature) is cold or warm, the bread may rise a little or a lot. The environment (oven) can also be hotter or colder than expected, leaving the bread burnt or underdone. When mixing the ingredients, we know approximately *how* the bread will turn out, and we may even have an idea of its taste. But the rest of the ingredients as well as the environment will determine *what* its appearance will be and *why*.

Similarly, you can think of the nine traits that Chess and Thomas (1977) found as different *ingredients* of a person's personality. These ingredients influence how an individual interacts with the world and within themselves. Each of the nine categories are listed here:

1. **Activity level:** This ingredient describes the child's overall activity level during daily life. Do they prefer to run, walk, or sit? Are they always engaging with their environment or passively taking things in? Activity level is rated as high, medium, or low.

2. **Biological regularity:** This category refers to how predictable a child's bodily functions and biological needs are. Does the child sleep and wake at the same time each day? Do they use the bathroom with predictability, or do they have difficulty regulating their digestive system? This trait is rated as regular, variable, or irregular.

3. **Approach or withdrawal:** This trait measures a child's initial reaction to new stimuli. Does the child like new experiences or people, or do they recoil from them? This is rated as approachable, variable, or withdrawn.

4. **Adaptability:** After experiencing something new, how quickly does a child acclimate and adapt? Can the child bounce back after a difficult or new situation, and how long does it take to do so? Adaptability is rated as adaptive, variable, or nonadaptive.

5. **Sensory threshold:** This trait describes how sensitive or insensitive a child may be to sensory stimuli. Does the child require lots of stimulation (hyposensitive) or very little (hypersensitive) for a response to be experienced? This trait is rated as high, medium, or low.

6. **Intensity of reaction:** In contrast to sensory threshold, this trait measures *how* the child reacts in response to certain stimuli. Does the child explode when experiencing a stimulus, or are they passive and nonplussed? This temperament category is rated as positive (high), variable, or negative (low).

7. **Mood:** This category measures a child's overall mood and emotional presentation. Is the child jovial and helpful, or do they present more like Eeyore—gloomy and pessimistic? This trait is rated as positive, variable, or negative.

8. **Distractibility:** This trait identifies the amount of stimulus a child needs to lose track of their train of thought. Can they remain focused, or are they distracted

by the simplest movement in a room? This category is rated as distractible, variable, or nondistractible.

9. **Persistence and attention span:** Finally, this trait identifies the level of persistence a child may exercise at accomplishing a difficult task. Do they give up easily when things are difficult, or do they persevere until the end? This trait is rated as persistent, variable, or nonpersistent.

Primary Temperament Constellations

Chess and Thomas (1977) noticed that children who had particular combinations of these nine traits had similar behavioral profiles, which they called *constellations*. They identified three important subgroups of children based on these constellations: difficult, slow to warm up, or easy. The children who were classified as *easy* were able to adapt easily to new circumstances, had regular biological functions, showed positive responses to new stimuli, and had a mild and overall positive mood. These children slept well at night, fed well, and did not find themselves in a lot of trouble with peers or authority figures. Parents and other adults would often comment on how easy these children were, giving this constellation of temperament traits its moniker.

Almost the exact opposite of the easy constellation were *difficult* children, who experienced high irregularity in their bodily functions, adhered rigidly to routines, were aversive to new experiences, and exhibited an intense overall negative mood. The parents of these children remarked how difficult it was to get these children to do normal things like sleep, eat, or potty train. These children often engaged in strong battles of will with peers and authority figures. As a result, this constellation of temperament traits was given its name due to the fact that researchers and parents found this group of children difficult to handle.

Finally, the last constellation of traits comprised children with varied responses within the nine temperament traits. Some of their responses leaned toward difficult, while others leaned toward easy. For example, these children initially responded negatively to new stimuli but then gradually adapted. As a result, these children were designated *slow to warm up*. Chess and Thomas (1977) found that approximately 40 percent of the children in the NYLS could be classified as easy, 15 percent as slow to warm up, and 10 percent as difficult. The remaining 35 percent were a mixture of these and other groupings that could not be fully explained.

Importantly, many studies have found a connection between these constellations and the risk of future internalizing or externalizing disorders. For example, children in the slow-to-warm-up category often exhibit anxiety or other internalizing disorders, while children in the difficult category tend to be more likely to develop disruptive behaviors (Achtergarde et al., 2015). In addition, children with a difficult temperament tend to respond more negatively to authoritarian parenting styles (Achtergarde et al., 2015), suggesting the need for a highly tailored parenting approach that fits the child's personality and that of the parents. This finding reaffirms that one size does not fit all when treating children with disruptive behaviors—and that it is key to understand the temperaments of *all* involved in order to fill in the pieces of the puzzle.

When I work with children who exhibit a DBD diagnosis, I make sure to assess where the child falls on each of the nine temperament traits so I can gain more insight into where some of the disruptive behavior is coming from and how I can help the parents and child interact better. I have found that most kids with DBDs have some manifestation of a difficult temperament, even if they don't meet full criteria for it. To help parents talk about their child's temperament traits, I use the following *Temperament Traits* worksheet, which asks parents to identify where their child lies within each of these nine traits. I find that this eases the conversation about different temperament constellations and how they apply to their child. When the parents and I are better able to identify challenges within each of these areas, we can come up with more targeted, effective interventions.

For instance, if a child presents with a DBD but is primarily hyperactive, biologically irregular, and adaptively inflexible, interventions that focus on improving regulatory functioning, enhancing executive functioning, and facilitating bilateral integration are likely to result in a significant decrease in disruptive behaviors. Educating and training parents on these trait challenges—as well as on the interventions that are likely to be most successful—will also help them respond in a more adaptive and flexible manner at home, leading to even greater decreases in disruptive behaviors. I provide a more thorough example of using this worksheet in chapter 4.

CLIENT WORKSHEET

Temperament Traits

All children exhibit many of the behavior traits outlined below. Choose one child to evaluate and place an X on the continuum below each trait that most closely matches your experience with this child.

ACTIVITY LEVEL
How energetic is your child during regular day-to-day activities?

Hyperactive (high) — **Mellow (low)**

BIOLOGICAL REGULARITY
How consistent are your child's eating, sleeping, and toileting habits?

Regular — **Irregular**

APPROACH OR WITHDRAWAL
How quickly does your child lean into new and unfamiliar circumstances?

Approachable — **Distant**

ADAPTABILITY
How rigid does your child prefer their routine, schedule, or daily activities?

Flexible — **Inflexible**

SENSORY THRESHOLD
How intensely does your child experience pain, smell, sound, or other senses?

Hypersensitive — **Hyposensitive**

INTENSITY OF REACTION
When experiencing difficulties, how strong do they exhibit their response?

Active — **Passive**

MOOD
What is your child's average attitude emotionally?

Positive — **Negative**

DISTRACTIBILITY
On average, how attentive is your child?

Distractible — **Focused**

PERSISTENCE OR ATTENTION SPAN
When faced with a long-term task, how determined is your child?

Persistent — **Nonpersistent**

Family Systems Theory

Around the same time Chess and Thomas (1977) were investigating the contribution of temperament to childhood outcomes, Murray Bowen (1966) and many others were experimenting with a revolutionary concept that came to be known as family systems theory. These pioneers of family therapy witnessed that when they viewed certain behavioral or mental health concerns from a family (or systems) viewpoint rather than from an intrapsychic viewpoint, interesting trends emerged. They discovered that much of the content that individuals and families were bringing to therapy could be connected to a few repetitive processes that perpetuated the underlying difficulties. This led to an explosion of new theories and interventions on how to work with mental health concerns by focusing less on content and more on process.

In family systems theory, a *process* is defined as a continuous pattern of emotional or behavioral interactions within and between individuals that contributes to or is influenced by the actions or emotions of others. In other words, process is about how family members are interacting with one another. On the other hand, *content* refers to the specific problems or stories that bring people to therapy in the first place—for example, poor conflict resolution, communication problems, defiance, hyperactivity, anxiety, and so forth. While content should not be ignored, systemic therapists pay more attention to the processes that families present with so they can identify what to do about the content. When a therapist says they are "systemically informed" or "systems focused," they generally mean that they tend to focus on process rather than content.

A quick anecdote from my experience as a second-level information technology support specialist during my undergraduate years highlights the need to be systemically informed (i.e., focused on process rather than content). I think about this event often when I teach others about family systems theory.

The customer called in complaining that he couldn't access the internet on his computer. Having had this conversation with other customers many times before, I focused first on process, as I had found that addressing issues systemically could prevent hours of unnecessary work. Therefore, my first question was simple: "Can you see anything on your screen?" The dialogue then proceeded as follows:

CUSTOMER: No.

ME: So, the screen is completely black?

CUSTOMER: Yes.

ME: Can you make sure the computer and the monitor are turned on?

CUSTOMER: Of course they are turned on. I know how to operate a computer.

ME: Okay, just checking. What we need to do first is just reset the computer. Can you turn it off for me?

CUSTOMER: How can I do that if all I have is a black screen?

ME: Just push the power button on the computer tower for about 10 seconds until it beeps, then let go.

CUSTOMER: It's not beeping.

ME: Okay, can you make sure the computer is physically plugged into the wall outlet?

CUSTOMER: Of course it's plugged in. It was working just fine yesterday, and I didn't unplug it.

ME: Can you check it, just to make sure?

CUSTOMER: Fine. It's plugged in.

Having exhausted my first line of process-focused questions, I decided to then focus on content. I believed that he was getting power to the computer, so I instructed him through another two hours of troubleshooting steps. I asked about his internet service provider, whether he had paid his bill, whether his computer was connected to the router, and other such questions. At the end of the two hours, I was totally at a loss as to what was happening. I had done everything that needed to be done, and we should have been able to get him back on the internet. He was frustrated; I was frustrated. I went back to more process-focused questions and asked him to look at the back of the computer tower and describe in very fine detail all the cables he saw plugged into the tower. I then had him follow every cable exactly to where it was plugged in. Everything was plugged in where it should be. I then asked him to identify the power cord and follow that cord.

ME: Follow that cord to where it goes. I just want to make sure it's going to a good outlet.

CUSTOMER: Okay...

Suddenly, the line went dead. I thought he had accidentally unplugged the phone. I called him back. He didn't answer. I left a message and said I wanted to make sure we were able to get him a resolution to his problem, gave him my direct number, and said I would investigate things more and call him back the next day. About five minutes later, one of my coworkers tapped me on the shoulder and told me to look at that customer's account. I noticed that the customer's service ticket was closed. Confused, I read the note left by my coworker: "Customer called. Stated he was embarrassed and didn't want to talk with the previous technician. Customer stated that we could close the ticket; the computer is now working. Stated that the computer needed to be plugged into the electrical socket." Even though the customer thought I was patronizing him by asking him to check whether the power was on, had he focused on answering my process questions, we would have discovered that the computer was unplugged toward the start of the call. This focus on process could have saved both the customer and me hours of time and frustration.

The first two questions I asked this customer—"Can you see anything on the screen?" and "Can you make sure the computer and the monitor are turned on?"—were a litmus test to identify whether there was power to the computer and whether there was a problem with the connections. A surprisingly large portion of my service calls were resolved after asking those two questions. Many first-level technicians would bypass these simple steps because they had a frustrated customer on the line, and they didn't want to make them more upset by "questioning their intelligence." Often, the easiest solution is overlooked because of its simplicity.

When we don't look at concerns from a systemic viewpoint, we are sure to miss something. When working with families and children with DBDs, it is imperative that we get as much information as possible to achieve a coherent and comprehensive assessment before we dive into interventions. Practically, this means I will work with the family, the school, medical providers, occupational therapists, probation officers, and others who regularly interact with the child. Without doing so, I'm going to miss something that could be essential for helping the family find some relief from the behavior problems their child is facing. This can be frustrating for family members, especially parents who often interpret my systems view as blaming *others* for the problems their child is experiencing. However, taking a systemic view lays no blame on any individual. Rather, it sees the child's issues as a delicate interaction between all individuals. It considers the fact that environment, nature, and nurture all play a part in how each of us develops and is socialized.

Principle Systemic Processes

There are three specific processes to consider when working with children and families who experience disruptive behaviors. While these three processes do not encompass the entirety of family systems theory, they are extremely important to understanding how to effectively intervene with DBDs.

Circular Causality

One process that commonly takes place in families where DBDs are present is circular causality. Circular causality describes a process in which interactions take place in a feedback loop that is not cause and effect but reciprocally interconnected. For example, if a father has a rough day at work and comes home grumpy, his mood will impact his interactions with his partner and children. Suppose that he interacts with one of his children in a negative way because the child did not clean their room. This negative interaction prompts the child to play, read, or listen to music (and not clean the room), which further aggravates the father. The father can't sleep because he is upset that his child is being defiant, lazy, *and* disrespectful. When the father wakes up to go to work the following day having had little rest, he struggles to accomplish his job tasks, leading to him coming home grumpy again, restarting the circular pattern.

A content-focused approach would attempt to tackle this problem from a linear, cause-and-effect lens. For example, the therapist might attempt to work on either the child's defiance, disrespect, and laziness or the father's sleep patterns, self-regulation abilities, and work habits. If the linear approach attempted to increase the child's willingness to clean their room but didn't focus on the rest of the feedback loop, the father may still come home grumpy and find fault with their child for something else entirely. This is like a fast-paced game of whack-a-mole where the provider or family is searching for "the problem" and exerting all their energy fighting it without really solving anything. In systems language, this content-and-symptom-reduction-focused approach only accomplishes first-order behavior change.

In contrast, a circular causality approach would conserve energy by addressing everyone's contributions to the system. Dad needs to work on his mood, and the child needs to clean their room. Dad needs to work on regulating himself to sleep better, and the child needs to know when it is appropriate to read, play, or listen to music. Unless the entire process is impacted, systemic change won't occur. This systemic change results in second-order, paradigm-shifting change. In first-order change, behavior may change for a short time, but like in whack-a-mole, new issues will crop up.

The very nature of circular causality eliminates the blame from any one person and distributes it across the entire system. However, when discussing abusive patterns or abusive individuals, it is not appropriate to distribute the blame upon the victims being perpetrated against. It is not correct, for instance, to say that a father would be justified in physically abusing their child because he came home grumpy from work. That blame lies solely on the shoulders of the father. It is also not correct to say that because a child is messy, the father's abuse is justified. That, again, is the sole responsibility of the father. Observing interactions with circular causality in mind does not eliminate personal responsibility; however, it acknowledges that behaviors may have multiple origins to address.

Paradoxical Interdependence

The next essential process when intervening with families and children with DBDs is paradoxical interdependence. This process identifies how every action of each member of a system has a direct or indirect impact on the actions and emotions of every other member of the system. The paradox arises from the fact that the actions of one family member that are intended to change another often end up creating either the exact *opposite* change or some derivative behavior that is seen as unhelpful.

A real-life example of this process occurred in the family of a 10-year-old client named Jimmy, who exhibited severe defiant behavior at home. When Jimmy's mom reached out to schedule the appointment, she described how Jimmy would stand on the edge of his bed and urinate all over his sheets right after she had put fresh, clean bedding on it. He was also getting in trouble more often at school. I met alone with his mom for the intake, and when I got to the end of the session, I casually asked, "So when did you and Jimmy's dad get divorced?" Her answer astonished me: "Oh, we aren't divorced. We're happily married." She looked at me, confused. "Why did you think we were divorced?"

You see, during the entire intake process of calling my office, scheduling the appointment, and filling out the paperwork, she had never mentioned anything about Jimmy's father. I asked to schedule another session, but this time with both Mom and Dad, even before I saw Jimmy. She was a little frustrated by this suggestion, as she just wanted me to start working with Jimmy, but she nonetheless agreed to it. My joint session with both parents was very different from the one with just Mom. The mother and father sat with a large gap between them, barely looked at each other, and didn't look anything like "happily married." When Dad described what he viewed as the cause of Jimmy's behaviors, he blamed them all on the mother's permissive parenting and said that all Jimmy needed was a "swift kick in the butt"—not therapy.

When I finally had a few sessions with Jimmy, I discovered that he was a very sad and anxious child. He expressed through his play that he could never do anything correctly and didn't know how to get love or acceptance from his parents. As a result, he would pee on his bed when he wanted his mom's attention. He had learned over time that when he urinated on his bed, she would pick him up off the bed, sit him on a chair, and teach him how to clean his own bedding. This took dedicated time out of his mom's schedule, and Jimmy had her undivided attention.

And there it was—the paradoxical interdependence. Jimmy was dependent on love, care, and concern from his parents. Jimmy's mother wouldn't yell when he peed on the bed; instead, she would take him and teach him rather than punish him, as Dad would have preferred. Whereas Dad was critical, Mom was permissive. Mom was dependent on the need to nurture. Dad, busy with work, was dependent on Mom's ability to manage the house, take care of the kids, and attend to his emotional connection needs. Although Jimmy's mom had been focused on child-rearing when Jimmy and his siblings were born, as they got older and became more independent, Mom had started a part-time job outside the home. She was considering transitioning to full time right about the same time Jimmy's behaviors began.

Seeing a need to work concurrently on Jimmy's behaviors and the state of his parents' marriage, I started couples therapy with them. After about six sessions of couples therapy and seven sessions of individual therapy with Jimmy, his behaviors suddenly stopped. His parents were able to get on the same page regarding discipline for Jimmy, and they began working on strengthening their relationship as partners versus as parents.

An important note of caution should be stated here. By acknowledging the interdependence between family members, I in no way blamed Jimmy's mom for going back to work, or his dad for his harshness, or Jimmy for his maladaptive request for comfort. Mom, Jimmy, and Dad were not independently to blame; the interactional cycles they had developed were. If I were to tell the mother that she was to blame for Jimmy's behaviors because she didn't harshly punish Jimmy for peeing on the bed and because she went back to work, it would not accurately describe the situation. She would be hurt, Dad would feel vindicated, and Jimmy would find a new behavior to manifest. The overall systemic interactions needed correcting, not just the individual behaviors of the family members.

Triangulation

Lastly, triangulation is a systemic process that is also present in families experiencing DBDs. Triangulation occurs when a person is drawn into a conflict between two people in a system, thus creating a triad. In Bowen family systems theory, a triad is considered the smallest stable relationship in the system because a dyad cannot fully sustain the weight of the conflict (Bowen, 1966). Therefore, as stress becomes too difficult to manage, it is transferred to a third party (the triangulated person). When the third party is drawn in, they often experience the weight of their own stress, the stress of the person triangulating them, and the stress of the original dyadic relationship. This can be extremely uncomfortable for the third party.

Triangulation can take many different forms. It can involve a caregiver parentifying their child by telling the child about their adult relationship concerns, or it can involve a child exhibiting behavioral concerns so their parents don't have to deal with their own relationship concerns (as in Jimmy's case). When children are triangulated, by choice or not, families tend to see them as the sole problem within the family. Many parents come to therapy with the idea that if the child were "fixed," it would solve the problems for the whole family. Child therapists with this mindset tend to ignore other systemic concerns occurring in the home, but neglecting the systemic concerns will not allow for second-order change to occur.

When children develop DBDs, it is important to assess whether triangulation may be occurring, as this will better equip you to identify interventions that lead to lasting second-order change. When you know what you are looking for, it is easier to detect triangulation. Look for the following three signs: (1) the child is being blamed for "all the family's problems," (2) the child is too knowledgeable of the parents' relationship problems, or (3) the child is tasked with too much caregiving within the family. Shifting parental relationship stress onto the child can result in significant increases in externalized and internalized problems.

Mesosystemic Work

Although Murray Bowen (1966) is considered the founding father of family systems theory, it was Urie Bronfenbrenner (1977) who expanded on family systems work by proposing that families are part of an ecological system. His ecological systems theory introduced the concepts of micro-, meso-, and macrosystems, among others. When providers work with the family as a unit, it is typically considered *microsystemic work*. Other examples of microsystems include schools, neighborhoods, and extended family.

As important as microsystemic work is, it is also important to identify the mesosystems in play, as children with DBDs experience difficulties within *all* their systems. Therefore, providers who only work within the family microsystem can limit their reach and their clients' progress. As a systemic therapist, I have worked directly with principals, teachers, aunts, uncles, grandparents, and sports coaches to help these mesosystemic individuals understand my work with the family and child. Interacting with mesosystems helps reinforce the changes the family and child make.

Coercion Theory

One of the most important discoveries in the past century for treating children with DBDs is Gerald Patterson's theory of the coercion cycle (Patterson et al., 1984; Patterson, 2016). Seeking to understand how and why DBDs develop, Patterson observed interactions between parents and children. What he discovered was an intricate process of aversive (i.e., unwanted) stimulus resistance by both parents and children. When an individual is faced with an aversive stimulus from another individual (such as a whining child or a demand from an adult), they can decide to resist or yield to the stimulus. If they continue to resist the stimulus, the stimulus may subside or increase in intensity. If it intensifies, the original individual may again decide to yield or resist. This pattern continues until one of the individuals yields or the behavior subsides. Patterson called this process the *coercion cycle*. As you'll see, sometimes this cycle is harmless and helpful, while other times it is detrimental and destructive.

A common example of this cycle plays out in the age-old case of a child asking for a toy or candy at the store: Imagine you are at the store with your child. You may be tired from your normal daily business and just want to get done with shopping as soon as possible. Already on your last nerve, your child sees a candy bar they want. At first, they simply ask, "Can I have that candy bar?" You are thinking of the best interest of your child and know that if you say yes, they will want to eat it right after you purchase it. You still haven't fed them dinner and want to make sure they have a nutritious and well-balanced diet. Happy to help your child become the best possible version of themselves, you say, "No, sorry. We still need to eat dinner, and today is not a candy day." Your child, not to be outdone, sees the weariness on your face and opts to increase the intensity of their request. "But, Dad, I really WANT this candy bar NOW!" Almost a yell, the intensity and volume of your child's demand starts to get to you. You feel the eyes of other shoppers on your back. You can almost hear them saying to themselves, *Ooh, just give him the candy bar*, *You'd better not give in*, or *What a rude child. Doesn't this parent know how to discipline?*

You and your child are now locked in a battle of wills. Who will win? Ironically, once this process has begun, you have both already lost. As this cycle builds upon itself over time, it is more likely that future interactions start at an escalated position rather than a simple request and subsequent denial. The next time your child sees a candy bar at the store, their first request comes out as a whine, and your initial response (denial) may not be based as much on proper nutrition as it is reacting to that whine. As this process continues, you will become less patient and more reactive to their behavior, and they will be less considerate in their requests.

Unfortunately, this cycle is natural and occurs in *all* relationships. It begins at birth, as all the interactions between a parent and their infant are inherently coercive as defined by this theory. For instance, the only way for an infant to communicate their needs is to make a fuss or cry. A hungry infant cannot simply say they are hungry (aversive stimulus for the child)—at least not yet. They start by fussing a bit and trying to signal their biological need. If that doesn't work, they may escalate to crying (aversive stimulus for the caregiver). When the caregiver hears the crying, they want to make it stop. They may look for other clues about what the infant needs, eventually settling on feeding them. When the infant learns that crying gets them food, the next time they are hungry, they won't start by fussing but by crying.

This escalation in demand from the infant is the beginning of the coercion cycle. When the parent learns that feeding ends the crying, they won't start by fumbling around with other needs—they'll tune right into feeding the child. Because they have found a response that stops the crying, they are able to stop that part of the coercion cycle. Eventually, the infant and parent learn how to read each other to get their needs met. As seen in this dynamic, the coercion cycle is healthy and necessary! It teaches the parent and infant to understand and attend to each other's needs. The problem begins after the child learns to speak, yet they (and other family members) continue to communicate their desires through escalated behavior rather than verbally, which perpetuates the coercion cycle beyond what is healthy. To help parents understand how the cycle works, you can use the following *Coercion Cycle Diagram* handout.

CLIENT HANDOUT

Coercion Cycle Diagram

The following flow chart describes the process of the coercion cycle in families. When the coercion cycle overruns a family, the child tends to use any previously escalated aversion behavior that worked in the past, which in turn encourages punishment acceleration and continued escalation of corrective behaviors by the adult.

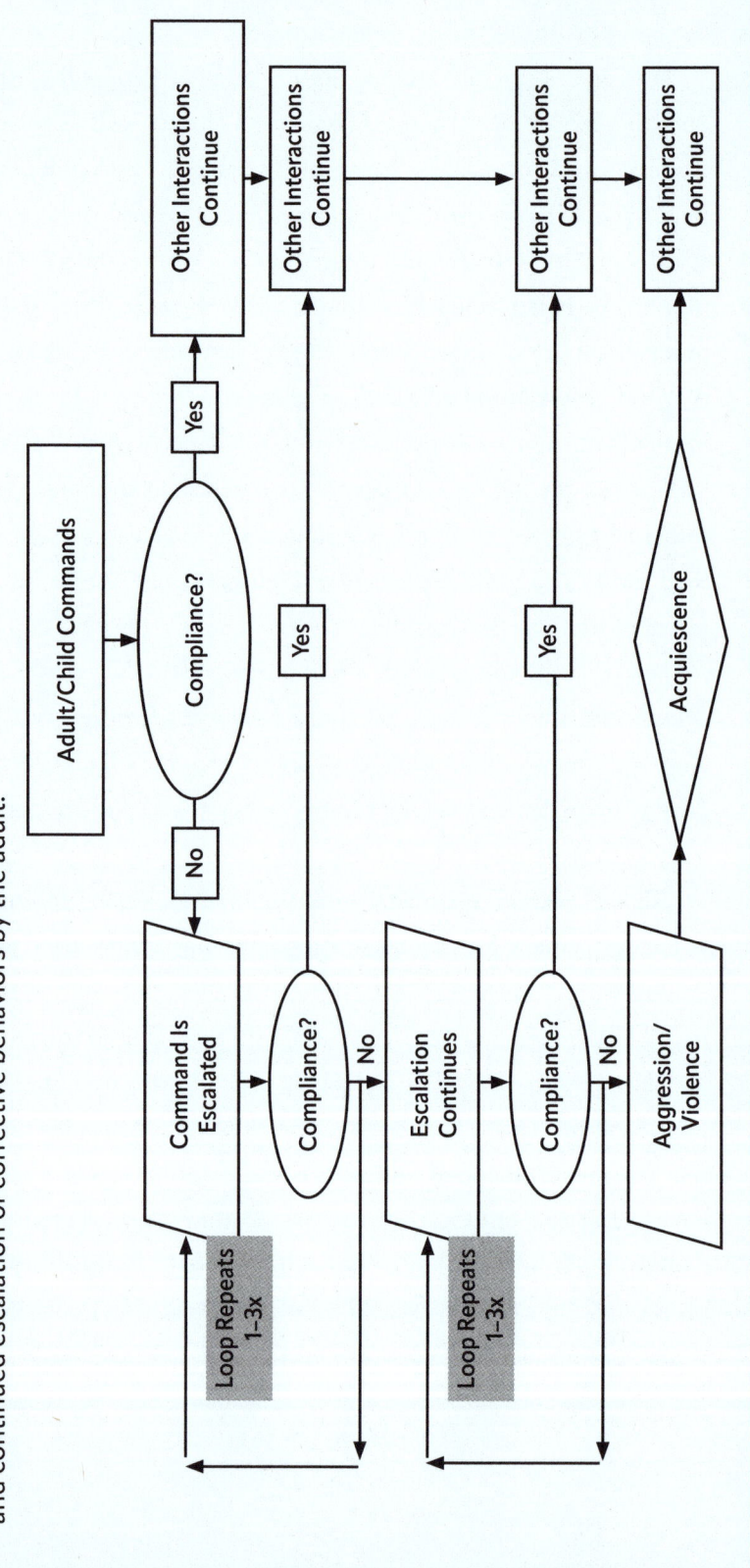

Intervening in the Coercion Cycle

Smith and colleagues (2014) identified that when children are between the ages of two and five, the first clues about potential disruptive behaviors can be observed by detecting the coercion cycle within the family. If these dynamics can be identified, then parents, caregivers, teachers, and providers can intervene early enough to reduce the coercion cycle and dramatically curb disruptive behaviors, as shown in the following example about my son William.

William was a very precocious young child but very quick to anger. He began speaking earlier than our other children and wanted to be considered a grown-up. When he was three, we started having him do chores. He was responsible for putting his clean clothes away after they had been folded. Many times, my wife and I would find clothes stuffed under his bed, behind a chair, or on the closet floor. While we attempted to teach him how to put his clothes away properly, at some point he began to escalate. Gradually, we got tired of his angry outbursts and stopped holding him accountable for his chore. By the time he was five, he was beginning to use anger and escalation to get out of almost everything. If we told him to put away his shoes or to stop hitting his sibling, he would yell at us and get us engaged in a battle of wills until we eventually gave in and went to take care of our other children or do some household task. William had mastered using the coercion cycle to evade responsibility and consequences.

One day, as I was explaining the coercion cycle to a client, I realized how much William had been using it on me. I was determined to use the skills I had learned and advocated for my clients to use to help my own family. That weekend, I decided to implement one of the interventions I teach my clients (see *Effective Commands* in chapter 7). Our family had planned to see a movie at the theater. William loved going to the theater. He relished the big bucket of buttery popcorn and the giant screen. It was one of his favorite activities. We told all our children that to go to the movies, everyone had to do one chore. We assigned the chores to each of them and set out to get ready for the movie. As I inspected each of their chores, I mentally prepared myself for the explosion I predicted would come from William. I warned my wife about what I was going to do and started up the stairs to check William's job. As I opened the door to his bedroom, it was plain that he had not completed his chore. We had tasked him with picking up his toys and making his bed, a job that should have taken him three to five minutes to complete. Toys littered the floor, and William was reading a book on his unmade bed.

I said in a firm, kind voice, "William, the movie starts soon. We need to leave in five minutes to get there on time. When you finish your room, we can leave."

He looked up at me and said, "Okay." Then he turned and kept reading his book. I didn't say anything else, just sat on the rocking chair and waited. As I waited, William began to squirm a bit in his seat. He was not expecting me to sit and watch him clean. Five minutes passed, and my wife shouted that it was time to go. William smiled, stood up, grabbed his coat, and walked toward the bedroom door.

"Where do you think you're going?" I asked. "You still haven't cleaned your room."

"Mom said it's time to go. We can't miss the movie. I'll clean it when I get home," he replied.

In a twist he was not prepared for, I called my wife on my cell phone and said, "William still isn't finished with his chore. Why don't you drive the van with the other kids, and we will meet you after William has finished."

As soon as I said this, William blew up. "WHAT? You can't do that! We HAVE to go with the family. We won't be able to get any popcorn."

I calmly replied, "William, I know you want to go to the movie, and I want you to go to the movie. Unfortunately, you chose not to do your chore, and when you chose not to do your chore, you chose not to go to the movie with the family. We can join them as soon as you are finished."

He looked at me in shock. He couldn't understand how or why I suddenly cared about his room. He proceeded to pick up his toys and started throwing them at me. I remained seated in the chair, having prepared myself for this explosion. I was determined to wait him out, and he was determined to win this battle. As the time ticked by, I occasionally reminded William that we still could join the family and would only miss the first 5, 10, 20, or 30 minutes of the movie. He would alternate between screaming about how horrible of a father I was and how much he hated me and sitting on his bed reading his book. Throughout this time, I was seated on a chair in front of the bedroom door to ensure he couldn't leave, and I alternated between reading my own books, emotion coaching his frustrations, or listening to music. Eventually, two hours passed, and I was still sitting on the chair, and he was still trying to escalate to get out of his room.

When he heard my wife and his siblings come into the house through the garage, he dissolved into tears and wailed; he had missed the whole movie. He escalated even further at this point and began throwing his mattress off the bed and tearing off his sheets and blankets. By this time, his bedroom was way worse than it had been when

I originally asked him to clean it. At this realization, he became even more upset and aggressive toward me. I was just as determined to hold my boundary and ensure the coercion cycle was eliminated.

Finally, five hours after I originally sat down in his room, William looked at me, said he was sorry, and started to clean up his room. It took him 30 minutes to completely clean his room. After it was cleaned, I thanked him and praised him for the work he had completed, and we joined the rest of the family downstairs for dinner. This instance was the first of many such incidents where I had to pick my battle and stick to my plan. While I haven't been perfect at not backing down, I have never again had to wait him out that long.

William, now a teenager, has told me that after that experience (and a few others like it), he realized that I would never give in. When he sees me get comfortable, he knows his battle is already lost. Had this change not happened for William at age five, I would have a much harder time getting him to comply, especially now that he is four inches taller than me.

Unfortunately, if this cycle is not interrupted soon enough, it becomes an entrenched dynamic, and significant changes occur within the child and caregiver. In particular, five emotional, cognitive, and behavioral changes are hypothesized to happen when the coercion cycle is allowed to persist (Patterson & Forgatch, 2010). These changes likely contribute to increased resistance to change, which limits the success of interventions. The five changes are (1) overly inclusive classification, (2) negative attribution, (3) punishment acceleration, (4) nonresponsiveness to positive social stimuli, and (5) emotion dysregulation. I discuss these five changes in further detail here.

First, families steeped in coercion tend to overly classify behaviors as defiant or delinquent, which often leads to harsher punishments and a degradation of the relationship between the adult and child. Second, these families tend to assign negative attribution to everything the child does and are unable to identify any positive traits about the child. Gottman (2011) would call this contempt. Naturally, the next change is acceleration in punishment. When adults are unable to see any positives in a child and are quick to classify behaviors as defiant, punishments tend to follow quickly. This tends to look like a quick succession of demands and corrections by adults before many children are even able to process the instruction. Fourth, children stuck in the coercion cycle stop responding to positive praise, social interactions, or reinforcement, which can lead them to seek out deviant peer groups where they are more likely to feel accepted. Finally, when coercion dynamics are fully entrenched in the system, emotion dysregulation takes place in both the children and adults involved, leading to quick escalation of negative interactions and a cascade of emotional reactivity between the adult and the child. Each phase of treatment explained in this book aims to address these changes that take place due to entrenched coercive family dynamics.

To help parents better understand the changes that take place from continued use of the coercion cycle, we can compare it to the gradual shift from seeing a person live and in color to only seeing a black-and-white photo of that person. The change is gradual, but at some point, how the child is viewed becomes static, like a photograph. For example, the first change in the cycle (*overly inclusive classification*) causes a slight tint or contrast change in the hues of color seen. While not fully black and white, the color of the image of the child is skewed so that parents see more reds, greens, or blues. Here, there is still time to intervene by simply adjusting a few settings. However, as the coercion cycle continues, the sharpness begins to fade, leading to a *negative attribution* of the child's behavior. As the rest of the changes accumulate—from *punishment acceleration* to *nonresponsiveness to positive social stimuli*, and eventually to *emotion dysregulation*—all color has faded. Now the image of the child, as well as the child's image of their parents or other adults, is seen only in black-and-white terms. There is no depth to the view of one another's personalities, just a static facsimile.

It's as if a series of filters have been layered over the photo, further distorting the child. The ISPT treatment described in this book essentially removes those filters, one by one, until the original photo is recognized for the imitation it is, and the child can be seen again. In the next section, I provide an overview of this treatment by walking you through each component of the BISON acronym that represents the five phases of treatment. Subsequent chapters expand on these components in greater detail.

Integrative Systemic Play Therapy: An Overview

Before using the interventions in the ISPT approach, it is important to assess each family system to identify the child's main temperament traits, determine how entrenched the coercion cycle is, and explore how the caregivers view the child and the behaviors. After your initial observation, it should be pretty clear how deeply the family is entrenched in the coercion cycle and which intervention would be most helpful at the start. Once you determine this, the BISON phases of treatment address each of the relational system changes that occur from continuous use of the coercion cycle:

- Bio-emotion regulation (emotion dysregulation)
- Individual play (nonresponsiveness to positive social stimuli)
- Successful communication (punishment acceleration)
- Organized play (negative attribution)
- Nurturing play (overly inclusive classification)

As a note, it is not always necessary to start intervening with the bio-emotion regulation phase, provided that the child and family already know how to regulate their emotions and don't experience emotional flooding. The assessment results will guide your approach, which may be to begin with a different phase or a combination of phases. Once the family completes treatment, as evidenced by reductions in the coercion cycle and successful reversal of relational system changes, it is best to regularly check in with the family to sustain progress.

Phase B: Bio-Emotion Regulation (Emotion Dysregulation)

When the coercion cycle is deeply entrenched in the adult-child relationship, both the child and adult experience changes to their ability to calm down, they escalate more quickly, and they explode emotionally more often. If the relational system has experienced this transformation, adults must have a good understanding of the factors that interfere with their ability to regulate their emotions and behaviors. This is crucial for the other phases to work. It's also important to educate children about their own regulatory functioning. When they discover that they have greater power over their bodies than they realize, it can change the dynamic of how they respond to adults who are unable to regulate themselves.

The bio-emotion regulation phase is all about teaching the adults and child about emotion regulation. I use a variety of tools to accomplish this, including HRV biofeedback, play-based techniques, and mindfulness. The goal is to help them gain a little bit of regulatory functioning before moving into other phases of intervention. They don't have to be perfect to move to the next phase, but if they are unable to regulate themselves at all or have significant difficulties doing so, other phases are not likely to be successful.

Phase I: Individual Play (Nonresponsiveness to Positive Social Stimuli)

When children don't respond to positive reinforcements, positive peer associations, or rewards, it is likely because they have experienced significant use of the coercion cycle. The changes in the child and family may not be to the extent that emotion dysregulation is occurring, but they are no longer responding to positive social interactions. The individual play phase builds responsiveness to positive social stimuli by using aspects of CCPT. The goal is to allow the child to experience full acceptance of who they are, without the expectation to be anything else, by an authority figure. The therapist provides a space where the child can experience a relationship characterized by unconditional positive regard without fear of reprisal or correction (i.e., noncontingent interactions). If the child (or associated adult) is not yet experiencing emotion dysregulation, this intervention phase can prevent it.

Phase S: Successful Communication (Punishment Acceleration)

When the coercion cycle occurs to the point that adults are more likely to punish with harsh punishments for minor infractions (think "three strikes" or "zero tolerance"), children begin to experience less drive to obey commands and requests. They start to see each request as an ultimatum, choosing instead to express their individuality, which is then experienced as defiance. The successful communication phase shocks the interactions in the system and creates mild confusion in the child because their behavior is not eliciting the same response. This disorientation permits both the adult and child to put aside predetermined notions of how interactions will be and allows them to rebuild their relationship. This, in turn, increases the chance for the child to exhibit obedience and compliance. When combined with praise and noncontingent interactions, the coercion cycle stops gaining ground.

Phase O: Organized Play (Negative Attribution)

As you've learned, negative attribution means that adults attribute destructive origins to a child's actions, sometimes thinking that nothing can be done for their child. Organized play, a form of directive play therapy, creates a neutral atmosphere for the child to be who they are, combined with direct instructions to help adults discover who the child is. When the child is seen for who they really are, the adult is more likely to see them in a positive light, giving them the benefit of the doubt to other actions outside the playroom. In addition to creating a neutral atmosphere, this phase allows the adult and child to self-identify problematic communication or behavior patterns. An example of an intervention from this phase is parent-child LEGO® play: The child leads the LEGO building by instructing the parent from behind a cardboard wall. The parent and child must use positive communication patterns to succeed. You'll learn more about strategic LEGO building in chapter 8.

Phase N: Nurturing Play (Overly Inclusive Classification)

While unlikely, if a family seeks therapy at the very beginning stages of the coercion cycle, that means the only observable change to the parent-child relationship is overly inclusive classification. In other words, parents are quicker to see behaviors as "problematic" rather than typical child behavior. When adults see their child as only performing badly, there is less opportunity for the child to return to favor. Nurturing play counters this change by cutting the coercion cycle out of the picture. The provider teaches the adult how to respond to problematic behavior without using the coercion cycle. The nurturing play phase also allows the parent to see the child's behavior from a neutral and noncoercive framework.

Troubleshooting, Graduation, and Maintenance

Throughout ISPT treatment, the provider keeps tabs on everyone's progress in the child's micro- and mesosystems: the parents' marriage and parenting skills, the teacher's attentiveness to using skills in the classroom, the school's willingness to address systemic concerns, and the child's possible recidivism. By the time all necessary phases are completed, and the parents and child are reporting positive results, titrating graduation can begin. I usually begin by scheduling clients every other week. After at least two months without backtracking, we go to once a month. After about three months of successful appointments, we meet on a six-month basis. I find it best not to go more than six months without contact to ensure that I continue a therapeutic relationship with the family. If difficulties arise, I can address them far more quickly this way than if negative changes progressively build up due to the family's continued return to the coercion cycle. At the end of this chapter, you can find a *BISON Treatment Overview* handout that summarizes the entire ISPT approach for parents.

Key Takeaway

DBDs result from a complex interplay of various biological, environmental, familial, and emotional factors. Without an integrative systemic approach, many children are left undertreated, and the root cause of the disruptive behavior is not addressed. By using an integration of behavioral, systemic, biological, and emotional theories, a more comprehensive approach is possible.

CLIENT HANDOUT

BISON Treatment Overview

This treatment is designed to quickly and effectively treat the underlying factors that contribute to disruptive behavioral disorders like oppositional defiant disorder (ODD), conduct disorder, and disruptive mood dysregulation disorder (DMDD). Each phase can be completed on its own or in combination with other phases. As I work with your family and other treatment partners (e.g., schools, justice departments, extended family), you will be involved every step of the way. If you have any questions during any of the phases or during the treatment, please do not hesitate to ask me. I want to make sure you understand this process completely. Only through open collaboration and communication will we achieve the best outcomes for your family.

Assessment:
Before treatment can begin, I will conduct a thorough assessment of your family. During this process, I will ask questions about your child's developmental history, when the disruptive behaviors began, and how your family functions. I will then have several meetings with just your child alone, with your child and siblings if necessary, and with the whole family. Once the assessment sessions are completed, I can tell you which phase of the treatment will be best to start with.

Phase B: Bio-Emotion Regulation:
This phase is all about teaching you and your child how to better regulate your emotions. I use a variety of tools to accomplish this, including biofeedback, different play-based techniques, and mindfulness. The goal is to help you have the foundational skills for other phases of treatment to work.

Phase I: Individual Play:
The overall goal of the interventions in this phase is to allow your child to experience what it's like to be fully accepted for who they are. In our sessions together, I will provide a space where your child can feel totally accepted without fear of reprisal or correction. Then you will be given the same skills to accomplish this at home. When your child experiences unconditional positive regard in this way, it increases the chance of behavior change and better compliance.

Phase S: Successful Communication:

With the foundation laid from the other two phases, the interventions in this phase rewire your family's communication systems to reduce the coercion cycle and increase behavioral compliance and cooperation. When combined with the unconditional positive regard from the previous phase, the coercion cycle stops gaining ground.

Phase O: Organized Play:

This phase continues to build the relationships formed during the previous phases by creating a neutral atmosphere where the child is accepted, while directly intervening with problematic behaviors. It also allows you and your child to self-identify problematic communication or behavior patterns, which increases your ability to intervene on your own.

Phase N: Nurturing Play:

This final phase of treatment empowers you as the main change agent in your child's life. This happens as I teach you how to continue to respond to problematic behavior without using the coercion cycle.

Troubleshooting, Graduation, and Maintenance:

Throughout treatment, there may arise issues or concerns that could slow down the progress of change. This may include the need for individual therapy for one or both parents, couples therapy, parent training, or collaborative care with treatment partners. Anytime these concerns are identified, I will let you know, and we will work together to ensure a quick resolution. Graduation takes place when all phases are completed successfully. After graduation, we will schedule follow-up sessions every four to six months to ensure continued progress.

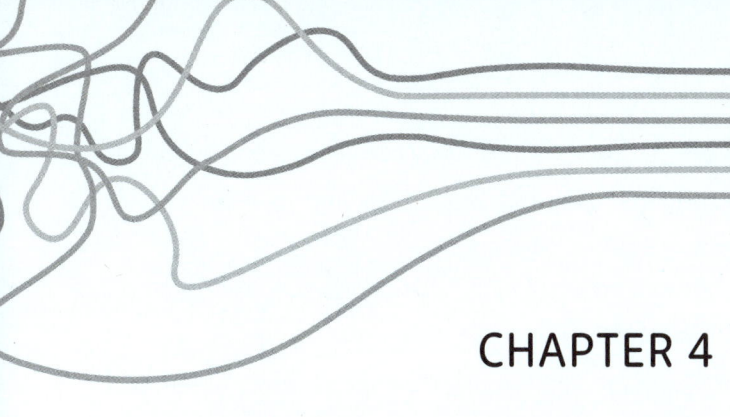

CHAPTER 4

Assessment: Identifying and Tracking Coercion

Effective interventions require thorough assessments, which should include a semi-structured interview, empirically supported measurements, and direct observation of systemic dynamics. While I use several empirically supported procedures, my assessments are largely a result of my own clinical experience in identifying how best to catch things more quickly at the beginning. Assessments can take one session or five, depending on the severity of the presenting problem, as well as the cooperation of the caregivers and clients involved. It's important to take as much time as you need because the assessment will give you a more accurate understanding of how rooted the coercion cycle is within the family. You must establish a systemic viewpoint from the beginning so that everyone recognizes their role in the treatment process. This systemic viewpoint begins with the intake session.

Intake Session

Intake looks similar for most families. Generally, if the child is 12 or younger, the first sessions are with the caregivers, and the child is absent. I only include the child if the reported behavior seems severe, and the child is at least 10. Otherwise, I meet with only the active caregivers in the first session. An active caregiver is anyone who plays at least a 45 percent parenting role in the child's life.

Having all active caregivers present in the first session establishes the reality that the provider is not just going to "fix" the child while the parents drop them off at the office but that the provider will work closely with everyone throughout the treatment. This establishes the mentality that you are creating a treatment team, and all active caregivers are an important aspect of that team. Meeting with all active caregivers is a tall order for many of today's families and therapists and may often mean that you need to be available in the evenings or early mornings.

Standard Intake Procedure

After the consent paperwork, we first focus on reframing the concerns from a relational perspective—meaning that interventions will use the relationships (of the child to the therapist, and of the child to the parent) for healing and reducing behavior problems—then on understanding the history of the problem and what has been tried before. Usually I begin with something like:

> *I am trained as a family therapist, which means that I will be looking at the interactions among the whole family. Although I will see your child individually at times, I will always be considering what is going on with your child and how it impacts the family—as well as what is going on in the family and how it impacts your child. This will require that I have sessions with you as parents, with or without your child and with or without their siblings, and with the whole family. Working with the family this way increases the success of therapy and speeds up the recovery process.*
>
> *[I add this if the child already has a DBD diagnosis.] The research says family therapy and parent training are essential for a positive outcome. We will meet in three to four sessions to discuss what that will look like specifically, but between now and then, I'll send you some resources to help you understand my approach and recognize what you can do to improve the process. My goal is to teach you the skills and tools you need so you won't need to continue coming to therapy once our work is complete or at least will only need to occasionally consult with me.*

Providing this acknowledgment at the beginning of the therapy relationship helps caregivers understand that you will need their involvement. Remember that therapists who are not trained in family systems therapy often purposely exclude parents from treatment due to their philosophical beliefs about who the client is and what creates presenting problems in people's lives. However, as I stated in chapter 3, ISPT is a systemic approach that requires a systemic viewpoint. For this reason, I provide more intentional and upfront systemic reframes throughout each phase of treatment to remind caregivers of this viewpoint, but starting gently helps increase their acceptance of the approach. I find that many parents report back that they are glad to be included in the process.

During the rest of the meeting, I ask some iterations of the questions on the *Therapist Intake Guide* to gather history, educate parents about the etiology of DBDs, and reframe the problem into a systemic perspective. Another option is to use the following *Biological and Environmental Factors Flowchart*. Begin by explaining that there are three environmental factors that affect the development of DBDs: biological, familial, and societal. The arrows in the image depict the potential directionality of these various factors. For example, family and societal environmental factors could impact the child and family throughout the entire developmental trajectory of the child and family. The arrows in the genetic and prenatal boxes explain the directionality of these factors on the newly forming child. The rest of the arrows show mutual directionality (between parents and children) during the major stages of development that may increase the likelihood of a DBD.

Some factors, such as genetics and epigenetics, are beyond our control, so it is important to help parents understand how these factors play into the developmental track of their child. For example, maternal trauma, mental health concerns, and family history can all impact hormones during pregnancy. Even a father's family history of trauma and stress can play an important role in the development of sperm. In addition, a family's country of origin and the experiences of violence or oppression they experienced in that country, all of which are largely uncontrollable and unavoidable, play an important role in DBD development.

Moving into the prenatal history needs to be done carefully and strategically. At no point during the intake do you want either parent to feel like they are solely responsible for their child's behavior. This is where asking questions about pregnancy is a bit less direct but obtains the necessary information. It is also just as important to identify and ask questions about the current family environment. You need enough information to know whether the parents need additional supports like couples therapy, parent training, individual therapy, or executive functioning coaching.

This flowchart allows you to keep track of all these variables and identify the best place to begin treatment. It is *not* a diagnostic tool and shouldn't be given to parents without explaining how the image is helpful in developing a treatment plan. The key takeaway for the graphic and these precursors is that ISPT considers the contexts of the family and is nonblaming. At no time are the parents, child, or family at fault. Sometimes, it is just an unfortunate mixture of nature, nurture, and environment that creates the perfect storm.

THERAPIST HANDOUT

Biological and Environmental Factors Flowchart

FAMILIAL ENVIRONMENTAL FACTORS

Caregivers
- Relationship discord/stability
- Alliance of parenting style
- Work stress
- Financial stability
- Extended family support
- Presence of harsh discipline
- Supervision of child(ren)
- Consistency of discipline
- Coercion cycle dynamics
- Conflict management
- Abusive relationship(s)

PRENATAL

INFANCY

Caregivers
- Mental health
- Attachment style
- Sleep quality

Child
- Temperament
- Physical health
- Sleep quality

EARLY CHILDHOOD

Caregivers
- Emotional regulation
- Stress tolerance
- Sleep quality

Child
- Frustration tolerance
- Delay of gratification
- Sleep quality

MIDDLE CHILDHOOD

Caregivers
- Tolerance of social connection
- Physical involvement with child
- Sleep quality

Child
- Cognitive abilities
- Social skill development
- Emotional regulation
- Sleep quality

ADOLESCENCE

Caregivers
- Tolerance for separation
- Frustration tolerance
- Social support
- Executive functioning skills
- Sleep quality

Child
- Personal confidence
- Social connection (negative vs. positive peer association)
- Timing of puberty entrance
- Sleep quality

BIOLOGICAL FACTORS

EPI/GENETICS

Bio-Mother
- Family history of mental health concerns
- Trauma
- Congenital deficits

Bio-Father
- Family history of mental health concerns
- Trauma
- Congenital deficits

Bio-Mother (Prenatal)
- Exposure to constant stress
- Substance exposure
- Maternal nutrition
- Maternal health
- Development disruptions

SOCIETAL ENVIRONMENTAL FACTORS

Country
- Violence
- Oppression
- Economic instability
- Government instability

Community
- Violence
- SES
- Access to nutrition
- Access to education

School
- Violence
- Negative attribution
- Void of play
- Harsh discipline

Copyright © 2025 Michael R. Whitehead, *Treating Children with Disruptive Behavior Disorders.*
All rights reserved.

THERAPIST HANDOUT

Therapist Intake Guide

The following questions are a general guide to ensure that you get enough history in the intake session to get an extensive systemic view of the family. You may use any, all, or none of these questions depending on your clinical judgment and the client in front of you.

General Questions:
- What brings you in today?
- What prompted the decision to seek therapy now?
- What have you tried in the past to overcome these concerns?
- What do you have as natural supports?
- Have you seen a medical doctor for these concerns?
- Have you had any blood tests regarding these concerns?

Child of Birth:
- When you found out you were pregnant with this child, what do you remember feeling?
- How was the pregnancy?
    - Were there any difficulties?
    - Were there any complications?
    - What did you find most enjoyable about this pregnancy?
    - Was the child carried to full term?
    - How did labor start?
- How was labor and delivery?
    - Were there any difficulties?
    - Were there any complications?
    - What did you find most enjoyable about the labor and delivery?
    - Was everyone present that you wanted to be?
        - If not, who wasn't there?
        - How did you feel about their absence?
        - How do you feel about it now?

- How long were you in the hospital after delivery?
- How was your experience in the hospital?
- Did you breastfeed?
    - How did you decide to breastfeed or not?
    - How do you feel about this decision?
    - How was the transition to breastfeeding?
    - What was most enjoyable about breastfeeding?
    - What was least enjoyable?
    - How long did you breastfeed?
    - What went into the decision to stop?

Child of Adoption:
- When did you decide to adopt?
- What were some of the reasons for adopting?
- How was the adoption process?
- How old was the child when you adopted them?
- What do you know about their biological parents and family?
- Did they spend time in foster care or an orphanage?
- What do you know about their time spent in foster care or orphan care?

General Milestone Questions:
- When did this child start crawling?
- When did they say their first word?
- When did they start walking?
- When did they start speaking in sentences?
- If there are siblings, how did the child adjust to the siblings? How did the siblings adjust to the child?
- When did you start noticing the concerns you are wanting us to work on?
- What alerted you most about these concerns?
- What have you tried to fix them?
- What has worked?
- What hasn't worked?

Intake Procedure for Clients Age 13 and Older

For identified patients 13 and older, the intake procedure includes the child. I don't ask "What brings you in?" when both the parents and the child are present so that the child doesn't feel blamed. I go over my typical informed consent, adding information on the importance of adolescent privacy during therapy and asking the parents to honor this privacy. I then ask to meet with the parents for about 20 minutes while the child waits in the lobby. I get a quick overview of the child's developmental trajectory and history of the problem. Then I meet with the child alone for about 20 more minutes to start building rapport. I ask questions about their likes, dislikes, hobbies, and family environment. I ask why they think their parents are having them come to therapy. If I have time left, I will meet with the parents and child together to talk about the structure of the next few sessions and schedule the parent follow-up session.

I also follow the 13 and older intake procedure when the child is at least 10 years old and the parents report that the child has engaged in the following behaviors to any degree:

- Suspended or kicked out of school at least once
- Involved with the juvenile justice system
- Deliberately and flauntingly broken the law
- Involved in gang-like behaviors or systems
- Deliberately, and repeatedly, physically hurt a family member

It is vitally important to begin the rapport-building process with children who have severe destructive behaviors such as these. These parents and their children often feel hopeless. Almost everyone has given up on them, and they believe that there is nothing that can be done to help them. The parents are socially isolated because of their child's behavior, and if they are still romantically involved, their relationship is often hanging by a thread. If there are siblings, they have been terrorized by the identified patient's behavior, and they likely want nothing to do with the therapy process. Any sense of blame on the parents or release of responsibility on the child is going to drive these families away from treatment. The delicate balance of multidirectional partiality is essential for these families.

Joining Sessions

The next three to four sessions continue the assessment process while building rapport between the provider and the family. With minor exceptions, I structure the sessions as outlined below to maximize the transition from an individual focus to a systemic focus.

Child-Only Sessions

Immediately following the intake session, I tend to meet with only the identified patient (i.e., the child). Typically, for children between 18 months and about nine years old, I use CCPT (see chapter 6). I identify the major play themes that the child exhibits in the session and distinguish between active and passive defiance. A child who runs into the room and disregards my presence and the first three rules of the playroom is more likely to be actively defiant. A child who looks like they are trying to follow the rules but doesn't respond when a limit is set or responds with extreme hesitation is likely passively defiant. I'm looking for how long it takes the child to acclimate to my presence and my boundaries. I count in my head to identify how long it takes for a child to comply with my request. I may time them to see how long they can sit still or stay focused on one task or area of the playroom. I usually end this session by speaking with one or both parents to share my observations and prep them for the third or fourth session, when I will see them without the child.

The second session is similar, but I involve a little more directive play therapy. I may use a game like UNO, chess, checkers, or Perfection to observe how they engage in cooperative play and whether they tend to cheat or are willing to play according to the rules of the game. Again, I'm paying attention to the major themes present in the play and how quickly they may or may not respond to my commands. I may use tricky puzzles that appear simple or have missing pieces to see how the child responds to frustration-inducing tasks. I want to see how much regulatory capability they have and whether they can tolerate frustration well. If I have enough information, I will fill out the *Temperament Traits* worksheet from chapter 3 and keep it in the file to show the parents in the next session. Here are some examples of how I rate the child's temperament depending on their behavior in the playroom with me:

1. **Activity level**
    a. Hyperactive: The child is all over the playroom and seems to be "bouncing" off the walls. They are constantly talking or playing.

b. **Mellow:** The child seems to have low energy and sticks to one or two areas in the playroom.

2. **Biological regularity**
   a. **Regular:** The child seems to be hungry at the appropriate times, uses the bathroom without assistance, and appears alert. Or the parents reported during the intake that there were no interruptions in the child's developmental milestones.
   b. **Irregular:** The child seems hungry soon after eating, looks tired at unexpected times, or requires a parent's assistance to use the restroom. Or the parents reported during the intake significant concerns with toileting and feeding issues.

3. **Approach or withdrawal**
   a. **Approachable:** The child appears to be friendly and eager to get to know me. They do not hesitate to enter the room without their parents. Their parents seem like an afterthought.
   b. **Distant:** The child is shy and unwilling to engage with me in the lobby or go into my playroom without their parents.

4. **Adaptability**
   a. **Flexible:** The child is unfazed with changes that take place in the playroom. I set a limit, and they are easily able to follow that limit, even if it seems illogical.
   b. **Inflexible:** The child is rigid in their expectations. Any deviation from those expectations creates dysregulation.

5. **Sensory threshold**
   a. **Hypersensitive:** The child's behavior seems to intensify around bright lights, loud noises, or physical touch.
   b. **Hyposensitive:** The child doesn't respond typically to common sensory disturbances (e.g., loud noises, bright lights).

6. **Intensity of reaction**
   a. **Active:** The child reacts to changes or differences in the playroom with extremes. They escalate quickly and intensely.
   b. **Passive:** The child is unresponsive to changes or differences in the playroom. They are muted in their response.

7. **Mood**
    a. Positive: The child has a generally pleasing demeanor and appears content.
    b. Negative: The child generally appears to be negative, muted, angry, or sullen.

8. **Distractibility**
    a. Distractible: The child tends to float all over the playroom as if they cannot remain focused on any one thing at a time.
    b. Focused: The child tends to stay focused on tasks throughout the playroom and is not easily distracted.

9. **Persistence or attention span**
    a. Persistent: The child remains determined to accomplish a frustration-inducing task until they can complete it or until time runs out.
    b. Nonpersistent: The child gets easily discouraged and gives up quickly on new tasks.

I end the session by debriefing the parents on our session and typically assign them homework, which can involve asking them to think about their child at a younger age or having them identify other systems (e.g., school, daycare, probation) that may need to be involved in the treatment, to prepare them for their parent-only session.

Parent-Only Sessions

If I have enough information to formulate a treatment plan, typically after three to four child-only sessions, I will start meeting with only parents or other caregivers and let them know what I have found out about their child. I will explain which phase of the treatment we may need to start with and give an estimate of how long they can expect therapy to last. I use the rest of this session to introduce them to the *Temperament Traits* worksheet. After giving each parent a copy of this worksheet, I have them examine each of the nine temperament traits and put an *X* on the side of the sheet they think matches their child. I will then take out my copy of the worksheet and put all our worksheets on a table facing the parents.

I use the information from the worksheet to explain how their child may have helped create the coercion cycle in their family and explain the coercion cycle in detail, including how these nine temperament traits reinforce the cycle and incite disruptive behaviors. I then ask the parents to identify themselves on these nine traits to better understand what they bring to the dynamic of coercion. Some parents have questions about the worksheet and may require support to fill it out. Use the previous descriptions of the temperament traits if parents need assistance, as well as examples from your experiences with the child to help clarify your choices. Having this worksheet filled out before this session as a direct result of your observations and experience with their child will help them understand that you "see" their child and, consequently, them.

In the following section, I provide a clinical example of the assessment process—beginning with the child-only sessions and proceeding all the way through the initial parent-only session—to illustrate how this looks in practice.

Case Example: *Kehlani*
Child-Only Session 1

My playroom is typically set up the same way for each child. Each toy is placed on a shelf with similar toys—for instance, aggressive animals (e.g., snakes, alligators, lions, tigers) are all on one shelf, while docile animals (e.g., cows, chickens, dogs) are on another. This way, when the child enters the room, they are greeted with an organized, calm, and deliberate setup. I also set it up so that toys are typically along the wall and there is a large space in the center of the room, allowing the child to bring the toys into the middle and play with them at their choosing. My room also has a couch with a bunch of pillows that children like to use to create forts or jump on when they need to expend energy.

This was how the room was set up when I first met with Kehlani, a small seven-year-old girl who came to therapy for disruptive behaviors occurring at home and school. She had been expelled from her elementary school due to unmanageable behaviors and constantly hit her mother at home. Kehlani looked shocked with joy when she walked into my office and saw all the toys at her disposal.

I introduced the playroom to Kehlani in the same way I do with every child: "Kehlani, in the playroom, you can play with any toys in a lot of the ways you want to. There are only three rules: I'm not for hurting, you are not for hurting, and the toys are not for breaking." I waited for a response, a nod, or some sort of acknowledgment of what I had said, but she didn't offer anything. She just looked at me, then at the door, then back toward the toys in the room. Taking this as acceptance of the playroom rules, I slowly closed the door, and the session began.

Looking toward me, she put her arm out, swiped her arm across the top of the toy shelf, and waited for me to say something as toys crashed to the ground.

I reflected her actions by saying, "You didn't want the toys on the shelf, so you swiped them onto the ground."

A little bit taken aback by my response, she swiped the second shelf with a little more vigor, which sent toys flying across the room. I again reflected her actions and waited for her next response.

Not getting any angry or reactive response from me, Kehlani ran toward my couch. As she climbed atop the couch, she began grabbing the cushions and pillows and hurtling them toward me. In my attempt to limit her behavior to keep myself and her safe, I opened my mouth to say, "Kehlani, remember I'm not for hurting and you are not for hurting..." but before I could get her name out, she started yelling. She yelled so loud that I could barely hear myself. As I closed my mouth, her yelling stopped. When I attempted again to set the limit, her yelling started again.

Throughout the pillow throwing, I was catching pillows and doing my best to keep my cool; Kehlani was observing me. She was tracking my movements almost as much as I was tracking hers. For example, I noticed she was breathing more heavily the longer the session went on. She would also modulate her voice according to my position in the room. The closer I got to her, the louder she yelled. The closer I got to the door, the quieter she got.

This continued for 30 minutes as I contemplated how to tell her our session time was up. I was afraid that if I tried to open my mouth to issue the lead time warning about the end of the session, she would just yell. This was our first session, and I didn't want to yell just to be heard to get her to leave the office. I also didn't want to open the door and risk her running out without me properly closing the session. I was worried that she would be able to outlast my 45-minute session, which would not be good for reducing the coercion cycle.

As we reached the 40-minute mark, Kehlani plopped down and sat on the couch. She looked around the room and saw some games on a shelf she hadn't yet swiped. I tracked her eyes and said, "You see the games over there. Did you want to play a game?"

Kehlani excitedly said, "You have UNO, my favorite game. Can we play that?"

Looking at the clock, I noticed we were out of time. "You'd like to play UNO. Unfortunately, we only have five minutes left of our session. We can play one game of Connect Four, or you can leave early. Which do you choose?"

She was upset with the time limit and my boundary. "I said I want to play UNO."

I attempted to empathize with her by saying, "You are upset that I said we can't play UNO. I know you would like to play UNO. We just don't have enough time for that.

Here is Connect Four." I set it on the table and continued, "We can play one round of this game, or you can leave the session early. Which do you choose?"

With that, she stared me in the eyes, swiped the Connect Four game off the table, yanked the door open, and stomped out of the room.

I gently stepped around the toys on the ground and followed Kehlani out of my office. Thankfully, Kehlani's grandparents were in the lobby with her parents. Kehlani rushed toward them and said, "I never want to come back to this stupid place again. He wouldn't even let me play UNO."

I smiled at Kehlani and said, "Thank you for coming today. I hope you choose to come back next week. I'd love to play UNO next time you are here." I then looked up at her mom and dad and said, "Can I speak with you two for a few minutes? It's okay if Kehlani and her grandparents leave; I just want to explain what we did today."

The parents arranged for Kehlani and her grandparents to go home and followed me to my office.

Mom gasped when she saw the floor. "What on earth happened in here?"

Dad's face started turning red. "I'm going to get Kehlani to come back here to clean up this mess."

I caught Dad's attention and said, "Please don't. I want to go over with you what happened here and explain my process a little bit. It's important that Kehlani not clean anything up, at least right now."

Looking a little embarrassed and somewhat dejected, they both reluctantly walked around the toys on the ground toward the couch. As they sat down, I noticed that their eyes were looking all over the ground. I could tell that they were trying to understand how any of this was therapeutic.

"Kehlani is a very persistent person," I started. "She can stick to one thing for quite a bit of time. She is also very determined. When she wants to do something, she doesn't stop until she is good and ready."

"Tell me about it!" Dad exclaimed. "She's been that way since birth."

"So, you're telling us you can't do anything to help," Mom blurted out unexpectedly.

"Oh, I didn't say that. I just wanted you to know what happened here. She is extremely determined and observant. I do think there are things I can do that will create more harmony in the home, but the first thing is to recognize that we must use what Kehlani has to our advantage. She is going to test us throughout this process, and we all need to understand what we are bringing to the table," I explained.

I continued, "She doesn't have an endless supply of energy, even if it seems like it. She has limits, and she diverts to other activities when she is exhausted. I will need another session or two to get my bearings straight with her, but I think I know what we have to do. I'd like you both to make sure you can make it to the parent session in about three weeks so we can go over the treatment plan."

"We'll be here; don't worry," Dad stated.

"Great, thanks. Now do either of you have any questions?" I asked.

"Nope, I just hope you know what you are doing," Mom said.

Child-Only Session 2

I heard the yelling in the waiting room during the last few minutes of my session with another client. Kehlani was my next appointment, and I suspected that she was still upset about coming back to my office. Sure enough, when I opened the door, Kehlani was in her mom's arms. Mom was gripping Kehlani around the waist, visibly embarrassed and exasperated but trying to maintain her composure. While her dad was trying to check in, I noticed that he was trying to ignore Kehlani's yelling.

"Kehlani, I'm glad to see you came back," I said, as I greeted the parents and approached her.

She quickly turned her head and buried her face in her mother's shoulder, muffling an exclaimed "NO!" at my approach.

I responded, "It seems like Kehlani doesn't want to come into my office today. Dad, would you like to speak with me for a few minutes while Mom and Kehlani sit in the lobby?"

As Dad turned toward me to give his answer, Kehlani blurted out, "NO! It's MY turn."

Looking surprised, Mom loosened her grip on Kehlani as she wriggled out of her arms and launched herself into my office.

"Okay then!" I remarked enthusiastically. "Looks like I get to meet with Kehlani after all." After closing my door, I said, "Kehlani, last time you were here, you wanted to play a game, but we didn't have time. Would you like to start by playing a game today?" She smiled and nodded her head. "Wonderful! I'd like you to take a seat on my couch and sit quietly for as long as you can. I'll time you, and afterward, we can play the game." She walked to my toy shelf and started dumping the toys on the ground.

As I sat in my chair, I reflected her actions. "You want to put the toys on the ground instead of playing the game."

She proceeded through the room touching shelves and saying, "I'm going to knock these over. Are you going to stop me?"

I repeated, "You want to knock all of those off the shelf."

After about three minutes of this behavior, she sat on the couch and looked straight at me. "Aren't you going to time me?" she asked.

I replied, "Oh, you want me to time you now. You want to play a game after you sit on the couch."

She nodded vigorously.

I said, "Okay, I'm starting the timer now. Sit as still and as quiet . . ."

She interrupted me and said, "I'm ready for the game." She was only able to sit for four seconds. I took note of that and asked her which game she would like to play. She selected UNO.

"Okay, to play a game in my office, we have to follow the rules of the game. Do you know the rules?"

"Yes, DUH!!! I'm not stupid."

"Okay, sometimes people don't know how to play these games, so I wanted to make sure."

"Well, they must be dumb then! Who doesn't know how to play UNO?"

I try to ignore statements like these. When children are accustomed to the coercion cycle, these statements are used to engage adults in debate and to create conflict. Most of the time when adults engage with these statements, the battle has already been lost, and increased escalation is almost a guarantee.

I counted out the cards and asked whether she would like to go first. Without hesitation, she placed her first card down. I placed down a skip card, which led to her saying, "Those cards don't count if it's just two people, so it's my turn."

I put my hand over the card and said, "I know you don't like that I used a skip card, and you would like to not have skip cards used in here. However, if we are going to play the game, we have to play by the rules."

She snatched up the draw pile, threw it at my face, and said, laughing, "52-card pickup!!!" She returned to the couch and started jumping up and down while throwing pillows at me. The remainder of the session was much like the first and ended similarly.

I gave her my first lead time warning by saying, "We only have five minutes left of our time today."

Kehlani continued exploring my room, a bit in shock that I hadn't forced her to clean up the UNO cards.

After a few more minutes, I said, "Kehlani, we only have one minute left." As soon as I said this, she pointed at some Play-Doh on one of my shelves and exclaimed, "Let's play with Play-Doh! I never get to use Play-Doh."

I reminded her that we were out of time, and she said, "I'm not leaving this room until we play with the Play-Doh." I reminded her one more time that our time was up by saying, "Okay Kehlani, we are out of time. You may either walk out, or I will have your dad carry you out." She insisted she wasn't leaving.

Recognizing the importance of following through, I opened the door and called out to her dad. As soon as I opened the door, she shot up out of her seat and walked out. I briefly told the parents I had enough information to meet with them and would only need them present at the next session. Kehlani was starting toward the front office door, and I didn't want to risk her leaving our office without her parents, so I told them I would update them about this session at our parent session. I filled out the *Temperament Traits* worksheet after finishing my case notes and saved it for the following session.

Parent Session

As I prepared for Kehlani's parent session, I made three copies of my filled-out *Temperament Traits* worksheet along with a few blank copies so I could walk Mom and Dad through my observations of Kehlani. When I opened my door to the lobby, I noticed that not only were Kehlani's mom and dad present, but so were her maternal grandparents. Suspecting that they had misunderstood my plan, I looked around for Kehlani. They quickly picked up on my confusion, and Mom remarked, "Oh, sorry, we brought my parents today. We were hoping that they could sit in with us so they can also hear what you have to say. They do a lot of caregiving for Kehlani and wanted to know how they could help. I hope that is okay with you."

I replied, "That's totally fine. In fact, I'm glad you asked them to join you. The more people who join our treatment team, the better chance we have of being successful with Kehlani. Let me go get some extra chairs, and we can all head into my office."

After asking some of my colleagues for a few of their chairs, we entered my office. My portable table was set up in front of the couch with my filled-out *Temperament Traits* worksheet face down on the table and two blank copies face up, positioned where I had assumed the parents would sit. Mom and Grandma took the couch, Dad sat next to Mom in a chair, and Grandpa sat next to Grandma in another chair.

"Had I known you all were coming to today's parent session, I would have had more blank copies so everyone could fill one out. I don't want to use our time making more copies, so let's get started. Mom and Grandma, I would like you two to work together on one sheet, and Dad, if you can come around to sit next to Grandpa, I'd like you to work on a sheet together."

"Sure. What are we supposed to do with this?" asked Dad.

I went over the generalizations of temperament theory and explained the terms listed on the worksheet. "Now, I'd like you to place a mark on the line next to where you feel Kehlani falls with each of these traits."

After they finished, I asked them to compare their results. Their completed worksheets are pictured in the following images.

Mom and Grandma's Completed Worksheet

CLIENT WORKSHEET

Temperament Traits

All children exhibit many of the behavior traits outlined below. Choose one child to evaluate and place an X on the continuum below each trait that most closely matches your experience with this child.

ACTIVITY LEVEL
How energetic is your child during regular day-to-day activities?

X---
Hyperactive (high)   Mellow (low)

BIOLOGICAL REGULARITY
How consistent are your child's eating, sleeping, and toileting habits?

--X
Regular   Irregular

APPROACH OR WITHDRAWAL
How quickly does your child lean into new and unfamiliar circumstances?

--X
Approachable   Distant

ADAPTABILITY
How rigid does your child prefer their routine, schedule, or daily activities?

--X
Flexible   Inflexible

SENSORY THRESHOLD
How intensely does your child experience pain, smell, sound, or other senses?

X---
Hypersensitive   Hyposensitive

INTENSITY OF REACTION
When experiencing difficulties, how strong do they exhibit their response?

X---
Active   Passive

MOOD
What is your child's average attitude emotionally?

--X
Positive   Negative

DISTRACTIBILITY
On average, how attentive is your child?

X---
Distractible   Focused

PERSISTENCE OR ATTENTION SPAN
When faced with a long-term task, how determined is your child?

--X
Persistent   Nonpersistent

Dad and Grandpa's Completed Worksheet

CLIENT WORKSHEET

Temperament Traits

All children exhibit many of the behavior traits outlined below. Choose one child to evaluate and place an X on the continuum below each trait that most closely matches your experience with this child.

ACTIVITY LEVEL
How energetic is your child during regular day-to-day activities?

X---
Hyperactive (high)   Mellow (low)

BIOLOGICAL REGULARITY
How consistent are your child's eating, sleeping, and toileting habits?

-----------------X---------------------------------------
Regular   Irregular

APPROACH OR WITHDRAWAL
How quickly does your child lean into new and unfamiliar circumstances?

---X-------------
Approachable   Distant

ADAPTABILITY
How rigid does your child prefer their routine, schedule, or daily activities?

---X----
Flexible   Inflexible

SENSORY THRESHOLD
How intensely does your child experience pain, smell, sound, or other senses?

---------------------------X-----------------------------
Hypersensitive   Hyposensitive

INTENSITY OF REACTION
When experiencing difficulties, how strong do they exhibit their response?

-----X---
Active   Passive

MOOD
What is your child's average attitude emotionally?

-----------X---
Positive   Negative

DISTRACTIBILITY
On average, how attentive is your child?

-----------------X---------------------------------------
Distractible   Focused

PERSISTENCE OR ATTENTION SPAN
When faced with a long-term task, how determined is your child?

-----X---
Persistent   Nonpersistent

As they compared the marks they had made on the worksheets, they talked about why they had rated Kehlani the way they did. We focused on the observations that were similar at first. Both parents agreed that Kehlani was very hyperactive. They used examples like "She is always on the go" and "We can't ever get her to sit down, even for just a quick second." They both rated her as inflexible and used the example of her not wanting to come back to therapy. She liked her routines and hated that her day was disrupted by having to visit me. They also agreed that Kehlani was reactive. When something didn't go her way, she escalated quickly.

I then asked them to talk about the marks that were not similar. Dad reported that Kehlani was more focused and more persistent than Mom and Grandma had reported, because he said he had seen her stay focused during fishing, an activity that she enjoyed doing with him. I noticed that Mom and Grandma's observations were in the extreme for every temperament trait and asked for their thoughts about this.

Grandma explained, "Well, we see more of her than does either Grandpa or Dad. We do the brunt of the caregiving for Kehlani, and we deal with her explosions and aggressive behavior more than they do."

I looked at Mom, who seemed a bit shutdown and distant. I asked, "What's going on for you, Mom? You look a bit shell-shocked."

"Yeah . . ." Mom started, then said, "Is there anything that can be done for Kehlani? These guys don't seem to see the real her, and I'm beginning to worry that you don't either."

"That is a great question. Thank you for asking. After my second session with Kehlani, I filled out this worksheet myself based solely on my brief time with her. Here is what my worksheet looks like," I said, as I flipped it over.

I went on to explain, "As you can see, all of us have a different experience with Kehlani. For Mom and Grandma, she is very extreme. For Dad and Grandpa, there are some extremes but also some positives, and her behavior can be less overwhelming. My observations are kind of a mixture of both. Kehlani is 100 percent all these worksheets. We only get a better view of the whole person of Kehlani when we combine our observations."

My Completed Worksheet

CLIENT WORKSHEET

Temperament Traits

All children exhibit many of the behavior traits outlined below. Choose one child to evaluate and place an X on the continuum below each trait that most closely matches your experience with this child.

ACTIVITY LEVEL
How energetic is your child during regular day-to-day activities?

Hyperactive (high) —X————————————————— Mellow (low)

BIOLOGICAL REGULARITY
How consistent are your child's eating, sleeping, and toileting habits?

Regular ————————————————X——— Irregular

APPROACH OR WITHDRAWAL
How quickly does your child lean into new and unfamiliar circumstances?

Approachable ———X————————————————— Distant

ADAPTABILITY
How rigid does your child prefer their routine, schedule, or daily activities?

Flexible ——————————————————X— Inflexible

SENSORY THRESHOLD
How intensely does your child experience pain, smell, sound, or other senses?

Hypersensitive ———————————————X——— Hyposensitive

INTENSITY OF REACTION
When experiencing difficulties, how strong do they exhibit their response?

X——————————————————————— Passive
Active

MOOD
What is your child's average attitude emotionally?

Positive ————————————————X——— Negative

DISTRACTIBILITY
On average, how attentive is your child?

X——————————————————————— Focused
Distractible

PERSISTENCE OR ATTENTION SPAN
When faced with a long-term task, how determined is your child?

Persistent ————X——————————————— Nonpersistent

I continued, "By identifying which of these traits are problematic for Kehlani, we also get a clearer picture of which overall temperament constellation best fits her. Of the three temperament groups most children fall into—easy, slow to warm up, and difficult—Kehlani can be classified as difficult. This is not to say she is defective or that calling her difficult means anything derogatory. It is just the name given to a group of traits that we have all just attributed to Kehlani."

I explained, "The information from the intake and the first two sessions with Kehlani helped me conceptualize where she likely falls on this worksheet. You reported during the intake that Kehlani has a hard time going to bed at night and is still having toileting accidents at night. I indicated this by marking the 'irregular' biological trait. These biological irregularities could be genetic or medical. It is important to rule out any medical concerns with a doctor before we try addressing them specifically."

Continuing down the worksheet, I said, "Kehlani appears very inflexible and only wants to do what she wants to do. She didn't care what I wanted to do, nor did she ask my opinion about things to do in the session. She also had a hard time focusing when asked to do so. However, there were times that she showed persistence in doing things she was interested in. For example, she would continue to yell and modulate her voice whenever I got closer to her or started opening my mouth. She also continued to throw pillows at me without a break for most of the session."

I kept explaining my experiences with Kehlani in those sessions. "She is very reactive and doesn't seem to experience any sensitivities around sounds or lights. She kept her voice loud, even though my room echoed a lot, and she would stare at the lights as if investigating something about them. She appears approachable but quickly withdraws and is distant when any demands are made of her."

Her parents and grandparents looked at me like I wasn't telling them anything new. Dad asked, "So what does all this mean? How are we supposed to help her?"

"Great question," I replied. "I'd like you all to look at the worksheets for another minute. Dad, can you tell me whether you and Kehlani are the same on any of those traits?"

Looking at Mom and Grandma's worksheet, he said, "Well, I guess she and I are persistent at times."

"Can you explain that more to me?" I asked.

"I really like to fish. Fishing is not a sport for the impatient. You have to be persistent and focused. When I take Kehlani fishing with me, she is extremely persistent. Sometimes, she can outlast me in waiting for a fish to bite." Dad got a quizzical look on his face as he looked at his and Grandpa's worksheet. "Strangely, though, this seems to be the only time she is persistent," he said and pointed at his own mark on the worksheet that indicated she was not persistent.

I asked Mom, "What are some ways that you two are similar?"

She looked at all our worksheets, then with a smile, said, "It looks like all of us think that she is distractible. This has been a good thing and a bad thing in my life. I struggled in school, but I learned some skills through those struggles. I learned to ignore anything that wasn't important. With the distractibility comes almost an innocence or ignorance about things going on around me. I can shift my focus fast and still get a lot done. I've seen her do this as well. She could be playing with LEGO bricks, then switch to a game, then to a book, but pick up right where she left off with the LEGO."

We continued looking at all the temperament traits, viewing them from a strengths-based lens rather than a deficits-based lens. By the time we were finished, each of Kehlani's caregivers had a different perspective about who she was. They started looking at her behaviors as clues to her strengths.

After exploring their view of Kehlani's temperament traits, I used the *Coercion Cycle Diagram* from chapter 3 to explain the coercion cycle. "I notice that when I give Kehlani a command to do something, she is very resistant to doing it or will pretend like she is going to do it, and then she seems to test me by doing something else. Does this happen at home?"

Mom instantly replied, "Yes, it's so annoying, and it happens all the time. We can't get her to do anything, so we just give up."

I nodded and continued, "This behavior is best described as a pattern called the coercion cycle. The coercion cycle is a naturally occurring dynamic in every relationship and does not tend to cause difficulties or defiance when it is only rarely present. Unfortunately, many children who have similar temperament traits as Kehlani become masters of using the coercion cycle to control their circumstances."

I pointed at my worksheet and said, "Let's take her adaptability trait, for example. She expects things to be a certain way, and anything that deviates from that expectation is considered unwanted. To get out of an unwanted situation, she escalates her behavior in the hopes that you will give in. During our last session, she wanted to play UNO. She didn't like that I played a skip card. At first, she stated that the card was not valid in hopes that I would let it slide. When I didn't give in, she picked up the cards and threw them all over the room. It is very likely that before we even start to try to play UNO again, she will throw the cards."

"That explains it!" Dad blurted out.

"What do you mean?" I asked.

Dad continued, "UNO is her favorite game. When we got home after the last session, she complained about not being able to play UNO with you, so she asked me whether I could play with her. When I played a draw two card, she suddenly picked up the draw pile and threw it across the room."

I looked at all of them and said, "Yes, that would make sense. She was not willing to allow for her unwanted experience to happen again."

By this time, Mom was looking more and more discouraged and said, "So, what do we do? This all seems impossible."

We went through several more examples of the coercion cycle, both from my office and from home. We identified moments when her temperament traits would likely induce more escalated behavior, as well as traits that wouldn't. For homework, I encouraged her parents to spend some one-on-one time playing with Kehlani, specifically focusing on a temperament trait that reflected one of her strengths, without giving any direction or correction. They decided to go fishing, since Dad previously identified this as one of her strengths.

Having given them the first homework assignment, I explained the BISON phases. "The first thing we need to focus on for Kehlani is biological regulation. I accomplish this through a series of techniques that can best be summed up as bio-emotion regulation. When Kehlani can effectively regulate her emotions in the room with me, and you are seeing some of the same at home, we will shift into the individual play phase. This phase provides an environment for Kehlani to relearn how to be accepted for who she is. Having learned how to regulate, she will experience greater confidence in who she is as a person, and my work during this phase will teach her how to accept limits from adults. During these two phases, my work will primarily be with Kehlani, with brief check-ins with you all before and after each session."

I continued, "When she can accept at least five of my limits during an individual play session, I will want to meet with you only to work on the successful communication phase. This phase is when I will teach you skills that have been shown to increase compliance and decrease the use of the coercion cycle. During this phase, there may be times when I'm meeting with Kehlani one part of the week and you all another part of the week. This combination helps us maintain progress as my role continues to shift from therapist to coach. When you all experience an increase of compliance with Kehlani and are feeling confident in how you are viewing her traits, we will move into the organized play phase. This is where I fine-tune my interactions with Kehlani, teaching specific skills and addressing any additional problematic behaviors. Usually, this is when we address frustration tolerance and strengthen compliance."

I then explained the last phase of the BISON approach. "When Kehlani is experiencing increased compliance at home, at school, and in my office and can tolerate frustrations without exploding, we will move into the nurturing play phase. Here is where my role moves from coach to consultant. I will teach you how to provide individual play with Kehlani at home, which will strengthen your bond with each other and increase opportunities for compliance and positive interactions."

Looking relieved and a little intimidated, Mom said, "Okay, so there is a path forward. It sounds like we will be doing some work on ourselves as well."

I nodded, "Yes. Kehlani does need help, but we've seen that by addressing the biology of the child and the environment they interact in at the same time, progress is faster and more sustained."

"So, what are we going to do about the school?" Dad asked.

"I'm glad you asked," I replied. "I would like to get a release of information so I can visit with the school and teach them the same skills I teach you and Kehlani as we move through these phases of treatment."

"You got it," Mom and Dad said simultaneously.

After this initial assessment with Kehlani and her caregivers, I contacted her school counselor and her teacher to get the process started with them. As we moved through each phase of treatment, I worked closely with each of them to ensure they also followed the same guidelines her caregivers were. For Kehlani specifically, this work consisted of me sending emails, handouts, and YouTube videos that illustrated what I was teaching her caregivers. Occasionally, the school counselor and teacher would ask questions or request clarifications on how to implement an exercise or activity I recommended.

When Kehlani's caregivers left my intake session, they had a plan mapped out and a renewed hope that things would get better. Overall, Kehlani's treatment ended up lasting 12 months due to various interruptions of service throughout the process, but after 12 months, she was a completely different person in sessions, at home, and in school.

Key Takeaway

The key purpose of the assessment process is to gain a full view of who the child is and what circumstances may have led to the development of their DBD. Without this comprehensive view, you may be left chasing different symptoms that continue to reappear seemingly out of nowhere. The assessment also provides you with an opportunity to answer questions that come up and explain to the parents how the treatment will proceed. Parents like to know that providers have a plan to work from so they aren't left feeling directionless.

CHAPTER 5

BISON Phase B: Bio-Emotion Regulation

Children with a difficult temperament, or who have experienced biological or environmental stressors, are more likely to experience emotion regulation difficulties. As a result, they may become emotionally flooded and react with fight-or-flight behaviors when they encounter a perceived stressor. John Gottman (2011) referred to this heightened state of distress as *diffuse physiological arousal (DPA)*. If someone has a child who is naturally prone to DPA—for example, as a result of difficult temperament, anxiety, autism, or a sensory processing disorder—then escalation is likely to happen more often and more severely over time. One common understanding is that when individuals constantly experience DPA, they become incapable of rational thought or logical processing (Gottman, 2011). Indeed, when children are emotionally flooded, it is not helpful to expect them to think logically about or control their behavior. Explaining this to parents can be difficult, so to help them empathize with their child's explosive behaviors, I connect each parent to a pulse oximeter and ask them to visualize the following scenario:

> *Imagine you are on your way home from work. You had a long, difficult day and are looking forward to sitting down alone and reading your favorite book or watching your favorite TV show or sports team. As you pull into your driveway, you think how relaxing it will be to recover from the workday doing something you enjoy.*
>
> *The moment you enter your home, however, you are met with several demands from your family members. It turns out that your spouse is sick and hasn't been able to get out of bed the whole day, one of your children needs you to take them to*

the store to get supplies for a school assignment that is due the next day, you hear your other child screaming from the basement that there are two inches of water on the ground, and then suddenly a baseball comes crashing through your living room window.

Imagine how your body would feel amid this chaos. What would you address first? How would you respond to each of your family members? If any of them said, "Just breathe," "It's not so bad," or "What are you freaking out about?" then how would you feel? What would you want to do?

This exercise allows parents (and me) to see the real-life biological regulation taking place, just by imagining a scenario. Often, parents' heart rates exceed 100 beats per minute (bpm) by the time I mention their spouse is sick. This threshold of 100 bpm is typically seen in the research literature as the line where flooding takes place (Gottman, 2011, p. 131). Once that line is crossed, even once, it can take up to 45 minutes to get back to baseline and out of DPA. Trying to reason with someone when they have experienced DPA will only make the flooding worse and lead to conflict and relationship disconnection.

Assessing Regulation

While we can't address everything that plays a role in an individual's ability to regulate effectively, there are certain factors we must pay attention to. These are represented by the acronym DEBRIS: **d**evelopment, **e**nvironment, **b**iology, co-**r**egulation, **i**njury, and **s**leep. When the debris is cleared, regulation returns, and other interventions can start to be effective. Therefore, you will want to assess and treat each of these factors before moving into other phases of treatment. If you try to move forward before clients are able to regulate themselves, it can lead to early termination or subpar outcomes. While the child is the primary focus, each parent may also have regulatory difficulties to address. In the following section, I review each of the DEBRIS components in greater detail.

Development

When looking at a child's emotion regulation abilities, you want to consider their cognitive, emotional, and social developmental trajectories. If the child's development in these areas is delayed in any way, their ability to regulate may be compromised. For instance, we know that infants and young children are incapable of solo regulation; they need the co-regulating presence of a loving adult to teach them self-regulation skills. If a child is developmentally delayed, they may be stuck in that co-regulatory state and need the assistance of an adult, even if they physically look older. When presented with difficult tasks or demands, this child will not have the skills or knowledge to carry out said task on their own, leading to dysregulation and, in turn, disruptive behavior.

The child's emotional development also plays an important role, as children with better emotional intelligence are less apt to experience disruptive behaviors and defiance. They can better tolerate frustrations and tend to persevere when dealing with difficult tasks. Importantly, a child's emotional development depends on the adults in their life being able to co-regulate with them and serve as "emotion coaches" who help them understand and manage big feelings (see chapter 7).

Therefore, it is important to identify where the child is based on typical child development and milestones. Dee Ray's (2015) book, *A Therapist's Guide to Child Development*, is an excellent resource to help therapists and parents understand typical developmental needs and areas of concern.

Environment

The child's home, school, and community environments all play an integral role in determining the extent to which a child is able to regulate or whether they engage in disruptive behaviors. Children who experience stressful environments tend to develop coping skills specifically adaptive to those environments but not to others. For instance, a child who lives in poverty with several siblings will learn to fight and claw their way for attention and nourishment. While this scarcity mentality is necessary for their survival at home, when they are at school or in the community, it serves to increase defiance, opposition, and disruptive behaviors. They feel the need to fight for and defend their very existence, especially if the authority figure challenges their way of being.

The same can be said for a child who grows up in a community where violence and oppression are rampant. What is adaptive in their community (e.g., being alert, defensive, independent) looks like opposition and defiance in another setting. For example, if someone asks the child what their name is, it could trigger a response that is typical and expected in their home community (e.g., "Who needs to know?" or "None of your business!") but looks extremely rude, disrespectful, and abrasive in another environment—and this behavior then gets labeled as defiance.

When assessing environmental factors, make sure to identify any moves the child has experienced throughout their early life. Ask the parents about the communities they have lived in and about racial and socioeconomic identities that could play a role in their environmental experiences. Ignoring this factor could lead to delays in moving successfully through the other phases of intervention.

Importantly, James and colleagues (2021) discovered how impactful the home environment is on specific neural pathways within a child's brain. When children are exposed to consistent parental criticism, their responsiveness to rewards and punishments decreases. Essentially, when this occurs, no number of rewards or punishments will be effective in changing the behavior of the child. While more research needs to be done to verify this, it stands to reason that when children are exposed to consistent criticism in any environment, these neural pathway changes would occur. Therefore, it is important to assess for this during the intake process and continuously throughout treatment. Whenever consistent criticism is aimed at the child, it will be important to remind adults of the impact this will have on how fast treatment will progress. A research spotlight is included in the appendix that you can use to help adults understand this.

Biology

In addition to a child's temperament, other biological factors impact their regulatory capacity. This includes a family history of depression, anxiety, and other mental health disorders. Children with these family histories may be more genetically predisposed to developing mental health concerns themselves, especially if their family member's concerns have not been addressed properly. For instance, if left untreated, a parent's anxiety or depression could lead to maladaptive coping skills (e.g., substance misuse, overworking, oversleeping, poor nutrition). If the child then starts exhibiting depression or anxiety themselves, the parents may not be able to help the child learn adaptive coping skills. Therefore, it is important that you take time to understand the intergenerational influences that a child and family are experiencing, as this helps clarify the family's emotion regulation abilities and determine whether other adjunctive interventions (e.g., individual therapy for parents, couples therapy, parent training, medication) are needed.

In addition, biological factors extend to sensory processing concerns as well, which are best addressed through occupational therapy. A child with sensory processing concerns may exhibit sensitivity to light, sound, touch, or smell. You will discover some of this information in the parent-only intake session, but most of these sensory sensitivities will present themselves in the child-only sessions. If these biological components are not properly addressed, it will be difficult to make progress in regulation training.

Co-Regulation

This factor is mostly about assessing the parents and adults in the child's life for the ability to co-regulate. Remember that co-regulation is crucial for young children, who require the presence of an attuned and loving caregiver in order to learn how to manage their own emotions. However, when a parent is not responsive or attuned to a child's emotional state—perhaps even ignoring the child altogether—it can lead to distress, acting out, and even "defiant" behaviors as that child makes a bid for attention.

The best demonstration of this is the still-face experiment by Weinberg and Tronick (1996). During this experiment, a mother-infant pair were observed interacting with each other for a few minutes in as natural a way as they could in a research lab. The mother was then asked to turn her face away for a few seconds, then face the child again, but only use a still, expressionless face for three minutes. The result of this "still face" is that the infant quickly became increasingly dysregulated. After three minutes, the mother was asked to soothe the child and return to reciprocal and normal interactions. Researchers found that the infant's vagal tone and heart rate (which are thought to be markers of stress vulnerability) quickly returned to baseline when the mother attempted to soothe the child, indicating that the parent and child relationship was secure, and the child was able to downregulate after this stressful interaction.

When assessing the parents' co-regulation capabilities, identify the history of each parent and how they respond to stress. You can generally assess for this information during the intake session and in follow-up parent-only sessions by asking questions about stress tolerance and family history. Their childhood and relationship histories in particular affect their ability to remain calm and present in the midst of their child's difficult or destructive behavior. Remind parents that it is normal to become dysregulated by their child's outbursts—it is the way humans are designed—but if they feel like they need help managing their child's emotions, this is the time to recommend interventions like individual or couples therapy.

Injury (Trauma)

Any history of trauma (including emotional, physical, or medical trauma) can play a role in regulation. When someone has experienced chronic stress or trauma, their body learns to cope by developing strategies that make sense at the time but may not be helpful in other situations. For example, a child who has experienced repeated harsh physical abuse for discipline may learn to disconnect from their body during high-stress moments. While disconnection may be adaptive in those times, being disconnected from one's body during a fast-paced game of dodgeball could create problems. As another example, a child who has experienced a long-term illness (e.g., cancer) may learn to thrive on chaos and last-minute changes but become extremely dysregulated during boring, mundane tasks. Again, this strategy is very adaptive for dealing with the unknown of a long-term illness, but not so much when asked to sit still during a test or quiet reading time.

In some circumstances, an individual's nervous system has been stressed for so long that their vagal nerve—which is the nerve responsible for the body's parasympathetic nervous system response—is effectively reversed. Essentially, the individual has learned how to remain calm and focused during stressful moments, but when they're asked to be calm, their body becomes dysregulated. I have seen this with a few clients when I introduce the DPA exercise from the start of this chapter, and their heart rate *decreases* rather than increases. On the other hand, when I ask them to think of a calm moment or take a few deep breaths, their heart rate significantly increases and crosses the 100-bpm threshold.

These "reversal" cases can be confusing for the provider and family—thankfully, some prominent researchers (e.g., Perry, 2017; Perry et al., 2018; Porges, 2011) have figured out what is occurring and what to do about it. In particular, they've found that these reversals are adaptations that allow the body and brain to function during high-stress moments. Think of someone who is able to remain calm and collected in the midst of extreme chaos. This reversal is helpful for those moments for which it developed. However, the downside is that when those same people are asked to sit still and try to meditate, their heart rate will instantly jump, and they will experience dysregulation. We will explore this in more detail later.

Sleep

Finally, one often-overlooked factor that can impact anyone's regulatory capacities is sleep quantity and quality. When we don't get enough sleep, we simply aren't able to regulate ourselves. Our judgment becomes impaired, our mood becomes unstable, and our ability to focus decreases. Therefore, the evidence is clear that this ought to be one of the first factors you address, especially when working with kids (Astill et al.,

2012; Sikora et al., 2012; Walker, 2018). When assessing sleep problems, I recommend working closely with the family's doctor, as a sleep study may be merited to determine any irregularities that may require medical interventions.

When it comes to sleep quantity, I typically compare the child's reported number of hours of sleep to the American Academy of Pediatrics recommendations, which vary between 10 to 14 hours per day, depending on the child's age. As for sleep quality, I ask parents to track the child's drowsiness level throughout the day. If the child seems excessively tired during the day, it may indicate another underlying sleep concern. This will need to be addressed with a consultation from a sleep medicine professional.

CLIENT HANDOUT

Bio-Emotion Regulation

Several factors may impact a child or an adult's ability to regulate biologically and emotionally. To help people remember these factors, I use the acronym DEBRIS. As most families of children with disruptive behavior disorders (DBDs) know, debris cleanup can sometimes be a daily occurrence. Coincidentally, before we can help children with DBDs, we need to clear out, consider, or accommodate their bio-emotion regulation debris. When a child with a DBD is having a difficult time, ask yourself the following DEBRIS questions:

Development:
- Are this child's behavioral, emotional, or social expressions typical for their age?
- Do they have any developmental delays that can explain this behavior?

Environment:
- Do adults recognize this child's individual needs and make proper accommodations?
- What environmental factors (e.g., family conflict, oppression, poverty) can explain this behavior?

Biology:
- Are there any known bodily concerns that may explain this behavior (e.g., sensory seeking or sensory avoiding tendencies)?
- Is the child currently experiencing a biological need (e.g., hunger, fatigue, malaise)?

Co-Regulation:
- Am I able to co-regulate with this child at this time?
- Who else is able to co-regulate with this child when they need assistance?

Injury (Trauma):
- Has the child experienced any medical, environmental, or developmental injury or trauma?

Sleep:
- Is the child getting the recommended amount of sleep?
- Is anything else impacting the child's sleep?

Increasing Regulation

After assessing for DEBRIS, it is important to address the concerns that can impair the restoration of regulatory abilities—whether that involves referring the child to an occupational therapist or a sleep medicine doctor, recommending individual or couples therapy for the parents, or moving forward with the bio-emotion regulation phase interventions. If you are ready to proceed with the interventions in this phase, your work will involve helping the client increase their HRV through a variety of biofeedback and related tools.

In simplistic terms, HRV is calculated as the magnitude of variation in time between heartbeats. Importantly, HRV is thought to be a marker of how quickly your body can recover from stress, with higher HRV indicating greater stress resilience and lower HRV indicating lower stress resilience. In addition, many studies have found that HRV is associated with disruptive behavior, as children and adolescents with oppositional, disruptive, and aggressive behaviors have been found to exhibit lower HRV ratings at rest (Chiu et al., 2024; de Looff et al., 2022). This is especially true for children with autism or ADHD. What these findings suggest is that the lower someone's HRV rating, the more likely they are to experience emotion dysregulation and behavior disorders. In fact, most of the clients I see have an HRV rating anywhere from 15 to 30. While there are no hard-and-fast numbers about what a "good" HRV is, I use interventions to get my clients to about 60 HRV before graduation.

An interesting characteristic about HRV is that someone can have a low HRV (typically bad) at the same time as a low bpm (typically good)—and vice versa (Schoorl, 2016). Although the only true indicator of HRV is an electrocardiogram (ECG), many devices have been created that have been tested against ECGs with a high level of accuracy. These include the Scosche Rhythm 24 Heart Rate Armband with the mobile app EliteHRV or the HeartMath program with the emWave device. As these devices have become readily available, I have used them more and more in my practice. These devices have allowed me to identify when a client has a low bpm but is dysregulated (as evidenced by low HRV).

In the next section, I discuss four common regulation interventions I use with clients, several of which employ these devices. The first two are HRV biofeedback approaches that require the purchase of equipment and training in the use of that equipment. The last two are a combination of play therapy techniques that help initiate active mindfulness in the client, often mimicking the effects of actual HRV biofeedback interventions.

HeartMath

HeartMath is an HRV biofeedback system that requires specific hardware (e.g., emWave, Inner Balance) and software that is exclusive to the HeartMath company. They offer training and certification programs for health providers, coaches, and the lay population. The sensors attach to the client's earlobe or fingertip and work much like a pulse oximeter. The power of the system comes from the software that reads the data from the sensor. The software helps the provider and client see how coherent they are in real time. *Coherence* describes the state of the body when breathing, heart rhythm, and mental state are in sync with each other. Additionally, the software displays real-time heart rate, HRV, and power frequency of a heart rhythm.

All this data can be used to assist clients in learning self-regulatory behaviors and techniques. For example, when a child is connected to the HeartMath equipment, they are able to see their heart rate and rate of coherence in real time, as well as how their body responds to different topics of conversation or to different coping skills. HeartMath has specific exercises that can be taught by the provider to increase the likelihood of regulatory capability. One such exercise is called *heart-focused breathing*. This exercise uses specific language to encourage deep diaphragmatic breathing, while the child connected to the device is able to see how their heart rate and coherence respond. With continued used of heart-focused breathing and real-time observation of their biological response, the child gains greater confidence in the usefulness of this breathing exercise in other scenarios.

Combining these exercises with homework between sessions (e.g., heart-focused breathing, juggling, balancing) increases the speed of recovery and the progression toward other phases of treatment. Seeing the promise of this new approach, I became certified in the HeartMath approach using the emWave and Inner Balance devices to perform HRV biofeedback. If you are interested in getting trained in HeartMath, I recommend visiting their certification website, taking some of their courses, and trying the equipment and exercises for yourself (https://www.heartmath.com/certification/).

Mightier

Like HeartMath, Mightier requires the purchase of hardware—namely, an HRV monitor band, program subscription, and any tablet or smartphone. Mightier is a game-based app that uses HRV data within the game to warn players when they need to take a break. The game then offers the player a few options of calm-down techniques and reads the data from the armband to identify when the player is ready to play again. Each time the player becomes dysregulated, the game forces a pause, which then requires the player to use a relaxation technique to continue.

This is a more affordable, home-based program than HeartMath. Mightier also offers several different subscription models for families and clinicians, though I have unfortunately seen two downsides to the family subscription option. Some clients find the games uninteresting, and sometimes parents hand the child the tablet and let them play the game for longer than recommended. I allow kids to use the devices at my office two to three times per week for 15 to 20 minutes each. This helps keep the novelty alive and requires some accountability. If you are interested in Mightier, I recommend reaching out to their sales team to explore the options of using this tool in your office (https://www.mightier.com/clinicians) or referring parents to the website for the parent program (https://www.mightier.com/plans-1).

Beat Saber

While *Beat Saber* requires an investment in virtual reality (VR) equipment, which can be costly, I have found it to be as helpful with regulatory training as HRV biofeedback and other nondigital alternatives. *Beat Saber* is a video game played with a VR headset and controllers. The objective is to swing VR light sabers in a pattern, often crossing the body's midline, to the rhythmic beat of the client's choice of music. The interesting thing about using this intervention is that when a client's HRV is taken before a session of *Beat Saber*, their HRV is often low. However, after a 15-minute session, they achieve a higher HRV and remain in a regulated state for the rest of the session. You can find out more about this game at https://beatsaber.com.

Nondigital Alternatives

For providers who are unable to access the training or equipment mentioned above, the following ultra-low-tech alternatives work well, just not as quickly as the digital biofeedback options. I used these alternatives before I was trained in and had the ability to access the digital interventions. I also still use these alternatives with my clients when they don't respond well to the digital biofeedback options.

These alternatives include teaching children how to juggle, having them balance an empty egg carton on their head while they walk in a straight line, or creating a mini obstacle course with office furniture and having them navigate it while balancing an empty egg carton on their head. Any of these interventions help children participate in an active form of mindfulness. They need to be fully aware of their bodies and surroundings to catch juggling balls or balance an egg carton. To teach them juggling, I typically start in my office having them throw one ball in the air and catch it with one hand. I ask them to practice this at home each day for at least 15 minutes. Once they have mastered that, they switch hands. They should be able to successfully catch the ball in both hands before adding the second and third balls. This builds confidence and self-esteem, and it teaches the child how to regulate their body. Most of my clients are eager to practice juggling at home. Balancing an empty egg carton can do the same thing. It requires the child to slow down and decrease their movement to be able to successfully traverse an imaginary line or navigate an obstacle course with the egg carton on their head. Occupational therapy is another alternative for this phase, as occupational therapists have more tools at their disposal when it comes to helping children regulate their bodies.

Case Example: *Bruce*

Bruce was a seven-year-old boy whose parents brought him to my office because they were concerned he was a "psychopath in the making." He argued with teachers, ran away from home, and deliberately destroyed property. He would resist taking time to calm down; he seemed to always want to escalate things. His parents adopted him at age three and didn't know much about his biological family's medical background or what had occurred during his early developmental years. They suspected he had experienced significant trauma and attachment disruptions but couldn't point to any specific traumatic events. He was seven when they started treatment with me. He had been diagnosed with autism a few months prior to our first session and was on the verge of being kicked out of school, so my first session with him was interesting.

He walked into my office looking distant, as though he was half asleep. He seemed detached and withdrawn. He didn't speak much or look at me. I couldn't put my finger on what was different about him, but the room felt off. Not knowing much about his biological background or potential trauma history, I took my pulse oximeter out in preparation to assess his regulation. When the oximeter read his heart rate, he was deep in flooding territory (130 bpm!). This was surprising, since a child his age and with his presentation should have a heart rate of about 70–80 bpm. After this discovery, I encouraged his parents to check with Bruce's pediatrician to make sure there was nothing else going on and got the appropriate releases to consult with his medical provider too. The pediatrician had also recorded that Bruce's bpm was extremely high on most visits but otherwise did not find evidence of any underlying concerns. They had chalked it up to him having an overactive heart rate or being nervous at the doctor's office. As I consulted with the doctor about my treatment approach and what my plan entailed, they were intrigued and excited for me to continue monitoring his heart rate.

In doing so, I quickly discovered that when Bruce was fully involved in a high-stress scenario, for instance playing Perfection, his heart rate started to level out (falling to about 87–93 bpm). Having more confidence that he was not experiencing a medical issue regarding his heart rate, I suspected his vagal response was reversed. This often happens when the body experiences trauma or chronic stress. The body adapts to the chronic stress by reversing the normal vagal response to threat and safety. To further test this, I took Bruce through a few experiments.

Once he was connected to the HeartMath device, I said, "Bruce, I'd like you to think about sitting quietly in your favorite place. Just imagine that you have no worries or concerns. You can just sit and do anything you want."

As he imagined this, his heart rate started to climb from 120 to 130 bpm. His HRV was extremely low as well, around 20–30. I thanked Bruce for his compliance. I then asked, "Now I'd like you to think of the most frustrating and overwhelming experience you can think of, then imagine that you are taking an important school test at the same time."

Unsurprisingly, his heart rate gradually decreased from 120 to 105 bpm and finally to 89 bpm after three minutes. Not only was his heart rate lowering, his HRV was increasing to 35–40. I concluded his vagal response was, indeed, reversed.

When I explained this discovery to Bruce's parents, they looked at me stunned, then in horror. They began explaining how this seemed to be present at home. Dad said, "When things are chaotic and everyone is yelling at each other, Bruce seems to be unusually relaxed and at ease. At times, it even seems like he tries to get us all riled up at each other, then suddenly he is calm."

Mom said, "In his last experience with therapy, the therapist attempted to get him to do breathing and relaxation exercises, but instead of calming down, they put him in a full-on panic."

"That makes sense," I acknowledged. "I'm going to ask Bruce to try a few things before our next session. They may not make a lot of sense, but I just ask that you stick with them for a few weeks. It would also be helpful if you both could encourage him to do these exercises each day for about five minutes."

Dad looked a little puzzled and asked, "What are you asking him to do?"

"I'd like him to practice throwing this juggling ball and catching it with just one hand. It's okay if he doesn't catch it every time, I just want him to try, every day."

This was very different from his previous experience with breathing exercises, so at first, the parents accepted this exercise. They didn't yet see how it connected to helping Bruce not get into trouble at school, but they agreed to try it.

When he came back the next week, his parents reported that he was even more discouraged than he was before starting therapy.

When I brought Bruce in, I said, "Your parents tell me you are more upset and hopeless than before. What's going on?"

He whispered, "I can't do anything right."

"Can you tell me more?" I replied.

"I'll never be good at anything, especially juggling. You are just making me see how defective I am," he said as he handed me the juggling ball. "You can keep it. I'm not coming back."

"Can you stand up for me?" I gently asked Bruce.

Bruce stood up.

"Now, close your eyes."

"Okay, now what!" Bruce exclaimed as if he was waiting for me to show him another thing he couldn't do.

"Nothing. Just stand there. Are you able to stand there without your eyes open?" I asked.

"Well, yeah, that is easy."

"Shoot, maybe it was too easy. Here—put this egg carton on your head. Keep your eyes closed and balance it on your head," I told him.

"Okay. What now?" he asked.

"Wow, you are pretty good at that. Try lifting one leg off the ground," I encouraged.

Bruce kept complying and succeeding, all the while continuing to get intense praise from me for the work he was able to do. I kept trying to increase the complexity of the balancing, and he kept succeeding.

"Bruce, how did you get so good at standing and balancing?" I questioned.

"I don't know, I guess I've been doing it for seven years now, so maybe just lots of practice?" he suggested.

"Great. So, you are now an expert stander and balancer. Do you still trip and fall sometimes?" I quizzed him.

Instantly, Bruce's countenance fell, and he replied, "Yeah . . . I told you I can't do anything good."

"Oh, I didn't say that at all. Even I still trip and fall sometimes," I said, smiling.

"Really?!" Bruce's eyes lifted, and a small smile crossed his face. "But you are so old. You really should know how to stand by now," he joked.

"I know. Crazy, huh? I bet if you asked any adult whether they still trip or fall sometimes, they would all say yes!" I exclaimed.

"So, what does this have to do with me?" he asked.

I replied, "Well, how long have you been learning to juggle?"

"Just a few days."

"Okay, so we shouldn't expect perfection just yet, right?"

"Right! Okay, I'll keep trying," he smiled, standing taller.

"First, let me show you something really cool," I told him.

I pulled out my HeartMath device and connected Bruce to it. His heart rate was sitting at about 123 bpm. I asked him to follow the breathing pacer on the screen. He breathed in and out as the ball went up and down. After about two minutes, his bpm started to fall and leveled out at about 90 bpm. He was still not achieving coherence—that is, the ability to consciously get his breathing, heart rhythm, and mental state in sync with each other—but he was getting close enough that I wanted him to try juggling again. I disconnected him from the sensor and handed him the juggling ball.

He threw it up in the air and caught it with one hand 15 times. On his last catch, he looked at me with surprise. "Wait, what just happened? I couldn't catch this ball more than two times at home, but you have me follow that stupid ball on the screen, and now I can catch it?"

"Not exactly. Do you see this number?" I asked, pointing to his bpm.

"Yeah, 93. What does that mean?" he replied.

"It is a record of your heart rate in beats per minute. When I first connected you, you were at 123 beats per minute. Now you are at 93 bpm. It means you are in better control of your body. You controlled your body by following and breathing with that ball. Having control of your body allowed you to think faster and be more focused when you juggled. You did all of it."

Teaching Bruce how to juggle, showing him his HRV, and increasing his ability to regulate his body improved his confidence and sense of well-being, which allowed us to move to other phases of ISPT. In addition, by forming a close collaboration with Bruce's pediatrician, we were able to accelerate Bruce's progress because we were both on the same page and could reinforce each other's treatments with his parents.

When Bruce first came in, he was extremely dejected and discouraged about not having any friends. After completing the bio-emotion regulation phase where I taught him how to juggle, he practiced at home for six months as we continued with the other phases of treatment. He was eventually able to juggle three balls. Juggling was one way he developed emotion regulation skills and awareness of his body. I later learned that he would show off at school, and people stopped looking at him like a strange kid and wanted to get to know him.

After about seven months, Bruce graduated from therapy with a new sense of confidence and self-control. His teacher reported that he was no longer her biggest concern, and she, his parents, and Bruce were all thankful for his improved regulatory abilities.

Key Takeaway

The key takeaway from the bio-emotion regulation phase is that you can help parents and children understand that their emotional response is driven by biology and how they can impact it. When parents and children can influence their body's response, they gain confidence and accountability. It reminds parents that sometimes the way a child responds is automatic and not a full reflection of their child. When parents accept this, they begin to see their child for who they are again.

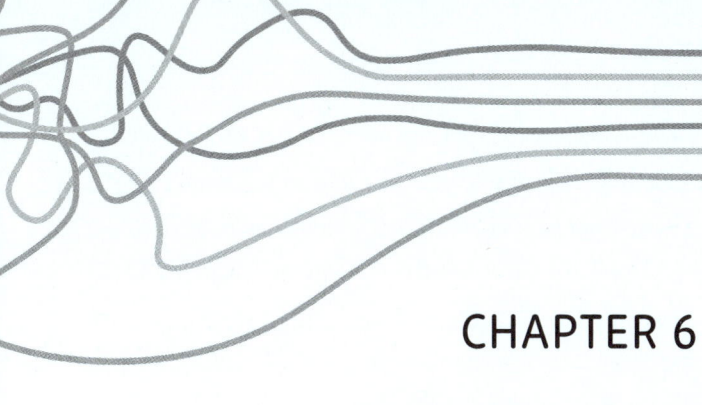

CHAPTER 6

BISON Phase I: Individual Play

The individual play phase is twofold, using CCPT skills in sessions with the child and instructing the parents on how to spend dedicated one-on-one time with their child. Built within CCPT is the paradoxical belief that children already know what they need to do to process their needs and concerns. Similarly, during individual play, the therapist provides a blank canvas and a safe space for the child to discover who they are without judgment, correction, or direction. The therapist believes in the child themselves. They allow the child to be fully who they are, without worrying about outside objectives or goals. The main goal is to allow the child to *be*. This allows the child to be seen, experienced, and accepted. The therapist introduces this concept to the parents and explains how to accomplish this at home with one-on-one time.

During this phase, the therapist provides a safe place, often a room full of toys organized in a particular way, that the child is allowed to explore and use in whatever way they need. It is best for a provider to be working toward their Registered Play Therapist™ (RPT) credential to provide the most accurate and effective version of individual play. If the provider is not working toward this credential, at least 50 hours of dedicated CCPT training and at least two to five observed supervised hours would suffice. The reason for this caution is that many providers use play-based techniques in their therapy but do not adhere to the rigorous guidelines of CCPT, which would only undermine this phase of treatment.

The concept of *paradoxical interdependence* is the driving principle behind the interventions for this phase. Remember that the principle of paradoxical interdependence recognizes that every action of each member of a system has a direct or indirect impact on the actions and emotions of every other member of the system. In this chapter, we'll return to the example of Jimmy—first introduced in chapter 3—to illustrate the interdependent nature between his behavior, his parents' marriage, and his desire for independence (as evidenced by Jimmy purposefully peeing on his bed). You'll see how individual play balances Jimmy's need for independence, structure, boundaries, and attachment.

Basic Skills for Individual Play and One-on-One Time

There are a few basic principles and intervention strategies that are used within CCPT for children with disruptive behaviors. While this is not an all-encompassing list of CCPT skills, they are the most pertinent to the client population of focus. I will explain each skill and describe how it impacts the coercion cycle and uses the systemic principle of paradoxical interdependence to restructure the family system and better accommodate a child experiencing disruptive behaviors. Each of these skills is also taught to parents after three sessions of individual play between me and their child. Conducting three sessions with the child before introducing these skills to parents helps me know which behaviors may show up during one-on-one sessions with parents and how to assist them through those behaviors.

Unconditional Positive Regard

The very first skill, and arguably the most important, used within this framework is a concept known as unconditional positive regard. This concept is the belief that there is something of worth in everyone. All humans deserve respect, love, care, and positive regard. No matter how difficult, disruptive, rude, or challenging a person may be, they deserve to be loved and accepted. To use this skill, you must search for and find something about the client you like. When you can find something you like about a client, it makes it easier to express that positive regard. This positive regard is something you must feel inside yourself toward the client.

In contrast, when you feel frustrated or upset with a child, you transmit this reality to the child. The child feels it too. You can probably think of times when you felt this way. Try to imagine a time when you walked into a room and the atmosphere was such that you could "cut it with a knife." It works the same way when a child can sense unconditional positive regard from you. When they feel your positive regard, they are more apt to come to therapy and more willing to do the work of individual play to resolve their challenges.

Tracking

The skill of tracking involves using your words and body to convey interest in what the child is doing. While the child plays with a toy or explores the room, you comment, much like a sports announcer would, about the child's movements and play. The difference here is that you do not label or name objects until the child has already done so. This allows the child complete freedom to use whatever toy they need for anything they want. A car can be a brick and vice versa. A highly skilled tracker will pay attention to the child's body language to read how much is too much and convey just enough interest that the child knows that they are seen and accepted in the room.

ACT Limit Setting

Even though the idea behind individual play is to allow the child to explore and play in a lot of the ways they would like and often need to, some limits need to be set. As I mentioned in chapter 4, at the beginning of each of my sessions with children, I introduce the playroom as follows: "In the playroom, you can do a lot of the things you would like to. There are only three rules: (1) you are not for hurting, (2) I am not for hurting, and (3) the toys are not for breaking. If there is another rule that needs to be set, I'll let you know."

Most limits in the playroom are some variations of the first three mentioned above. This allows the child ultimate freedom to explore and process as they see fit. When I have to remind them of a limit, or I need to set a new limit, I use the ACT limit-setting framework (Landreth & Bratton, 2005):

- **A**cknowledge the desire, feeling, or want of the child.
- **C**ommunicate the limit.
- **T**arget an appropriate alternative.

The following example shows this in action: "Jimmy, I know you would really like to shoot me in the face, but remember I am not for hurting. You can draw my face on the whiteboard and shoot that." The reason for this framework is that it allows the child to maintain dignity through the use of object-first language. Notice that I did not say anything like "We don't shoot people." This is exclusionary language and communicates to the child that they are not part of the collective *we*. He just had a desire to shoot me. If I were to convey the limit in this fashion, I would be telling him more of the same: You are not wanted, needed, or even a part of the group. By using object-first language ("I am not for hurting") and acknowledging his desire, I am communicating that it is okay to have those desires, he just needs to recognize and use appropriate alternatives. Paradoxically, I am not changing his internal desires but teaching him that he is acceptable as he is and can use appropriate alternatives to carry out his behaviors.

Encouragement

The final skill that is used in individual play is encouragement. Encouragement may seem straightforward, but this can be difficult for some providers unfamiliar with the specifics of this skill. Encouragement differs from praise in that praise comes after a child has completed a task and is often, unfortunately, focused on the result rather than the effort the child has put into the task (e.g., "Good job," "That picture is pretty"). Encouragement takes place throughout the process of doing a task and is focused on helping the child see themselves as capable. When a provider uses encouragement, it is often after the child has asked for help doing something. I typically respond with "How would you like me to help you?" This encourages the child to think through the task and come up with specific actions I can do to help.

Many times, children with disruptive behaviors are too impatient to tell me how they'd like me to help, so they continue to struggle and figure out different ways to accomplish the task. In these cases, I use encouraging words like "You are figuring it out," "You have an idea about how to do that," or "You figured it out by yourself." This helps the child gain independence and self-respect for their abilities. In doing so, the skill of encouragement uses the principle of paradoxical interdependence to help the child find strength and acceptance of their own self.

Explaining Individual Play to Parents

Possibly the most challenging aspect of using individual play is helping parents understand its effectiveness and explaining what is taking place in the room. Many parents have expressed their concern and frustration when I tell them that I plan to use play therapy with their child. I usually get some iteration of the following statement: "We've already tried play therapy. We want *real* therapy." In most cases where they have tried "play therapy," the provider was not credentialed as an RPT or did not have more than a cursory class about play therapy in their graduate training. Unfortunately, most providers who say they are doing play therapy do not have the required training to use it effectively. This is the reason for my caution about having a minimum number of education and supervision hours in play therapy before attempting to use this intervention.

When parents are concerned about my use of play therapy, I explain the interventions I will use in my sessions, such as unconditional positive regard, tracking, limit setting, and encouragement. I also give examples of situations in which I would use each intervention, including how it will help their child learn to manage their own body and behavior in a warm, accepting environment. After each session, I also meet with parents for about five minutes to explain what took place in the session. I go over the major themes of play that the child used during the session, explain how well they complied with my requests, demonstrate how to execute those requests so parents can try them at home, and discuss how many more sessions of individual play I think we will need before moving to the next phase of therapy.

It is imperative to involve parents every step of the way throughout this process. The more I talk to parents about their experiences with providers who treat DBDs, the clearer it is that parents want to be involved in their child's treatment. Many parents have expressed their frustration that they don't know what is going on in the room with the therapist, and they feel like nothing is getting done. When I tell parents from the start that they need to be involved, it is often met with a sigh of gratitude and relief. If parents are kept in the dark about what is happening in the playroom, they are more apt to end therapy prematurely and try to find a "real" therapist.

Introducing One-on-One Time

After three sessions of individual play with the child, I have a better understanding of how the child responds to tracking, limit setting, and encouragement. With this information, I can introduce one-on-one time to the parents as homework for them to complete with their child. Depending on the intensity of the case, I may still meet with the child individually and add a few sessions with the parents on another day of the week. During those parent sessions, I will go over the basic individual play skills, role-play with them how to use the skills, and ask them to set aside 20 minutes once per week to spend this time with their child.

Parents need to understand that during this one-on-one time, they need to be fully attentive to their child. There should be no agenda and no expectations. It is an opportunity for the child to be fully seen. When parents can do this with their child, it also changes how the child views the parents. The child is used to being corrected, taught, or disciplined, so when they are able to be seen and experienced by their parents for 20 minutes once per week without agenda or filter, it is a huge gift. The following handout can help you introduce this approach to parents.

CLIENT HANDOUT

One-on-One Time

Before you read the instructions on how to do one-on-one time, please take some time to understand the principle and rules behind this approach so you can understand why it is important and how it works.

The Principle:

Many times (not all the time), children use misbehavior and defiance to get the attention of their parents or caregivers. When parents pay attention to this misbehavior, the child learns that this is an easy and effective way to get a reaction (i.e., attention) from their caregivers. This creates a cycle that continues to get increasingly frustrating for both parent and child (the coercion cycle).

One-on-one time is a way to break this cycle by setting aside dedicated time to engage in child-directed play with your child. This is a type of play in which your child takes the lead, not you. Having this one-on-one time is especially important given the busy lifestyles that most families live. As technology has increased and as more limits are placed on the family from outside sources (e.g., school, work, daycare, bills, email), fewer and fewer families spend dedicated time together. A symptom of these limits can be childhood misbehavior. One-on-one time counters those limits and reassures the child that you are theirs and will always be there to care for them.

One-on-one time gives your child a space in which they are in total control, or in other words, a space in which you are completely attentive to them. When children get the chance to have 100 percent of your time focused on them, many behavior problems disappear. Using one-on-one time at home is much like using antibiotics: You don't stop when the "symptoms" (behavior problems) are gone. It needs to be continued so the symptoms don't come back.

Because this is your *child's* dedicated time, it is important to let them oversee it. Keeping this principle in mind will make it easier for you to be nondirective. Being nondirective is the key. Let your child lead you; take this time to learn from your child.

The Rules:

- **No teaching:** Do not use this time to teach your child. This will be difficult, but if you abide by this rule, your time will be well spent.

- **No correcting:** If your child says something is blue when it is really red, do not correct them. You will have time to do that the rest of the day. This is their time—learn from them.
- **No cleaning:** Do not make your child clean up after themselves. Again, *you* can clean up later, but this is their time, so let them enjoy it.
- **No hitting or hurting:** If your child becomes aggressive, inform them that *you* are not for hitting, *your child* is not for hitting, and the *toys* are not for hitting. If they continue after you tell them that toys are not for hitting, warn them that if it happens again, you will need to take that toy away. Follow through and put the toy away if the aggression continues.
- **Have fun:** Participate in the play with your child. This is a time for bonding, so have fun and take your child's lead.

The Instructions:

- Set aside a block of 20 minutes once per week for one-on-one time.
- Don't schedule the play time within the first 30 to 45 minutes after a major transition (e.g., coming home from school or a friend's house).
- If playtime is missed, reschedule it within the next 24 hours, giving a real scheduled time for the child to expect.
- Narrate the play of your child. As your child plays with a car, say, "You are rolling *that* across the floor." Only name the object when your child names it. If the child says that a toy car is a phone, say, "You are pushing *that phone* across the floor." Use *only* the words that your child uses.
- When your child looks like they want help, say, "You want me to [*action*] that? Why don't you try first?" Let them try for a few seconds until it looks like they really need your help. Then help *only* if they ask for it again. If they don't ask again, assume that they are content.
- Don't interrupt their play. If they don't engage you, just narrate their play while you play with toys near them.
- Stay in their metaphor. Let them lead your play. If they tell a story with their play, don't detract from their story; continue playing *in* their storytelling.
- When the time is almost up, give them a five-minute lead time warning. Give another warning when they only have a minute left to play.
- When the play time is over, leave the area and don't make the child clean it up. Get them busy with something else before you return to clean up.

Case Example: *Jimmy*

As you'll recall from chapter 3, Jimmy's mother brought him to therapy because he was urinating on his bed for no apparent reason. Let's explore more of his case, including how I used individual play with him.

After getting both Mom and Dad to come to the intake and explaining how I would work with the family, I started meeting with Jimmy individually using individual play. I went over the basic rules of the playroom and allowed him to explore. At first, he seemed a little confused. He seemed not to know how to play with the toys. He walked the perimeter of the room looking at the toys and occasionally at me.

"You are looking at the toys," I said. "You are unsure what to do with the toys." [**Tracking**]

Jimmy picked up a toy, looked at it, and placed it carefully back on the shelf.

"You were curious about that but decided not to use it," I said. [**Tracking**]

Eventually Jimmy picked up the game Hungry, Hungry Hippos and brought it to me. "Do you know how to play this game?" Jimmy asked.

"You are curious whether I know how to play that game. Yes, I do. Would you like to play it?"

Jimmy nodded his head up and down.

I explained how to play the game and asked whether he understood the rules. He nodded, and we played a few rounds of Hungry, Hungry Hippos.

After the third round, Jimmy hit his fist on the table, saying, "This is a stupid game. I'm always losing. It's not fair."

"You seem really angry about losing," I said. "I can see you want to hit something because of how mad you are. Remember, you and the toys are not for breaking. If you need to break or hit something, let me know, and I'll get you an egg carton to break." [**ACT limit setting**]

Jimmy looked surprised at my acknowledgment of his feelings and seemingly being okay with his anger. "Yes, I'd like to break something. Can I get something to break?"

I got him an egg carton, which he used to jump on, stomp, and tear into many pieces. "It looks like that was helpful for you to do. We only have five minutes left in our play session. Would you like to break something else or play another round?"

"No. I'm good. Thanks for not yelling at me," Jimmy said quietly.

Jimmy and I spent the remaining five minutes talking to each other as I put away Hungry, Hungry Hippos. As I walked toward the door, he asked, "Who's going to clean up the egg carton pieces?"

I looked at him and said, "No worries, I'll do that."

He looked at me confused and muttered, "Okay?" as he shrugged his shoulders.

I brought Mom back to the playroom and explained what took place and how I responded. She didn't seem surprised about his outburst and seemed even more skeptical that anything was going to help.

I empathized with her. "I know seeing this mess and hearing about his outburst is discouraging. I can also appreciate that you are worried that nothing is going to work. Can I ask you to do some homework between now and the next session?"

"I can try," she said dejectedly.

"That's all I want you to do. I want you to take out a picture you have of Jimmy between his birth and three months old, a picture of when he was between one and a half and two years old, and a picture of him when he was around five years old. Each day this week when Jimmy has been explosive or disruptive at home, I'd like you to take out one of these pictures and try to recall how you addressed his needs during the age of the picture. For example, if he yells at you or Dad, take a minute and look at his infant picture. Recall a moment when he fussed to get food or a diaper change. Imagine how you felt after you finished meeting his needs and how he responded to getting those needs met."

This assignment often helps parents reconnect with an earlier version of their child, which begins the healing process of the relationship. It may not always work if the parent can only remember difficult times with their child at these ages. The questions about early childhood development in the assessment can clue you in to whether this will work.

She looked at me a little confused but agreed to try.

The next session, Jimmy came straight into the room and got out Hungry, Hungry Hippos. "You know exactly what you want to do. You want to play that game again," I said.

"Yes, I want to see whether I can beat you."

"You want to beat me at the game. I'm sure you have figured out a new way to play."
[Encouragement]

We played the game for about 10 minutes. Jimmy won a few games, and I won a few games. Seeing that he looked upset, I said, "You look sad even though you beat me a few times."

"I'm just not good enough. I do bad things at home and school, and I can't do anything right. You were able to beat me even though I tried my hardest."

"You tried your hardest, and I still won. You want to find a way to be good at a lot of things. What did you do when you won? Try that strategy again." **[Encouragement]**

Jimmy sat for a moment to think about his moves when he won and declared, "Okay, let's try again."

Using the strategies he recalled from winning previous games, Jimmy won the last round and seemed extremely pleased with himself. He stood up and said, "Can I play with any of the toys here?"

"You are wondering whether the toys here are for you to play with. Yes, you can play with them in a lot of the different ways you want to."

Jimmy began exploring the room in depth, getting many toys out, and seemed to have a new energy and confidence. He even pushed a few boundaries that required me to use the limit-setting intervention. He complied with the limits set and continued to explore.

After the session ended, I invited Mom and Dad back to the room. When Dad saw the room, he exclaimed, "Oh no, what did he do?"

I replied, "You seem to think he did something wrong. Can you help me understand your concern?"

"Well, Jimmy never cleans up after himself. He totally trashed your office and just left. I'll go get him to clean it up," Dad said emphatically.

"Oh, no. Let me explain," I said.

I explained to the parents that in the playroom, it is important for the child to feel free to play with whatever they need to, and if I were to ask them to clean up after playing, they may restrict their play. I also explained that I have the toys in a particular place, and I would rather clean them up so I can put them back where they belong.

I told the parents, "I brought you back to let you see this because it is a good sign. For the past few sessions, Jimmy hasn't allowed himself to explore or play with any toys. Today, after playing a few rounds of Hungry, Hungry Hippos, he stood up and started playing with the rest of the toys. He even challenged a few rules and quickly complied when I reminded him of them."

Dad asked, "So how is this going to help him at home with all of his bad behaviors?"

"I'm so glad you asked. I'd like Jimmy to be given 10 minutes every day when he can go outside and just play. Just let him explore and try new things. Allowing him to have a few minutes each day when he can explore things with almost no limits will channel his energy in more constructive ways," I explained.

Jimmy's dad sat up a little bit and said, "Hmm. So, Jimmy has been asking me to build a pinewood derby car with him. Would that count?"

"Yes, but you would need to allow him to do most, if not all, of the work. Allow him to choose how it will look and how it will function," I clarified.

"That is going to be really hard. He doesn't like to lose. If he doesn't make it correctly, it's going to be the slowest car," said Dad.

"I know he doesn't like to lose. I'm working with him on that," I began. "In fact, I think today we made a little progress on that front. I'd really like to see how he does with building the car to his design and find out how he reacts to not winning."

"Okay, I'll try it," Dad said hesitantly.

I had another two sessions where Jimmy wanted to play Hungry, Hungry Hippos and then explored the room with all the toys. Throughout those two weeks, Dad was spending more time with Jimmy building the pinewood derby car, and some of his behaviors at home decreased. Finally, the session after the derby race took place.

As I went to the lobby to bring Jimmy back, his dad approached me and said, "Can I meet with you before you meet with Jimmy? I just want to fill you in on a few things."

"Sure," I said.

Dad started, "So, I did what you asked me to. I let Jimmy design, cut, paint, and build the car to his liking. He designed the ugliest and slowest car of the entire race. At first, I was encouraged that doing this was helping. His behaviors at home and at school decreased, and he was nicer to his mother."

He paused for a minute as if to let that sink in, then he continued, "The day of the race came—and remember how I told you that Jimmy hates to lose? He was eliminated after the first round, which led to him throwing an enormous fit and asking to leave immediately. As you had encouraged us, we stuck around and didn't give in to his aggression. As soon as we got home, he instantly went upstairs and started pissing all over the stairs."

"Okay, how did you respond to his outburst and his behavior at home?" I asked cautiously.

Dad replied, "I told him he was grounded and that he wouldn't be able to go to activities like that again."

I acknowledged Dad's concerns, then said, "What do you think Jimmy was trying to convey with his behavior?"

"He was probably really mad about losing, but it's not okay for him to piss all over the place when things don't go his way."

"You're right, and he has never peed in my office when he lost a game."

Dad continued, "I'm just telling you this because I'm going to sit in this session with you and Jimmy so I can see what he is actually doing in here. I want to make sure he is doing real work."

"I'm totally fine with that, as long as Jimmy is okay with it. I just ask that you observe and don't get too involved with Jimmy, unless he specifically asks you to get involved."

I checked with Jimmy and explained that I would like his father to join us for the session so he could observe how we interact. He assented and asked whether his dad could join him playing Hungry, Hungry Hippos. I agreed that if Jimmy wanted him to, he could.

When we brought Dad back to the session, Jimmy surprised me and didn't get the game but instead got the Nerf guns out. He instantly started pointing them at his dad. "Remember, Jimmy, in here people are not for shooting. It looks like you would really like to shoot the Nerf gun at your dad. You can draw a picture of him on the whiteboard and pretend you are shooting him."

Jimmy looked a little sad about not being able to shoot his dad but went over to the whiteboard and drew a picture of his mom and dad on opposite sides of the whiteboard. He started shooting at his dad only and would shout mean things about his dad as he was shooting. I could tell that his dad was starting to get a little upset about the things he was saying.

Just before Dad opened his mouth, I said, "Wow, Jimmy, something really has made you mad at your dad."

I stopped speaking as if to allow Jimmy some time to process and decide whether he wanted to say more about it. Silence filled the room for about 30 seconds, then Jimmy said, "Yeah, I'm very mad at Dad. He made me lose the pinewood derby race. He didn't help me build my car at all."

"What do you mean he didn't help? Can you explain more to me?"

"Well, he was there with me and would give me some tools and help me cut things out, but he didn't do any of the work. He made me do it."

"You mean kind of like how I made you think about how you won Hungry, Hungry Hippos?"

"Yes, exactly like that. I took my car, and I looked like an idiot. I lost the very first race."

"That sounds very sad. You really wanted to win that race. You thought you would be able to build a car that would win; instead, your car lost right away."

"Yeah . . . I can't do anything right."

"Who won the race, Jimmy?"

"One of my friends."

"Do you think you could ask him how he built his car so that next time you could have a better chance to win?"

"I guess I could do that."

"Before you lost the race, how did you feel about the time you spent with your dad?"

"I loved it. I hardly ever get time to be with him. It was great."

"You loved spending time with your dad, but you were angry and sad that you lost the race. You weren't angry or sad about spending time with your dad, am I correct?"

"Oh, no, not at all. I wish we could spend more time together, but now that the race is over, and we didn't get to advance, I won't be able to spend time with him until next year."

"So, you think that because you won't be at another race, you won't be able to spend more time with your dad until next year."

"Yeah."

"Thank you for telling us how you feel. I know that it is sometimes hard for you to do that."

Jimmy then got the Play-Doh out and asked me and Dad to join him in creating pinewood cars out of playdough. At the end of the session, I met again with Dad and was surprised by his change.

"Wow, I learned so much about Jimmy in here. I think he was so upset that the pinewood project was over because he thought I wouldn't spend time with him until next year. I think he pissed on the stairs because that would mean that his mom or I would have to clean up the mess with him. I'm going to ask him for more projects he would like to do. I'll ask his mom to find a few projects she can do with him too. Thank you for letting me observe that." Moments like this help parents see the value in individual play and solidify the reality that real work is being done.

In addition to conducting couples therapy with Jimmy's parents, I eventually had the opportunity to connect with one of his sports coaches. Despite his quick improvement at home and at school, his family took advantage of the maintenance check-in sessions (see chapter 10) due to his explosive and defiant behavior toward his coach. At the family's request, the coach came to my office to discuss how he could address Jimmy's behavior. I explained the principles behind individual play (e.g., unconditional positive regard, child-directed interactions) and bio-emotion regulation (e.g., self-regulatory behaviors). We discussed different ways the coach could use these principles during his coaching practices (e.g., giving Jimmy more choice in how to accomplish a certain exercise, using balancing or juggling during practices). Just as quickly as the coach started using these different interventions, Jimmy's behaviors began to improve.

Key Takeaway

The key takeaway from the individual play phase is to help the child recolor, or reframe, the view of themselves as the problem and experience acceptance from an adult. If this phase is needed, the child's view of themselves is that of a problem child or outcast. This view carries over from their family to school, the playground, and the neighborhood. They may have tried to escape this judgmental appraisal, but the way they interact with others continues to reinforce this opinion. This phase allows the child to reset their viewpoint and start to see who they really are.

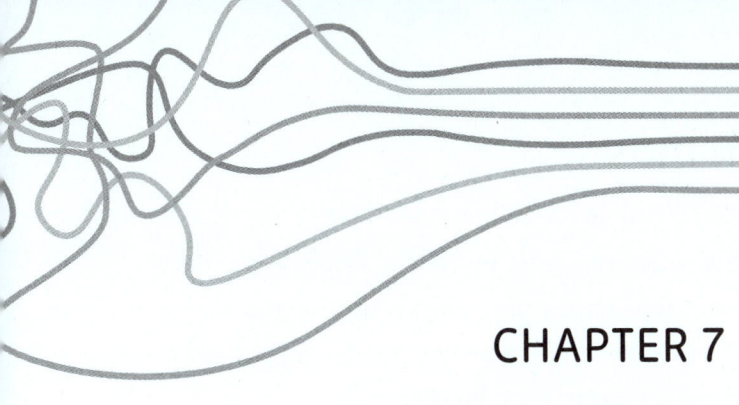

CHAPTER 7

BISON Phase S: Successful Communication

Punishment acceleration occurs regularly in families who have children with DBDs and are used to the reciprocal interactions of the coercion cycle (Patterson & Forgatch, 2010). This is usually observed by instant escalation on the part of the adult, who begins by issuing a command to stop the behavior and then suddenly moves to punishing the child for noncompliance to avoid the possible escalation of behavior. In this chapter, I discuss three direct interventions that address this change in the relational system: effective commands, emotion coaching, and family meetings. These three interventions encapsulate the successful communication phase of treatment.

The most important objective of this phase is the reduction and possible elimination of the coercion cycle dynamics within the parent-child relationship. The bio-emotion regulation and individual play phases are preparatory for this phase and set the foundational work of ensuring continued progress. When the child and parents can regulate themselves (bio-emotion regulation), and positive responses to positive interactions have increased (individual play), the successful communication phase will create a cumulative impact, rolling back the effects of the coercion cycle.

If families are not experiencing emotion dysregulation and the child is already responding well to positive social reinforcement, it may be appropriate to start treatment with this phase. Unfortunately, however, I have learned on several occasions that offering these interventions too soon leads to increased doubt, lackluster results, and deeper entrenchment of the coercion cycle.

Ineffective Commands

Before we dig deep into the effective commands intervention, how to use it, and the research behind it (and how well it works), we must understand ineffective commands. It may sound obvious that most adults prefer *not* to use ineffective commands, but we are notorious for using them. Take a moment to imagine the language you use when directing your child. It might sound like some of the following:

• "Billy, <u>let's</u> get ready for bed."	→ *Let's Command*
• "Erin, <u>why don't you</u> stop hitting your brother?"	→ *Unclear Command*
• "Luke, <u>can you</u> do the dishes?"	→ *Request/Question Command*
• "Frank, <u>I'd be really happy if</u> you picked up your trash." Frank ignores the request, so you follow up with "Frank, <u>that makes me</u> really sad."	→ *Manipulative Command*
• "Becca, <u>we don't</u> use that kind of language in our family."	→ *Exclusive Command*
• "John, you need to brush your teeth, take a shower, clean your room, <u>and</u> get your pj's on."	→ *Chain Command*

These are a sampling of the many types of ineffective commands that we adults naturally find ourselves giving to children. I address some of the more serious offenders below, along with how and why they may not be the most effective options.

Let's Command: "Billy, let's get ready for bed."

These commands include the word *let's* before the content of the command is expressed. Think of this phrase from a child's perspective. Your caregiver is telling you, "Let us go and do something." This phrase implies that you will be joining the child in this activity. For instance, "Let's go do the dishes." Most adults and older teens know intuitively that you are trying to get them to do something by themselves, but if the child you are dealing with is somewhat inflexible (see *Theory of Temperament* in chapter 3), this command will almost surely lead to confrontation or an explosion: "What do you mean *me*? You said *us*. Why do I have to do the dishes by myself?"

When working with children with DBDs, this command creates quite a bit of confusion, hurt, resentment, and relational distance. I encourage parents to do all in their power to eliminate this type of command from their vocabulary.

Unclear Command: "Erin, why don't you stop hitting your brother?"

It may seem clear to an adult what this command is trying to accomplish, but once again, think like a child. At first, the statement is a question ("Why don't . . .") followed by a command ("Stop"). To some children, this might imply that all they need to do is provide an answer to the question: "Because he's a jerk and took my toy." The adult may not respond well to such a statement, since now they're name-calling too. (And you—the adult—prompted the name-calling!) The child then responds with "But you ASKED!"

An unclear command sets up the child for massive confusion as to whether they need to comply, reply to the question, or just think about the statement. This command also sounds a bit like begging, which further confuses the child because now it sounds as if they are in charge: You, the adult, are begging them to do something. Without a clear direction to go with these types of commands, you set yourself and the child up for more conflict.

Request/Question Command: "Luke, can you do the dishes?"

This is one of my favorite commands to role-play with parents. Imagine that you are a child with a list of things you'd like to do in your day: play video games, hang out with friends, watch a movie, eat candy, and so forth. Suddenly, your caregiver approaches you and kindly asks, "Can you please do the dishes?" Most children, especially those who tend to have a strong personal agenda, are likely to say, "No thanks, I'd rather play my video games." This type of command can also begin with "Will you . . ."

Unfortunately, most adults are used to asking things of almost everyone in this manner. It's how I was taught to ask for things as a child. Not surprisingly, this generational difference (or temperamental difference, depending on whom you ask) is ripe for conflict with these types of children. There is nothing wrong with this command for easy or slow-to-warm-up children, but if a child has anything of a difficult temperament within them, this will surely lead to another power struggle. (For an example, see the story about my daughter, Abigail, in chapter 11.)

Manipulative Command: "Frank, I'd be really happy if . . ."

I don't see parents use this command as much, but it can be harmful. The root problem of this command is that it's indirect and makes the request all about how the child's response will affect the adult. It makes the child feel powerless in their ability to manage their own life because if they don't comply or respond appropriately, they are responsible for how the adult feels. Although we want to foster independence, strength, and autonomy—even while commanding a child to accomplish a specific task—this is different from telling a child how their action made us feel (e.g., "I feel sad when you yell at me"). The purpose of a statement like that is to teach children how their actions impact others, even though the adult is still responsible for their own feelings. A manipulative command, on the other hand, makes the child responsible for the emotions of others and uses that to try to get compliance.

Exclusive Command: "Becca, we don't use that kind of language in our family."

This is another harmful command that is used quite regularly. The intention is innocent enough: We want the child to understand what our values and expectations are by letting them know that some behavior is not in conformity with those values or expectations. When we ask a child to change their behavior using this type of command, we are essentially telling them "If you use that type of language, you don't belong in our family." It's obvious to the child that they performed an action that would get them expelled from the family or society. Even if the behavior is something they are unable to control (either because of biological or emotional maturity), the message still stands: They don't belong.

A better way to teach kids about values and behavioral expectations is to use object-first language as explained in the individual play phase. For example, "Becca, that language is hurtful, and people are not for hurting. Is there another way you can say what you feel?"

Chain Command: "... take a shower, clean your room, and get your pj's on."

To many adults, issuing chain commands seems easier and more efficient. We want the child to accomplish many tasks in as short a time as possible. Although this is an approach we can use as adults when we want to accomplish many tasks, many children with DBDs unfortunately have difficulties with working memory and executive functioning. When they are given a chain of commands in quick succession, they generally only remember the last one or two commands. Alternatively, they will zone out and give up trying to remember or execute any of them. There are many ways to help children gain greater working memory and learn to perform executive functioning skills, but until they have such skills, we as adults are setting them and ourselves up for failure.

Effective Commands

In contrast to ineffective commands, the successful communication phase of ISPT draws on the use of effective commands as a primary intervention. As the name of this intervention suggests, effective commands are *commands*. These are statements we give to others with the expectation that they will comply with our desires. Some parents and adults cringe at the word *commands* because we have an embedded cultural belief and desire to increase collaboration and kindness between adults and children. Unfortunately, children with difficult temperaments and who exhibit DBD behaviors need a firm, kind, commanding caregiver; otherwise, they will take advantage of any statements that are unclear or seem like requests.

As you'll recall from chapter 3, the coercion cycle begins and ends with escalation when an adult makes an expectation of compliance from their child. By using effective commands, we can improve compliance rates by 20 to 40 percent (Matheson & Shriver, 2005)—with children's overall compliance rate typically increasing to an average of 90 percent. Considering that the average observed baseline rate of compliance for children exhibiting DBDs is typically below 20 percent, this is an astonishing jump.

To give an effective command, you should be within an arm's length of the target child. It is best to begin by touching the child on the shoulder or knee to get their attention. Ensure that they are looking at you before issuing the command. With exceptionally challenging children, it is best to approach the child and be slightly below the eyeline of the child. This can prevent the child from viewing you as an authoritarian or dictator and make them more likely to comply with the command. Once the child is looking at you, issue a single command in a calm but firm manner: "Jeremy, I need you to [*issue command*] right now, please."

After you issue the command, you should step slightly away from the child (about six inches) and allow them to process the command. This means that you should remain silent, while still looking at the child, for up to 15 seconds. (No counting out loud!) Importantly, during these 15 seconds, the child may start escalating by yelling, screaming, debating, or negotiating. No matter what happens—short of violence*—you should ignore it all. Yes, this means even if the child is calling you all sorts of nasty names. During these 15 seconds, you should use self-soothing techniques to stay calm and grounded. This can involve using breathing exercises, visualizations, or nonverbal affirmations.

After these 15 (long) seconds, if the child complies, you should praise them in the following manner: "Jeremy, thank you so much for [*repeat the command or say 'doing what I asked'*]. I really appreciate your compliance." Should the child *not* comply with the command, repeat the command with a warning of a consequence. It is important that this consequence is small but impactful to the child (e.g., removal of TV time, going to bed early, no dessert, 10 minutes of a work chore). After repeating the command and the warning of a consequence, wait silently for another 15 seconds.

Again, if the child complies, praise the child for their compliance. You should *not* mention anything about how long the child took to comply or the fact that the child only complied *after* the warning of a consequence. Nothing negative about the child should be mentioned. *Only* praise their compliance. Should the child *not* comply after the second bout of 15 seconds is over, you should execute the consequence by repeating what the consequence is ("Okay, Jeremy, you have chosen not to have TV time tonight"). Then, walk away and do not engage with the child in argument or debate. If, after the child notices that you are serious about executing the consequence, they comply, you can thank them for complying, but it is imperative that you remain steadfast and follow through with the consequence.

The whole point of this intervention is to train the child to comply within 15 seconds of a command being issued. Using effective commands with children who have DBDs has been shown to accomplish this. Any deviation from this process tends to reduce the effectiveness of treatment because the coercion cycle regains its hold on the family dynamics. These interventions are designed to reduce and eliminate escalated responses.

---

* If violence occurs, ensure that you, the child, and anyone else are safe first. This may mean removing yourself or others from the room. Then, depending on the age of the child and the extent of the violence, different responses are recommended. These are explained in more detail in the troubleshooting section of this chapter.

Introducing the Intervention

As you can guess, there are many places in the intervention where parents or other adults may be skeptical or unwilling to give it a try. The best way to introduce it to parents is to role-play how it should be conducted. I usually use a timer to demonstrate how it feels for time to pass. Many adults are surprised by how long 15 seconds feels.

During the role-play, you need to bring out your best and most accurate portrayal of a disruptive child. If you have worked with disruptive children, it is pretty easy. If you are not used to working with disruptive children, just imagine the main character from *Dennis the Menace* or *Problem Child*, both of whom provide great examples of a typical disruptive child. Each time I have role-played as the child, the parents have remarked that they are quite surprised by how accurate my depiction is. The role-play is completed in the following way:

- Briefly describe the intervention and explain it in detail using the following *Using Effective Commands* handout.
- Ask whether the parents have any questions about the intervention.
- Ask who would like to role-play the adult as you role-play the child.
- Use a toy and instruct the adults to tell you, "[*Therapist's name*], I need you to put the toy on the table right now, please."
- After the parent gives this instruction, you, as the child, must wait for about 12 seconds before complying. During the 12 seconds, you should "talk back" to the parent. Yell, call names, or try to get the parent to engage in negotiation or debate. Do the best you can to engage the parent during the 12 seconds.
- After 12 seconds have passed, lightly slam the toy on the table and say, "FINE! There you go," or something along those lines.
- Debrief with the parents about their experience during this role-play.

After you have debriefed with the parents and answered any of the questions they bring up, invite them to try using this intervention with one single command they need to give at home. It could be to eat dinner, get ready for bed, or something else that can be accomplished by issuing one command.

CLIENT HANDOUT

Using Effective Commands

The following instructions explain how to use effective commands in order to get your child to comply with a task.

1. Get your child's attention:
    a. Approach your child before giving any commands.
    b. Touch your child on the shoulder.
    c. Establish eye contact.
    d. Try to be one to two inches below your child's eyeline.

2. State the instruction clearly:
    a. Using a clear, firm, kind voice, issue the command in the form of a statement: "[*Child's name*], I need you to [*command*] right now, please."
    b. Do *not* use questions or unclear commands.

3. Pause for 15 seconds:
    a. Allow the child to process your command by pausing silently for 15 seconds.
    b. Count slowly in your head.
    c. Self-soothe when the child talks back, yells, does not comply, or acts in a way that you do not approve of.
    d. Ignore all behavior, except for violence. (If they are violent, skip to step 7.)

4. If they do not comply, restate the command with a warning of a consequence:
    a. Using a clear, firm, and kind voice, issue the command in the form of a statement: "[*Child's name*], I need you to [*command*] right now, please. If you choose not to [*command*], you will lose 10 minutes of video game time today."
    b. Do *not* threaten or use a consequence you are *not* willing to follow through with.

5. Pause for another 15 seconds:
    a. Allow the child to process your command by pausing silently for 15 seconds.
    b. Count slowly in your head.

- c. Self-soothe when the child talks back, yells, does not comply, or acts in a way that you do not approve of.
- d. Ignore all behavior, except for violence.

6. If the child follows your command, praise the compliance:
    a. Say, "Thank you for listening."
    b. Do *not* criticize or correct the child's previous noncompliance.
    c. Do *not* mention any behavior that you dislike happening during the pauses.

6. If the child does not follow your command, follow through with the warning:
    a. Proceed to enact the consequence.
    b. Repeat steps 4 and 5 until compliance is achieved.
    c. Limit consequences to 24 hours.

7. If the child becomes violent, ensure everyone is safe by either removing yourself or others from the presence of the violent child. After everyone is safe, attend to the violent child in the following manner, depending on the age of the child:
    a. Six months to four years old: Gently hold the child in a way to prevent them from hurting themselves or you. While holding them, calmly emotion coach and validate their emotions.
    b. Four years to nine years old: Hold the hands or feet of the child in a gentle but firm way, kneeling in front of the child in a way that maintains your safety. Proceed with emotion coaching and validating the emotions of the child.
    c. Nine years and older (depending on the size of the child): Maintain a safe distance from the child, and do not engage in physical contact unless the child is harming themselves. If they are harming themselves, do what you can to safely prevent intense harm. Attempt to redirect their expression of violence to an appropriate alternative. Use emotion coaching to try to understand what provoked the violence.

Troubleshooting Effective Commands

Take a moment to think about this intervention. Is this an intervention you have used in your life? Have you personally experienced its utility and effectiveness? If not, it'll be difficult to convince others to try it or to navigate skepticism presented by parents and other adults. So, before you use this intervention, try it yourself and troubleshoot the bugs that arise from your own use.

When parents or other adults express skepticism about this intervention to me, I ask them what their concerns are and then walk them through how this intervention is intended to work. Here are some of their more common skepticisms or concerns they have encountered when attempting this intervention:

1. **The child starts screaming or is violent toward themselves or others when this intervention is attempted:** This is usually an indication that the child is unable to regulate themselves when given a command. They are so used to the coercion cycle dynamics that they are unable to cognitively understand the command. This indicates that more regulatory biofeedback is needed before starting this intervention. If the child does express violence, it is important for the adult to attend to the safety of all those in the presence of the violence. Once that violence is attended to, they can intervene with the appropriate steps depending on the child's age and size. (See step 7 of the *Using Effective Commands* handout.)

2. **The adult is unable to disengage during the silent portion of the intervention. They tend to get sucked into an argument or debate with the child when they should be regulating themselves:** This is an indication that some regulatory work is needed for the adults as well as the child. Biofeedback could be a good option, or they may need some individual therapy for a few sessions before trying this intervention again.

3. **There is nothing that they can "take away" or "punish" the child with because their child "doesn't care" about anything:** This usually occurs when the family is entrenched in the coercion cycle and overuses punishment to deal with all aspects of behavior. This is one of the reasons that the child-centered play interventions from chapter 6 (individual play phase) are prescribed before this intervention. If the adults continue to see this as a concern, redirect them to continue to use nondirective, noncontingent play times at home.

4. **One parent buys into the intervention, and the other parent doesn't:** Typically, when one parent starts this command structure with a child but the other parent isn't convinced about its utility, they will jump in and try to discipline the child during the 15 seconds when behaviors should be ignored. This undermines the process and increases the likelihood of triangulation. This indicates the need for some couples therapy to help both parents get on board. It may take a few sessions of couples therapy to help both parents understand the necessity of the ignoring portion of the intervention. The provider should role-play with each parent a few times to make sure they both understand the process.

5. **The child simply won't stay put when the parent tries to initiate the effective commands structure:** This typically occurs early on with this intervention and can be quite frustrating for parents. If this is a concern, I usually have them start using this structure very slowly with commands that take place when the child is a "captive audience." For example, at the dinner table, as the child has a fork or spoon full of food and are lifting it toward their mouth, the parent should quickly say something like "[*Child's name*], I need you to take a bite of your food for me right now, please." Almost instinctively, the child will continue eating their food, just a little confused as to why their parent is now "commanding" them to do so. After the child has "complied," the parent should finish by saying, "Thank you, [*child's name*], for doing what I say." It could easily be introduced this way at school as well. For example, as the child is about to sit in their chair, on the way down, the teacher can say, "[*Child's name*], I need you to sit on your bottom right now, please," following up with the same appreciation for compliance. This can be done multiple times a day for about a week or two before trying other scenarios where the child may have "escape potential." More often than not, the child will become used to the protocol and will begin to comply without running away.

6. **Adults are worried that by *not* mentioning misbehavior that takes place during the silent portion of the intervention, they are letting the child get away with bad behavior:** This is a common concern, especially for adults who come from a behavior modification background. I help them understand that this intervention is *not* about changing behavior; instead, it is about communicating in a way that the child is able to hear and understand. So often, when children are given commands or requests, their fight-or-flight

system automatically kicks in. They perceive the command as a threat to their personal and emotional safety. If we discipline during this process, we are essentially telling the child that they shouldn't trust their bodies, and they are being punished for having a normal nervous system response. The process of ignoring the negative behavior during the silent period is to prioritize an emphasis on compliance and good behavior. Children thrive on positive praise and encouragement. In fact, recall from chapter 5 the research about reward and punishment pathways for children. The more we improve the relationship with the child, the more likely rewards and consequences will work. Until then, and within the successful communication phase, negative behavior should be ignored.

Emotion Coaching

Emotion coaching is a parenting skill that allows children to express and understand their own emotions (Gottman & DeClaire, 1997). This skill, when combined with the use of effective commands, decreases the use of coercion dynamics to communicate. Briefly, emotion coaching consists of five key steps: (1) maintain an awareness of our own and the child's emotions, (2) recognize emotions and as an opportunity to connect with the child, (3) listen empathically and nonjudgmentally to the child's emotions, (4) name the emotions we *think* the child is experiencing, and (5) set limits or problem-solve if necessary. To teach parents how to use this emotion coaching with their children, I use the acronym ALERT to remember its steps: **a**cknowledge, **l**ean, **e**mpathize, **r**ecite, **t**rain.

Acknowledge

Acknowledge that all of us experience emotions. Parents have emotions. Children have emotions. The first step in emotion coaching is acknowledging that emotions are a natural and good part of our biology and lives. If we fail to acknowledge our own or the child's emotional experience, we will inadvertently encourage emotional dismissal.

Lean

After we acknowledge our human emotional experience, we need to lean into the emotion as a connecting force. This may be difficult to do if the emotion that the child is experiencing is anger or frustration. However, all emotions are expressions of our desire and our need to connect. When we lean into those emotional experiences, we strengthen our connections with the child by demonstrating to them that we see them for who they are and not for their behaviors. This unconditional positive regard allows the child to let down their defenses.

Empathize

Empathy is the ability to hear another person's emotional experience and imagine how we might feel if we were in their shoes. This also requires that we sit in nonjudgment while listening to the emotional experience of the child. We must recognize that their experience is just as valid as ours, even if we disagree with how they may perceive that experience.

Recite

After we can nonjudgmentally empathize with and lean into the child's emotional experience, we need to recite what emotion we believe the child is experiencing. We may be completely off base with whatever word we use, but that is not the point of this step. The idea behind it is to begin the process of helping the child understand different emotion words for the experiences they are having. When we allow the child to correct us if we are wrong, they gain more confidence in understanding their own bodies and see that adults are going to respect their perspective.

Train

Sometimes, after we have completed the first four steps of emotion coaching, we may need to set limits with the child or assist them with problem-solving. If the child has used behavior or violence to express their emotions, it is necessary to set limits on that behavior. It is appropriate to clarify that while emotions, desires, and wishes are acceptable, some behavior is not. If the child has expressed an emotion (e.g., anger) but requires help problem-solving the situation (e.g., they didn't do their chore, so they can't play with a friend), this is the time to walk the child through different problem-solving steps (e.g., have the child brainstorm ideas, talk about the pros and cons of each idea and how it might be implemented to solve the problem, allow the child to select the solution, agree with the child to readdress this problem in a week to see whether the solution worked).

When parents, teachers, and other adults use these steps, children show significant reductions in disruptive behaviors (Dunsmore et al., 2013, 2016; Rose et al., 2015; Wilson et al., 2013). Children start to be seen for who they are without being criticized or judged for their emotions, and parents start to see an increase in compliance. Additionally, the black-and-white beliefs that adults often hold about a child's behaviors (e.g., "They're doing it for attention," "They don't have any manners," or "They are just being lazy") begin to shift as they learn to recognize the spectrum of colorful emotions behind these behaviors. The following *Emotion Coaching* handout helps you introduce this approach to parents and other caregivers in the child's life.

CLIENT HANDOUT

Emotion Coaching

Below is a brief description of the five steps of emotion coaching. I have adapted these steps using the acronym ALERT to help you remember them. Another way to think about it is that when you are *alert* to the emotional needs of the child, you are able to reduce disruptive behaviors.

<u>A</u>cknowledge:

- This step requires that you acknowledge that you have emotions and that your child has emotions. When you can acknowledge your emotions and understand what they are, you can do the same for your child.
- This step also requires that you acknowledge that emotions are a normal part of being a human. Recognize that there are no *bad* emotions. They just *are*.

<u>L</u>ean:

- During this step, you lean into the experience of emotions as an opportunity to connect. If you do not lean toward the emotional experience, you create distance between you and your child.
- Leaning in means you look for emotional cues (e.g., frowning, irritability, smiling) and see them as opportunities to connect. Even anger or irritability is an opportunity to connect to your child.

<u>E</u>mpathize:

- Empathy requires putting aside your judgment regarding your child's emotions, and the ways they are expressing these emotions, and recognizing that the experience your child is having is authentic. The key to empathy is seeing the world from the eyes of another person.
- Using a basic framework of empathy can help. This basic framework looks something like "You feel [*feeling word*] because [*restate the concern*]..."

Recite:
- When reciting the emotion words your child is likely feeling, don't be afraid to be wrong. Use whatever word or words you think best describes the experience or expression that your child is having (e.g., anger, sadness, happiness, joy, love, frustration, anxiety, worry).
- Be okay with your child correcting you if you get it wrong. Remember this is your child's experience; your view may not be exactly their view.

Train:
- If your child has expressed a behavior that needs to be corrected, or has a problem that needs to be resolved, only do so after completing the first four steps.
- Walk them through their problem and help *them* create a solution.

More About Empathy:
- Empathy is *not* logical. The child's feelings may or may not be logical, but that does not matter. What matters is that the child is feeling it. For example:

  > Imagine you are late to an important meeting, and you are traveling above the speed limit on the highway but only slightly faster than the rest of traffic. But it's your unlucky day, and you are pulled over and given an expensive speeding ticket, which you cannot afford and also makes you late to your meeting. Later, when you call a friend about the incident, they respond, "Well, technically, you were going over the speed limit, and the officer was just following the law." This is a "logic" answer or response.

- Empathy is *not* argument or criticism. You do not have to agree with a person to validate their concern. Don't argue about feelings. For example:

  > Imagine the same incident as above, but when you call your friend to vent, the response you get is "You shouldn't be angry. The officer was just doing his job. It was your own fault; you were speeding, and you deserved to be embarrassed for being late!" This is an argument or criticism response.

- Empathy is *not* problem-solving. Problem-solving is easy, whereas validating someone's experience takes time. This time creates room for intimacy, and easiness is seen as nonconcern. For example:

  > With the same incident above, your friend starts giving you solutions like "You need to leave for work earlier so you don't speed," "If you asked your

boss for a raise, the money wouldn't be an issue," or "Maybe you should go to bed earlier so you aren't in a rush every morning." These statements try to solve the problem that your friend perceives led to your incident.

- Empathy is *not* an inquisition. People may not know why they feel the way they feel. Asking why only creates a distance and makes them feel defensive. Imagine your friend starts asking the following questions in quick succession:

    "Why does it make you mad that you were late?"

    "Why couldn't you just leave for your job on time?"

    "What was so important this morning that you were late to your meeting?"

    "Do you think the officer targeted you?"

    "I know how you drive. What is it going to take to get you to slow down?"

- Empathy *is* hearing the other person fully. Imagining the speeding ticket incident from above, an emotion-based validating response would be "Wow, that would have been so frustrating!"

Building Emotional Closeness:

- The image below demonstrates how using emotion coaching increases emotional closeness between you and your child.
- Try to see behavior problems as opportunities for closeness and try to validate the emotion your child is likely feeling at the time.

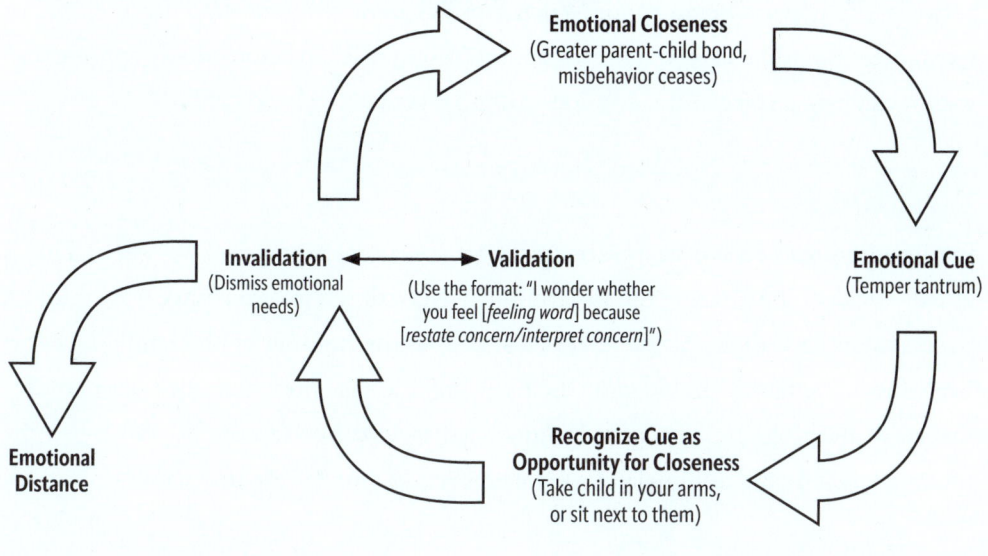

Family Meetings

The final intervention in the successful communication phase is the family meeting. To correct negative communication patterns, especially when the coercion cycle has been used, the family needs to use a more constructive process for discussing family problems. The idea behind all phases in ISPT is that the therapist will work themselves out of a job. Hence, teaching families how to conduct productive process meetings on their own is necessary.

There are many ways to successfully hold a family meeting since each family is different in its makeup, presenting concerns, and emotional and cognitive bandwidth. However, there are some basics steps you'll need to follow when holding a family meeting, which can be remembered with the acronym SAFE: **s**tructured, **a**rranged, **f**ocused, and **e**xpedient. Apart from these main steps, I encourage you to develop an approach to family meetings that is best for each of your own clients.

Structured

For a successful family meeting to take place, there needs to be an agreed-upon structure, defined by the parents, regarding how the meeting will be run. Will everyone be able to speak at once? Do people have to take turns? How will the family determine the agenda of the meeting? You can guide parents through this process of structuring their family meeting so that when they present the structure to their family, there is agreement between the parents beforehand. When families have children who are preteens or teens, they should be involved in this conversation (as is developmentally appropriate) so they can have a voice in the decision-making process.

Arranged

Family meetings need to be prearranged and consistent from week to week. This is usually decided upon during the structuring conversation. However, once it is arranged, there should be little to no event that can eclipse the holding of the family meeting. Everyone in the family should clear their schedules for the predetermined day and time that these meetings are arranged. Parents need to lead by example by sticking to the meeting schedule and holding all family members responsible for attendance.

Focused

Without an agenda, family meetings can feel like lectures or wasted time. Each agenda should accommodate the prearranged time frame that the meeting is scheduled for. Parents need to communicate to the children how items can be added to the agenda, and each item should be discussed equally to demonstrate commitment to the process.

Expedient

Family meetings should not be prolonged past the prearranged scheduled time. This also needs to be determined with an understanding of the developmentally appropriate attention span for each child. If a child is unable to sit for 20 minutes, and a family meeting is scheduled for 90 minutes, it will not be a successful family meeting. The parents should consider the child with the shortest attention span and ensure that the meeting length does not exceed 75 percent of that child's attentional capacity. For example, if a child has an attention span of 10 minutes, the meeting should not exceed seven and a half minutes. This may limit the number of items that can be discussed each meeting, but consistently holding even a five-minute family meeting will result in more productive behaviors and interactions within the family.

The handout on the next page provides guidelines regarding the SAFE structure that you can provide families.

CLIENT HANDOUT

Conducting Family Meetings

An important step in creating family harmony and eliminating the coercion cycle is by conducting regular family meetings. Family meetings allow every member of the family to voice concerns or identify issues that need to be resolved. They also can be used for managing the complex scheduling needs of families, such as planning vacation or tracking sporting events that children are involved in.

It is important to have a format to use when conducting family meetings. I suggest you use the SAFE format. This acronym helps families remember all the essentials of holding family meetings, as well as the underlying reason for them: to *safe*ly discuss concerns.

Structured:
Family meetings must have a structure. A structure can include who talks first, who decides when others can talk, how issues will be brought up, and how decisions will be made. Generally, the parents decide on the structure. However, as children age and become teenagers, they should be included in the decision-making process.

Arranged:
Additionally, family meetings need to be arranged and scheduled. Everyone in the family needs to attend the arranged meeting for it to be effective. The arrangement of the meeting can accommodate the needs of all family members, but the result must be a dedicated time and day for when the meeting takes place.

Focused:
Without a focused agenda, meetings will typically become nothing more than complaint or lecture sessions. Along with the structure that is built, there should be a way for concerns to be added to the agenda. Agendas ensure that the meetings stay focused and decisions are made.

Expedient:
A meeting without a scheduled end time is not likely to be successful. All meetings must have a dedicated time length for which they are held. Once the time is up, the meeting should end. The agenda items that do not get addressed should be carried over to the next meeting.

Case Example: *Carol*

Carol was an extremely defiant teenager. She was referred to my office due to her failing grades, her violent behavior toward her peers, and her screaming matches with her mother and stepfather. Her stepfather was ready to kick her out of the house at any moment due to the increasing disturbance Carol brought to the family. I worked with Carol and her mother for three months during the bio-emotion regulation and individual play phases before her mom and stepdad could start the successful communication phase. At almost every session for those three months, Mom asked me, "When are we going to work on getting Carol to listen?" It took determination on my part and a good therapeutic relationship to convince Mom that we would get to it.

During the bio-emotion regulation phase, I was able to demonstrate to Mom with the HeartMath device that Carol was doing better with her ability to regulate during difficult interactions. At first, when I challenged Carol during our sessions, her heart rate would spike, and she would be unable to think clearly. However, after several sessions and consistent practice of heart-focused breathing at home, she was able to engage in difficult and challenging tasks with only minor changes in her heart rate. As we moved to the individual play phase, Mom started to spend one-on-one time with Carol once a week, sometimes reading books or talking about school gossip. Sometimes, they would go for a walk and discuss Mom's hopes for Carol's future. By the fifth week, she was better able to regulate, and her teachers started to report better cooperation in class.

At the end of our 11th session, I told Mom it was time to teach her and her husband how to get Carol to comply. I scheduled a session when they both could attend, and when they came in, I started with "So, do you both think you have what it takes to get Carol to comply? This is going to require quite a bit of strength from both of you to be able to accomplish this." They looked questioningly at me, believing that I was overexaggerating the difficulty of the task I was about to give them.

"On average, what percentage of the commands you give Carol does she comply with?" I asked them.

Stepdad was quick to answer, "No more than 15 percent, I'm sure."

"More like 5 to 10 percent," Mom countered.

I replied, "Okay. So what percentage of commands would you assume a 'typical' teenager complies with?"

Again, Stepdad was quick to answer, "My kids complied with at least 75 percent of my commands, and they weren't the best, so somewhere around 75 to 85 percent."

Mom nodded in agreement.

I shocked them both by saying, "What if I told you the real number is near 50 percent?"

Mom blurted, "That would be a dream. If we could get Carol to comply with just 50 percent of our commands, I'm sure our home would be much more peaceful."

"Okay," I replied. "What is one command you think she would comply with about 50 percent of the time you ask her?"

After about 15 more minutes of discussion about the correct command to start with (we decided on getting ready for bed) and describing the need to be clear, concise, and direct with the command, I asked who would like to do the first role-play.

Mom volunteered. Stepdad expected immediate compliance and did not tolerate disrespect, so I was very clear that he needed to remain quiet and observant during the role-play. I got my most annoying toy out and told them to ask me to put it on the table.

"Michael, I need you to put that toy on the table right now, please," Mom stated very carefully, calmly, and directly.

I ignored her at first. Within three seconds, she repeated the command *and* Stepdad stepped in and said, "Listen to your mother."

Already they had failed the first task of remaining quiet and waiting for 15 seconds. I stopped the role-play and said, "Okay, let's talk about what just happened. Mom, you didn't wait 15 seconds; you reminded me within three seconds. And Stepdad, you jumped in right after Mom issued the reminder. Tell me what was going on for each of you."

I empathized with their concerns, redescribed the intervention, explained the importance of the 15-second silent period, and asked them to begin again.

"Dr. Whitehead, I don't think you understand. THIS. WILL. NEVER. WORK."

I took a deep breath and paused for a moment as I looked Carol's mother in the eyes. "Mom, all I want you to do is try it. Just give this tool a try and let me know how it goes. I'm not expecting miracles. I just want to make sure we go through all our options before trying something more drastic."

This time, Mom remained silent for five seconds before I started yelling, "I can't believe how stupid you are!" Both parents flinched but remained steadfast and silent. I then muttered under my breath, "Bitch . . ." Still nothing from them. At 12 seconds, I slammed the toy on the table and said, begrudgingly, "FINE! YOU WIN!"

Both parents looked like they had just run a marathon. Both were breathing heavily, seemingly exhausted from this 12-second experiment.

To be clear, I don't casually or regularly call my clients names, let alone swear at them. However, to help parents of these kids really understand how to use this intervention, it is important to use the language that their own children would use. Act as much like their own child as possible. This requires two things: a strong working alliance with the parents and an intimate knowledge of the way the child and parents interact.

I debriefed with Carol's parents by asking, "What was that role-play like for you? How long did I defy you?"

Carol's mom replied, "It felt like forever! I was transported to my living room, and you were Carol. It was uncanny. This is going to be so hard..."

After more troubleshooting and a few more role-plays until they completed the intervention perfectly, I ended the session. Carol's mom said, "Dr. Whitehead, *if* this works, I'm going to buy you a steak dinner. Just don't hold your breath."

As is the case with most of my clients, Carol's parents came back exactly one week later and exclaimed, "This was the most magical thing I have ever learned! I've been using it on *all* of our kids. If I'd known that this could get them to comply, I would have been doing this years ago! Why didn't you *start* with this technique?"

I answered, "I was just as skeptical as you were when I first learned about this intervention. The funny thing is, this technique has been available and in use since at least the late 1970s, yet I didn't even know about it until I was in my second year of my PhD program. I was totally unsure that the intervention would work until I started using it on my own children and fell in love with its outcomes. I've also found that unless we build the foundation by using the bio-emotion regulation and individual play phases, we don't get a lot of success."

In addition to working with Carol's parents on effective commands, it also became clear that treatment needed to address one particular element in her macrosystem: her cultural system. Carol had grown up in a very traditional religious culture, which she experienced as oppressive. To get a better understanding of her religious culture, her parents connected me with ecclesiastical leaders from their congregation. Having a better understanding of their beliefs, I was able to encourage her parents and religious leaders to use emotion coaching when they interacted with Carol. While this did not drastically alter how she felt about her religious tradition, having greater acceptance from her parents and leaders continued to soften her views toward them.

Key Takeaway

The key takeaway from the successful communication phase is to reshape the way parents and children interact with each other. They have been so used to using the coercion cycle that even simple communication with each other increases opportunities for defiance and opposition. When parents learn how to use effective commands and conduct effective family meetings, they start to notice different hues of color in their child. The child is no longer viewed from a black-and-white perspective, where they are all bad, but they begin to see the nuance in their responses.

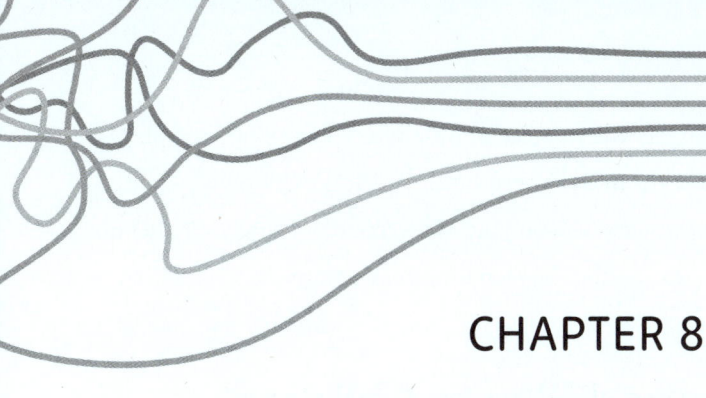

CHAPTER 8

BISON Phase O: Organized Play

In chapter 3, I introduced Murray Bowen's (1966) concept of triangulation and its effects on family systems. According to Bowen, triangles are the most stable relationship possible, despite how problematic they are, which is why a dyadic relationship (a relationship between two individuals) often needs an uninvolved third party to remain stable. Unfortunately, many times this means that the third party is often mistreated or experiences the stress of being left out.

Bowen (1966) theorized that how we function in relationships reflects our ability to remain true to ourselves while also remaining connected to another. He called this ability *differentiation of self*. Importantly, the higher someone's differentiation of self, the more able they are to remain in a stable dyadic relationship without needing to involve a third party. The lower their differentiation of self, the more likely they are to need to triangulate someone to dissipate the stress of the relational dynamics. Since triangulation significantly increases the incidences of disruptive behaviors, you will want to assess for and address triangulation effectively when working with families (Buehler, 2020; Jacobvitz et al., 2022; Murphy et al., 2017).

An effective way to address triangulation is to use organized play, which is a form of directive play therapy that combines different directive play therapy approaches. This can include cognitive behavioral play, Adlerian play, AutPlay, TheraPlay, prescriptive play, and systemic play. It is up to you to decide which approach is most appropriate for your client. Some clients may require an outside referral to an appropriately trained provider for this phase of therapy. Indeed, as with individual play, you should only use this intervention if you have at least 50 hours of educational training and two to three hours of observed supervision in directive play therapy. However, unlike individual play, organized play is led by the therapist, not the child. This makes it even more critical that you are trained to use this approach appropriately; otherwise, you may inadvertently infuse your agenda into the child rather than allowing the child to be seen for who they are.

Introducing Organized Play to Children

Children naturally adapt to and enjoy the nondirective nature of the individual play phase, so when you notice a need to introduce organized play, it can be a challenge for some kids. These children have often been told what to do (or not do) in many different environments in their lives, so when you introduce this new directive approach, it can feel a bit overwhelming to them. I tend to introduce organized play in the following way:

"Isabella, normally in here, I give you the opportunity to play in a lot of the ways you like to. Today, we are going to start something new. It is called *My Time* and *Your Time*. The way it works is that when it is My Time, we are going to do an activity that I want to do, and you will follow the rules according to my instructions. When it is Your Time, we will go back to the way things have been, and you will be able to play with the toys in the ways you choose. What would you like to do first, My Time or Your Time?"

This gradual shift to more directive play helps the child acclimate to the more in-depth triangulation intervention I will do later on. It also helps the child see that they still have some autonomy in the playroom. I give them time to do individual play and the power to decide whether it comes first or last. When fulfilling the directive play intervention, I'm able to target specific behaviors or concerns without being too blunt or confrontive with the child.

Common Reasons to Introduce Organized Play

Triangulation

If you witness hints of triangulation or see the child stay stuck in one theme of individual play for far too long (e.g., 5 to 10 sessions), this is a good sign to introduce organized play. I look for moments when the child may be using behavior to get the attention of one parent over another (e.g., Jimmy) or when the child's behavior dramatically changes and improves when individual play is introduced. Another indication of triangulation is that the child clearly favors one parent over another even after both parents are spending one-on-one time with the child as I recommend. I also look for moments during individual play when the child says something about one of their parents that could come from another adult (e.g., "My dad is bipolar" or "My mom spends too much money"). During individual play, a child might be playing with dolls or figures and let this slip out. For example, when playing with two figures in the sand, a five-year-old girl took an adult figure and a child figure and played out the following scene between the two:

ADULT FIGURE: Momma stays at work too long. I wish you had a momma who cared and was home.

CHILD FIGURE: I'm sad when you and momma fight.

ADULT FIGURE: I know, honey. I'm trying my best to keep her happy. You know how angry she is if dinner isn't made when she gets home. I always love that you hug me after she yells at me.

It doesn't take a trained therapist to know that this conversation is not ideal. The great thing about play therapy sessions is that they are windows into the way the child views the world. The concern is not whether what the child played out using the dolls took place exactly as she expressed. The concern is that she is somehow being triangulated between her parents. One parent is using the child to express her frustrations about the other in an unhealthy way. Or at least, that is how the child views the situation. When these frustrations are experienced by the child, she unknowingly or unintentionally starts to develop resentment toward either one or both parents.

Aggression

One of the most common themes revealed during individual play and addressed with organized play is aggression. This theme looks like a child who is always wanting to battle with toys and use aggressive toys (e.g., guns, knives, aggressive animals, aggressive human figures). They will typically use these toys in ways that are violent in nature, either toward the toys, the provider, or the child themselves. When I see this theme played out regularly in individual play without much change, I transition toward organized play to help the child work out the aggression in a different way.

Allowing children to express aggression in a strategic and nonviolent way allows them to be recognized by you, their parents, and the world for the power within them.

Another directive play therapy approach that addresses aggression is role-play. When I use role-play as an aggression-targeting intervention, I instruct the child that we are going to do a mixture of My Time and Your Time. I use themes and stories that they have played out in the session before and tell them a story.

This directive approach teaches children to negotiate and work out problems without using aggression. The child's aggressive theme may continue in or out of sessions for a few more weeks until they use some of the negotiation tactics demonstrated during role-plays with me and with their family and friends.

Defiance

As you would expect, children with disruptive behaviors often express themes of defiance. This theme can be a bit difficult to spot if you don't know what to look for. Generally, this theme presents itself as control. The child quickly catches on to the "child-centered" idea of individual play, and they start directing you to do nearly everything. Instead of asking for help, they command you to play in a particular way. The reason this control falls into the defiance theme is that, many times, defiant children have preconceived notions of how things should work or how others will view them. They expect others to act toward them in a certain way (generally in a negative or controlling way), so they prioritize their agenda over anyone else's. This is done in the hope that they can finally do things their own way. In the playroom, this can look like a child who chooses games and makes rules that control the outcome where they will win every round. Or they continue to play make-believe games with toys and make you, the therapist, always lose the make-believe game. There is nothing that you can do to win.

The organized play intervention I use when this theme presents itself is a combination of bio-emotion regulation and individual play. I let the child know that I want to find out how good they are at sitting quiet and still. I get a timer out and ask them to guess how long they can remain quiet and sit on the chair without moving. Alternatively, I see how long they can stand still enough to balance an egg carton on their head. No one wins; it's not a competition. It's all about them beating their last time. I record how long they can stay quiet and still and put it on the whiteboard in big block numbers. They get satisfaction whenever they beat their previous time, and they learn how to further delay gratification, which leads to greater emotion regulation and less defiance.

Anger

Another common theme for children with disruptive behaviors is anger. Many of my clients present with anger because they are being told that they are a problem that needs to be fixed. Anger tends to come out in their play quite regularly. This anger can look like control or aggression, but it is usually targeted at someone—many times a parent, sibling, or teacher. As with the case of Frederick from chapter 1, anger toward one parent can often be directed at the therapist. Each therapist must decide for themselves how much anger they are willing to tolerate and absorb. No one can tell anyone else what is an appropriate amount of anger to handle. My first rule in the playroom—I am not for hurting—prepares the child to understand that expressing violence in the playroom toward me is not okay. This does not mean that anger is not okay. As my body ages and takes longer to recover, I am less tolerant of absorbing the hits from children and more ready to issue the ACT limit-setting redirect to pretend another object is me, and they are free to hit that.

Some parents and providers may object to this idea, thinking that allowing any sort of angry expression may lead to greater violent tendencies. I have had adults tell me they are concerned their child won't differentiate between real life and play and will be more prone to hitting themselves or another child. In my experience, this has not been the case. In fact, when I absorb anger and allow it to be expressed in the playroom, I tend to see a precipitous decline of anger expressed violently toward others—especially as I reinforce the limit that people are not for hurting.

When anger is prevalent during play sessions, the organized play intervention I use could be best understood as redirection. Using Jenga blocks or large cardboard bricks, I ask the child to create a structure as high as they possibly can. I connect them to a finger pulse oximeter, and then I warn them that as they are building, I may wiggle the table or walk a little too close to their brick tower. I explain that I know that this will make them upset, but the point of the game is to keep their heart rate below 100. If they haven't participated in the bio-emotion regulation phase, I will explain to them what this means, why I'm measuring them, and why I'm asking them to stay below 100 bpm. If they have participated in the bio-emotion regulation phase, they will already know what I'm doing and will think of it as a game to beat.

As they approach 100 bpm, I tell them that they can put up their hand like a stop sign to "pause" the game to re-regulate. As they regulate and build their tower, they learn that it is acceptable to respectfully ask for more time to calm down and do things that others expect of them. If they breach the 100-bpm threshold, we stop the building and talk about their anger. Many times, they are angry with me and "this stupid game." At this point, I let them know that they can pretend that the tower is me standing in front of them, and they can kick "me" down. This usually results in lots of laughter, a drop in bpm, and their eagerness to try again.

Need to Win or Succeed

The last theme I typically see with clients who exhibit disruptive behaviors is competition. It usually encompasses a need to win or succeed. These children struggle with different aspects of their lives and often connect success with their own self-worth. As they see peers or siblings succeed in school, receive behavioral awards, or participate in prosocial interactions, they start to internalize the idea that they are failures. In the playroom, this comes out as extreme competitiveness, where they structure play to always win, or as severe behavioral outbursts when they lose.

The organized play intervention for this theme only works if the client has successfully completed the bio-emotion regulation phase and is able to maintain regulation during difficult or intense play sessions. For this intervention, I teach origami. The idea is to promote success and winning while at the same time encouraging self-regulation. Origami is an ancient paper-folding tradition in Chinese and Japanese culture. The goal of origami is to fold paper into shapes that resemble lifelike figures, often an animal or useful object. When using origami in directive play therapy, I recommend buying premade origami squares of different colors to add to the creativity and distinctiveness of the objects the children create. Origami captures their competitive spirit and gives them a feeling of accomplishment.

I teach children to make a boat, a balloon, and a transforming star. The three projects progress from easy to difficult and add on skills learned from the previous builds. The instructions are included in the following three handouts. After the client successfully builds the paper boat, we test it in a sink of water. I encourage them to build a few more of each at home and to teach their family members how to build them. By the time the client can build the transforming star, they are able to demonstrate delay of gratification, self-regulation, and perseverance—all hallmarks of adult success.

THERAPIST HANDOUT

Beginning Origami: Boat

The following steps detail how to fold a standard piece of paper (8.5 × 11 in.) into a boat. This is typically an easier project for clients who still have regulation concerns but could be challenged to increase their learning.

1. Make a folded "+" with a valley:

    - Fold the paper in half (portrait), making a long rectangle. Crease well. Unfold.
    - Turn the paper horizontally (landscape) and fold the paper in half. Crease well. Unfold.

2. Make a folded triangle:

    - Turn the paper so the crease line is in the middle of your body and the paper opens away from you.
    - Bring the right corner toward the middle of the crease, forming a triangle by not crossing the crease.
    - Do the same for the left side.
    - Fold the same paper in half horizontally. Crease well. Unfold.
    - Fold the right and left sides of the horizontal line together, using the "X" creases to form a triangle.

3. Make the boat base:

    - Keeping the flaps folded, slightly separate the bottom of the remaining horizontal edge from the other side. Fold this up toward the flaps.
    - Turn the creation over and do the same on the other side.

4. Seal the base:

    - Fold the base triangle over the triangle. You should have four folds to do.

5. Make the first square:

    - Gently pull up from the crease in the center of the triangle while holding the bottom crease, and flatten the paper. This will make a square.

Copyright © 2025 Michael R. Whitehead, *Treating Children with Disruptive Behavior Disorders.* All rights reserved.

6. Make the second triangle:
    - Slightly separate the bottom flaps and fold the top crease toward the top point of the square.
    - Turn over the creation and do the same with the other side.
7. Make the second square:
    - Gently pull up from the crease in the center of the triangle while holding the bottom crease, and flatten the paper. This will make a square.
8. Make the boat:
    - Gently pull the sides away from the center.

To see visual instructions of these steps, search the internet for "paper boat" or "origami boat."

THERAPIST HANDOUT

Intermediate Origami: Balloon

The following steps detail how to fold a standard origami square (6 × 6 in.) into a balloon. This is a more difficult project for clients and will require patience from the client and therapist.

1. Make a folded "X" with a valley:
    - Fold the paper diagonally in half, making a triangle. Crease well. Unfold.
    - Fold the paper diagonally in the opposite direction, making another triangle. Crease well. Unfold.

2. Make a folded triangle:
    - Using the same paper, fold it in half horizontally. Crease well. Unfold.
    - Fold the right and left sides of the horizontal line together, and use the "X" creases to form a triangle.

3. Fold outer flaps inward:
    - Make a smaller, internal triangle by folding the flaps toward the center, where the edges are aligned.
    - Do this for all flaps.

4. Create pockets:
    - Turn the creation so it looks like a diamond, with the flaps remaining from the previous step opening from the bottom. Fold the right and left corners to the midline of the diamond.
    - Turn it over and do the same on the other side.

5. Tuck in the flaps:
    - Tuck the leftover flaps into the pockets you just created.

6. Blow up the balloon:
    - Find the hole on the top of the diamond and gently blow, inflating the balloon.

To see visual instructions of these steps, search the internet for "origami balloon" or "origami water bomb."

THERAPIST HANDOUT

Advanced Origami: Transforming Star

The following steps detail how to fold eight standard origami squares (6 × 6 in.) into a transforming star. This is an advanced project for clients and should only be accomplished when a child has demonstrated sustained regulatory control. For the best effect, use two different colors of paper, four squares each.

1. Make a folded "+" with a valley:

    - Fold the paper in half (portrait), making a long rectangle. Crease well. Unfold.
    - Turn the paper horizontally (landscape) and fold the paper in half. Crease well. Unfold.

2. Make a folded "X" with a valley:

    - Fold the paper diagonally in half, making a triangle. Crease well. Unfold.
    - Fold the paper diagonally in the opposite direction, making another triangle. Crease well. Unfold.

3. Make a folded "house":

    - Bring the right corner toward the middle of the crease, forming a triangle by not crossing the crease.
    - Do the same for the left side.

4. Make a "half-house":

    - Fold the house together so the triangle flaps are inside the fold, making a half-house.

5. Make the star point:

    - Turn the half-house so the point of the house is facing left and you can see "inside" the fold.
    - Hold the top point of the house, slightly open the fold, take the top right corner of the house, and fold it inward. The star point should look like this:

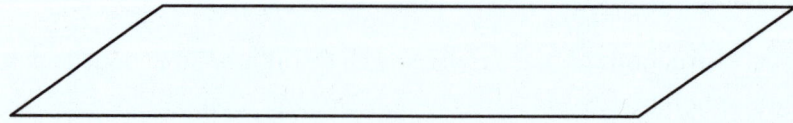

6. Repeat steps 1–5 with the seven other star points.

7. Make the star:
   - Put one star point resting in between the flaps of another (not inside the house).
   - Fold the corner flaps of the outer point into the flaps of the inner star point.
   - Repeat with all star points until they are all connected in a circular fashion.

To see visual instructions of these steps, search the internet for "origami eight-pointed ninja star" or "origami transforming star."

Introducing Organized Play to Adolescents, Preteens, or Older Children

While the reasons for using organized play don't differ with the age of the child, the *how* of doing it does. When working with teens and adolescents, the themes of play that I previously discussed (e.g., triangulation, aggression, defiance, anger, need to win or succeed) may show up as topics that clients bring up in session or key issues that occur at home or school. Without repeating the details of each theme, I will share some specific interventions below that can be used with teens, preteens, or older children during this phase.

LEGO Building

LEGO building can be used to effectively intervene for triangulation, aggression, or need-to-win concerns. Depending on the need, the intervention will be different. For instance, if using LEGO building to address triangulation or the need to win, you will want to use the *Strategic LEGO Building* intervention provided at the end of this chapter. This intervention encourages the use of a cardboard trifold barrier between the child and either the therapist or the parent. This barrier blocks the view of the structure that is being built by one person assigned as the builder, while the person assigned as the director gives instructions. This is typically a "no-win" scenario and teaches the need for effective communication.

Chess, Mastermind, or UNO

For teens, preteens, or older children who are aggressive—and who need extra interventions to train them to expect unpredictability or disappointment—I will play any of the following games, but only after they have demonstrated some regulatory abilities: chess, Mastermind, or UNO. Each of these games requires sustained attention, working memory, and regulation capabilities. When playing these games, we are stretching the muscles of regulation to help the child develop better abilities to manage aggression in other environments.

Experiential Exercises

By the time older kids are at the organized play phase, they may be more interested in walking outside during therapy, showing you a new skateboard trick, or sharing their new favorite song with you. To capitalize on this energy and use it to build greater regulation, you can use your own creativity to develop a directive intervention that is tailored to the client you are seeing. If you struggle to come up with creative exercises, *The Therapist's Notebook for Children and Adolescents* (Sori et al., 2015) is a great resource.

Case Example: *Isabella*

As I alluded to earlier, one directive play therapy approach that I use in this phase is strategic LEGO building. This intervention is aimed at addressing both the patterns of triangulation and negative attribution that can come from overuse of the coercion cycle. In the case of Isabella, both processes were happening.

When I started seeing Isabella, she was 12 years old. She had two brothers, an infant and a five-year-old. Both of Isabella's parents were women, and they lived in a more conservative community where their relationship was not as respected or honored. Isabella experienced discrimination at school due to her parents' relationship, which caused her to gravitate to a more deviant peer group throughout her elementary school years.

By the time she started therapy with me, she had experienced multiple school suspensions and was failing in school. To top it off, her parents' marriage was starting to suffer from the schedule of her working mother (Mom). Isabella had unwittingly become a sounding board for her stay-at-home mother (Madre) to complain about Mom's busy work schedule, the expectation that Madre have dinner on the table as soon as Mom got home, and how volatile Mom would get when stressed from work. Even though Isabella had been in therapy with another provider when she was seven, she would often refuse to come into my office. She would sit in the lobby and refuse to even look at me. Her parents were extremely frustrated with this behavior. They were bringing her to my office to get help, and she would sit defiantly in the lobby, in their minds wasting my time and their money.

I started by sitting next to Isabella in the lobby and asking her parents to wait in my office. Eventually, she looked at me and asked why I was sitting there. I told her that this time was for us to get to know each other, and if that meant I needed to sit quietly in the lobby with her, I was fine with that. Showing her the respect that she could decide for herself whether she wanted to be in therapy, I was able to get her to join me in my office. She tested me many times. Sometimes, I would go out to the lobby to get her, and she would be pacing outside of the building. In response, I would simply go to her and walk with her until she was confident that I wouldn't force her.

Having helped Isabella gain some self-regulation skills (through bio-emotion regulation) and self-confidence (through individual play), it was time to address the triangulation and negative attribution that Mom had toward Isabella. Because Madre was constantly triangulating Isabella by oversharing the concerns that Madre and Mom had with each other, Mom and Isabella's relationship was fracturing and was the focus of conflict in the home. Whenever Madre used effective commands, Isabella complied instantly. However, when Mom tried, Isabella dug her feet in and became extra defiant. This would lead to Mom and Madre arguing with each other while Isabella cared for her younger siblings.

I introduced the LEGO intervention to Mom by saying, "In the next session, I want just you and Isabella to come. I have an activity I want you two to try. I will need you to just be patient with me and Isabella through this activity. It may cause you to feel upset and uncomfortable, but it should help repair your relationship with her. I'm going to do this activity with Madre as well, but I want you to go first so you are aware of how communication patterns happen between you and Isabella."

When Mom and Isabella came for their session, I had a table set up with a small container of LEGOs on one side and the instructions for building the LEGO structure on the other side. Dividing the table down the middle was a trifold presentation board colored like a brick wall. The presentation board was just high enough that neither Mom nor Isabella could see above or around it to the other side when they were sitting in their own chairs. This activity can be accomplished without the presentation board via teletherapy or by having both the parent and child sitting back-to-back on the ground throughout the activity.

I gave them all the instructions on how to complete the activity (see the *Strategic LEGO Building* handout at the end of this chapter) and assigned Mom to be the director while Isabella was the builder. The following is a brief reconstructed narrative of what took place:

ME: Now, without telling Isabella what she is building, I want you, Mom, to walk her through the instructions as best you can to see whether she is able to construct the structure you chose.

MOM: Okay, Isabella, I want you to take the long black brick and have it facing down.

ISABELLA: [*Looking at me for help.*] Okay?

Mom: Now take the green four-dot piece and put it on the left side of the black brick. When you have that—

Isabella: WAIT. I still need to find the green piece. What does it look like?

Mom: It's green, and it has four dots.

Isabella: What color green?

Mom: What do you mean? Green.

Isabella: Is it light green or dark green?

Mom: Oh, I didn't know that there were two different colors. Sorry, honey. Light green.

Isabella: Okay, I have it. Now what?

Mom: Now take the blue piece that has two across and four down, and put it on top of the green and black bricks.

Isabella: [*Again looking at me with even more confusion.*] Okay?

Mom: Now turn the whole thing around and make sure that the blue piece is closest to the bottom.

Isabella: On the bottom? You told me to put it on the top. How do I do both?

Mom: What do you mean on top? Where is the blue piece now?

Isabella: It is on top of the green and black piece.

Mom: Perfect, now turn what you constructed so the blue piece is closest to the bottom.

Isabella: Okay? [*Turning the whole structure over, upside down.*]

Mom: You don't sound so confident. What are you confused about?

Isabella: Nothing. I think I got it. Let's just keep going.

Mom: Okay. Now take two red pieces that have four dots on the top and put them on the blue piece.

Isabella: Done.

Mom: Now take the white piece and put it underneath the whole structure.

ISABELLA: Hold up! What white piece?

MOM: You should have a white piece from the last step.

ISABELLA: No, you only told me to get two red pieces.

MOM: I think I skipped a few steps. I'm confused.

ISABELLA: So am I!

Mom and Isabella argued about what step they were on for another five minutes. By this time, it was time for us to start closing the session. I asked Isabella to show Mom what she had built. Mom was surprised to see what had been constructed. She showed Isabella the picture of what they were supposed to be building, and they both laughed and expressed frustration about how different it was. I asked Isabella what was most difficult about this experience for her.

She said, "Well, Mom didn't know what she was doing. She kept skipping ahead and not giving me all the instructions. Then when she gave instructions, they were unclear and confusing."

I summarized, "Okay, in previous sessions, you've mentioned that you often get confused when she tells you things at home. Was it anything like that today?"

Isabella corrected me, "Similar, but way worse. I got to the point where I wanted to give up. If she would have said she was done trying this exercise, I would have stopped too."

"Okay, so that was very frustrating for you," I clarified.

"Yes," she said.

I turned to Mom and asked, "What was your experience like?"

Mom took a deep breath and said, "I hate to admit it, but I found myself getting irritated by my lack of control over the situation. I was so lost and confused myself. I was sure that if I took the wall down, I could probably build this structure so much faster or at least help Isabella with it."

Isabella quickly jumped in and said, "Yeah, but that's what always happens. You ask me to do something, then if I'm not going fast enough, or it's not getting done the way you want it done, you just take over."

Mom's eyes softened, and she empathized. "I can see how that would be frustrating. You don't feel like I ever give you a chance."

I interrupted them before it could devolve any further. "Let me chat with your mom for a few minutes, Isabella, and then I'll bring you back."

I leaned toward Mom and asked, "Tell me what was going on for you just now. You seemed to have an epiphany today."

She replied, "Sometimes, when Isabella is not doing the things I ask her in the way I want, I think she is doing it on purpose. I feel contempt toward her. I think she is just broken, so I give up and take over. Today, I think I realized that some of this is me. I may not be communicating well enough."

"So, you don't think she is broken anymore?" I asked.

She corrected me, "I'm not sure about that. But I'm beginning to see what you have been saying. I now think I have a lot more work to do for myself than I realized. The truth is, I envy Madre and Isabella's relationship. She is our only daughter, and I wanted to have a classic mother-daughter relationship, and I think I've pushed her away with my perfectionism."

I thanked Mom for sharing her realization with me and for how vulnerable she was able to be in our session that day. I brought Isabella back and quickly debriefed with her and her experience.

Isabella confessed, "I think it was fun. I don't think my mom liked it. She doesn't like giving up control."

I smiled and asked, "If you were to do this again, what would you do differently?"

"I'd plan with her to come up with some key terms we could agree on. We were just not speaking the same language," she surmised.

"Can you try this at home with your mom again?" I asked hesitantly.

Isabella smiled and said, "Sure, if she'll let me."

"You don't think she'll let you?" I asked, confused.

"I don't know that she would want to put herself through that again." She smiled.

I ended by saying, "Okay, well, I'll check with her, and we can see how it goes."

In addition to addressing the triangulation that had fractured Mom and Isabella's relationship, I needed to do extrasystemic work with Isabella and her family. This work was twofold in nature, as it involved working with both macro- and mesosystems. The macrosystem work that I did related to the cultural environment Isabella and her parents were in. Because Isabella's parents were in a same-sex marriage, she experienced discrimination by many in her community. While this couldn't be altered directly (without them moving to a more accepting community), I did work with Isabella and her whole family to find groups and organizations where they could find acceptance.

The mesosystem work that I did required collaborating with Isabella's school. While Isabella was not as defiant as some of my other clients, she did occasionally have problems with her teacher. At one point, soon after the LEGO-building session, Mom reached out to express concern that Isabella's teacher was starting to see Isabella as a problem child. She and Madre asked whether I would attend a 504 meeting for Isabella to help explain the work we had been doing with Isabella. After explaining my approach to the school staff at the 504 meeting, Isabella's teacher and principal asked whether I could give a presentation to the whole school. Realizing that many of my other clients were also students at this school, I agreed. After giving my presentation, many teachers (including Isabella's) approached me and expressed how eager they were to use the tools I was presenting.

As Mom and Isabella built a relationship with each other, Isabella was more likely to withdraw herself from conversations where Madre was talking negatively about Mom, or Isabella would ask Madre to talk with Mom herself. The reason I asked Mom to instruct Isabella during this activity was to show Mom how unclear her communication can often be with Isabella. It is for this reason that I rarely have the child give the instructions first. If I ever have a child give the instructions, it is to help deepen the meaning of successful communication in the relationship and highlight the responsibility teens have in reciprocating this communication.

Key Takeaway

The key takeaway for this intervention is to get parents and children to see how they contribute to negative communication patterns within the family and to reduce the triangulation that takes place. With this intervention, the child starts to see the world with more hues of color instead of seeing only black and white. They begin to see the nuances of their parents' responses, which allows for greater opportunities to connect.

THERAPIST HANDOUT

Strategic LEGO Building

The following guidelines will help you facilitate the parent-child LEGO intervention during the organized play phase of treatment.

Activity Preparation:
- Gather pieces for at least two to three different structures.
- Include about 25 additional random pieces.
- Print off or copy noncolor instructions.
- Build a "wall" between participants.
- Assign "director" and "builder" roles to the participants.

Activity Rules:
- Participants cannot look over or around the wall.
- Take notes regarding your observations during the activity.
- The director must use any language possible to communicate instructions.
- The builder can ask any questions they can think of to successfully build the structure.
- When the structure is completed, or when designated time has passed, show the director the structure first.
- Debrief with both.

Activity Debrief:
- While the director has the structure, show the builder the completed picture of what it should look like.
- Discuss the differences that the builder sees between their completed structure and the picture.
- Discuss with both:
    - What went wrong (if the structures look different)?
    - What was difficult about this activity?
    - What could have made it easier?
    - How does this apply to life at home?

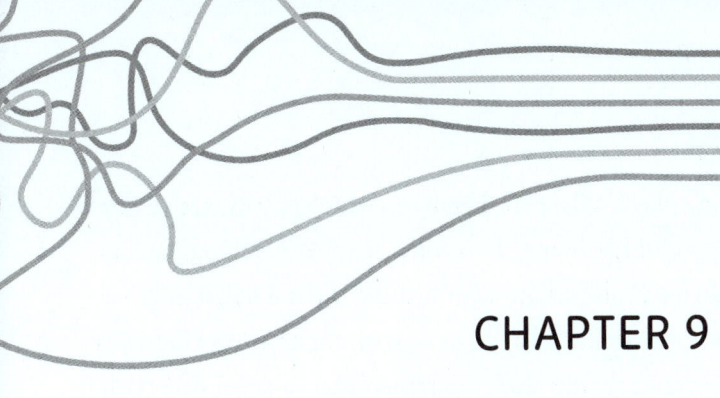

CHAPTER 9

BISON Phase N: Nurturing Play

The nurturing play phase is designed to directly address the systemic principle of circular causality. Recall from chapter 3 that this principle suggests that the actions of each person in a family are circular in nature. That is, interactions don't occur in a linear fashion but in a reciprocal feedback loop with many different possible causal pathways. The nurturing play phase also addresses the first relational change that occurs in a family as a result of the coercion cycle: overly inclusive classification. By providing different viewpoints of childhood behavior, new familial interactions, and alternative pathways for behavior correction, this phase helps eliminate the coercion cycle.

This final phase of therapy promotes the parents as being the main agents of change versus the therapist. It capitalizes on the established relationship between parents and children by bringing both parties into the therapy room together. As I discussed in chapter 2, the research clearly shows that directly involving parents in the therapy process and teaching them therapeutic skills increases the likelihood that treatment will be effective and also deepens the changes in the family. Sometimes, if the family's presenting problems are not too severe, starting with this phase is all that is needed to get the family out of the use of the coercion cycle and on the correct path of healthier relational dynamics.

Filial Play Therapy

The most basic version of nurturing play is filial play therapy, in which parents are taught how to use CCPT skills with their child at home. This often requires teaching parents the basic skills introduced in individual play, along with helping them understand that their *relationship* with their child provides the basic framework for this intervention. This means helping parents understand that as they strengthen their relationship with their child, the child's behaviors will decrease. This can be hard for many parents of children with DBDs because many times their relationships have been eroded from constant behavioral escalation due to the coercion cycle.

The nurturing play phase can be accomplished with any format of filial play therapy, so it is up to you to decide which format you prefer. Of the many models of filial play therapy, two have been formatted with fidelity to a manual: parent-child interaction therapy (PCIT) and TheraPlay. Both are considered evidence-based models and require a minimum level of training, supervision, and qualification to utilize. They differ primarily in the underlying theoretical frameworks that inform their approaches. PCIT is more behavior modification based, whereas TheraPlay is more attachment focused. Both are highly effective for treating DBDs, but it is often difficult to find providers who have the proper training. I know of many providers who haven't received training for either of these models due to the steep financial cost and time commitment required, which is why I recommend using either traditional filial play therapy or child-parent relationship therapy (CPRT) for this phase.

CPRT, which is more in line with the traditional model of filial play therapy, was developed by Garry Landreth and Sue Bratton (2005), and research continues to find it effective at treating typical child-focused problems (Cornett & Bratton, 2014; Hicks & Baggerly, 2017; Opiola & Bratton, 2018) as well as children with behavioral problems (Allen, 2020; Pishdadian et al., 2024; Shafi et al., 2019). Regardless of the model of filial therapy chosen during this phase, the most important aspect is to prioritize strengthening the attachment relationship between the child and their parent.

Managing Parental Resistance

Some parents are a little resistant at first to getting involved in their child's therapy, or they see filial therapy as blaming them for the child's problems. This is another manifestation of the circular causality principle. We, as humans, like to make things simple and have been programmed by society to look for and treat symptoms rather than recognizing the complex, systemic framework in which we operate. For instance, if I have a headache, the straight answer of taking Tylenol may temporarily lessen the pain, but if I don't find the source of the headache, I'll have to continue taking Tylenol every time it comes back. If my headache resulted from a combination of sitting posture and diet, just taking Tylenol is not going to solve the problem. Viewing this example from a circular causality perspective, I would track my food intake, pay attention to where and when the headache starts, and identify the level of pain I experience throughout my week. This would give me enough data to understand clearly the source of my headaches. Once I understand the various sources, I can adjust my behaviors to reduce continued occurrence of headaches rather than just treating the symptom. Similarly, when parents better understand the dynamics of circular causality and recognize that involving them does not equate to blaming them, they are typically eager to contribute.

Another way to help parents understand the need for their involvement is to explain a little about attachment theory so that they understand that children are dependent on adults for their survival during their infancy and toddler years and that parent-child dynamics that form during those years often create processes and cycles that are difficult to alter. When a child does not have a secure attachment with a caregiver, which may or may not be the fault of the caregiver themselves, disruptive behaviors often act as symptoms of a greater systemic problem.

Let's use an example of a parent suffering from facial paralysis to illustrate my point. Imagine that a parent is unable to engage in reciprocal, normal give-and-take facial expressions with their infant child because they suffer from facial paralysis. The parent doesn't experience any depression or anxiety—their face is just paralyzed. (This is a very hypothetical example, and I'm not even sure it could happen, but it is perfect for a nonblaming example.) Through no fault of the child or the parent, this can become a barrier to attachment building, as evidenced by the famous still-face experiment I described in chapter 5. Remember that this experiment helped us understand that infants are highly responsive to those back-and-forth facial expressions. When presented with a still face, many children experience distress, both physiological and emotional.

Therefore, if this facial paralysis barrier persists throughout infancy and toddlerhood, it can contribute to attachment distancing between the parent and the child. Again, the parent is not at fault, and neither is the child. I'm sure there are things that the parent and child could do to accommodate for the lack of facial expression play; however, the parent may start to feel distant from their child, especially if their partner is able to engage in that facial play. When that parent begins to distance, the child will feel it and is likely to experience that distance as something about themselves, not about the parent. The child then would begin to degrade themselves internally, leading to greater disruptive behaviors over time.

If this hypothetical family were to come to me for therapy, my number one priority would be to strengthen their relationship and provide education about attachment and parent-child dynamics. Once parents understand the basic tenets of attachment theory and acknowledge that the child needs them to be a secure base, relationship repair can begin.

Potential Roadblocks

While some of these roadblocks are present during previous phases of treatment, they become more pronounced during this phase due to the need for all sessions to be conjoint and the common need for the entire family be involved. More common logistical roadblocks include timing, childcare, office size, and therapist comfort and competence. Each of these roadblocks are described here, along with possible ways to address them.

Timing

One of the major obstacles to initiating and sustaining filial therapy is time. Most parents either work during typical clinic hours, or providers prefer not to see clients during evenings or on the weekends. Another complication is that scheduling sessions in the evening can be difficult due to conflicts with dinnertime and other activities the child may be involved in. I circumvent these barriers by providing evening appointments for families on some nights of the week. It is not necessary to work every evening; providing one or two days per week dedicated to families in this phase of therapy is sufficient. I preserve these time slots for family cases and only offer them to clients whose involved parents have committed to attend. If they later recant that commitment, we reschedule them in a daytime slot.

I also emphasize to parents and families at the beginning of therapy the importance of dedicating enough time to follow through with the full treatment. I use the analogy of taking antibiotics, explaining that as we get closer to this last phase of treatment, they will see a lot of positive changes in their child. They will be tempted to think that reducing the time commitment to attend therapy for this last phase won't matter—just like when you start to feel better after taking an antibiotic for a couple of days. If you don't fulfill the course of treatment, the risk of developing a medication-resistant strain of the illness grows. Similarly, if parents only fulfill part of the treatment for DBDs but fail to follow through with the last phase to become the change agents for their child, they risk developing increasingly more resistant disruptive behaviors that require an even higher level of care.

Helping parents and other adults see that this isn't just an unnecessary aspect of treatment but one of the most essential parts of therapy increases the chance they will follow through with this phase. Dedicating a portion of your evenings to accommodate families shows a level of commitment reflecting the seriousness of this phase. This is especially true when you hold families to their commitment to attend family sessions with the real possibility of them losing the evening slot to another family that is willing to do the work.

Childcare

Another common barrier to this phase is childcare for younger siblings. While it would be amazing to provide childcare to families needing it so they could attend a family session, this is improbable; however, as a real barrier, it is important to think of how to address it. When I'm faced with this barrier, I opt for parent swapping or whole family sessions. With parent swapping, I must determine which parent is most in need of relational repair with the child and focus solely on that parent-child dynamic for a short time. This allows the other parent to stay home with siblings for the interim. After a few sessions, we swap parents, and the one who was attending sessions now takes care of the other children, while the other parent attends sessions with the focal child.

The other possible solution is called *whole family therapy*. I'm an advocate for whole family therapy and will demonstrate a session that uses it later in this chapter. This form of therapy invites all members of the family into the room while playfully working toward the directive of eliminating the "problem child" lens. Choosing to conduct whole family therapy is individual to the provider. Not every provider has the training or skills to work with an entire family in one room at the same time. If you would prefer this option but don't think you have the experience or competence to do so, see the solutions to the *Therapist Comfort and Competence* barrier in this section.

Office Size

Another unfortunate reality we face as providers is the layout and size of our offices. Sometimes, we can rearrange our offices to meet our clients' needs, but more often than not, we have to adjust our clients to fit our office needs. This can be a major barrier to conducting whole family therapy, or even filial therapy.

If you don't have the space, the only work-around may be to teach filial therapy skills to parents using CPRT, a model of filial therapy that works more like parent training. With CPRT, parents are brought in, preferably as a unit, and taught the basic skills of CCPT. They are then tasked with conducting and recording a 20-minute play session at home with their child of focus. They are to bring the recording back to the therapist for review. The therapist and the parents watch the video together while the therapist provides feedback and teaches more advanced versions of the skills used in the play sessions. The purpose of this training is to strengthen the parent-child relationship, and it takes place over the course of 10 weeks.

Therapist Comfort and Competence

Finally, a big barrier to this phase is the therapist's comfort and competence level. Not many providers are trained in whole family therapy or in play therapy. Most therapists are given basic therapeutic skills in their graduate programs, and their experience is dependent on the clients assigned to them and their choices of internships. As a result, when they begin working with children with DBDs, they find themselves overwhelmed and unprepared.

When I have spoken with other providers about this approach, I am often confronted with varying degrees of concern because I'm (1) not just focusing on the child or (2) not focusing on the whole family the entire time. From a classical perspective, family therapy should involve as many family members as are willing to engage in the therapy process. However, many family therapists are often trained to focus their attention on the couple. The belief is that by improving the couple's relationship, the child's behavior will improve. While this does happen to some extent, it does not address the underlying processes that are building up within the family and contributing to disruptive behaviors. On the other hand, child therapists often don't get enough training or experience working with couples and find working with couples unpleasant. They focus all their attention and energy on working with the individual child.

These dichotomies create a problem for parents looking for a provider who can work with DBDs. They are either told, "You the parents are the problem, so come to couples therapy and parent training" or "Your child is the problem, so leave them here and I'll fix them." As this book shows, neither approach is helpful nor correct on its own. Therefore, if you find yourself wanting to take on these cases or that some of the work you are doing is missing some of the marks, it is imperative that you find yourself a good systemic supervisor. Having a solid grounding in systems thinking and systems therapy will improve outcomes for these types of families.

If you are a child therapist who is not trained in play therapy, seek out a Registered Play Therapist-Supervisor™ (RPT-S) to assist you in providing general play therapy and filial play therapy. It would be best to find an RPT-S who is also well trained in conducting whole family therapy or couples therapy. The Association for Play Therapy (https://www.a4pt.org), the American Association for Marriage and Family Therapy (https://www.aamft.org), and the Coalition of Associations for Systemic Therapy (https://www.coastmft.org) are great places to search for qualified supervisors.

Case Example: *Noe*

Noe was an eight-year-old boy who was the oldest child of his five siblings. His mother and father were both exasperated with Noe's behavior. Much like the other clients described in this book, he was extremely defiant, rude, and hard to handle. During earlier phases of treatment, Noe was exhibiting defiant behaviors with his teachers and on the verge of getting kicked out of his school (as is the case with many of my clients). I tried to encourage his teachers to use effective commands with Noe, but they were a bit reluctant due to the belief that it would take too long and wouldn't work as promised.

After continuous attempts and requests, I was eventually able to schedule a time to observe Noe in his classroom, where I observed him for three hours while he interacted with his teacher and peers. During this observation, I was attending to how his teacher executed requests and commands, how quickly he responded and the nature of his response, what his relationship with his teacher and peers was like, and most importantly, what the predecessors to his defiant and oppositional behaviors were. After my observation, I was able to determine that Noe's teacher was expecting compliance within three seconds of issuing a command, would not attend to his emotional cues, and seemed to miss behavioral cues that would precede an outburst. I shared my observations with the teacher, along with some handouts about emotion coaching. Not surprisingly, when the teacher began regularly using emotion coaching with Noe at school, his behavior problems were significantly reduced.

Once we had successfully completed all the other phases of treatment, it was time for Noe and his family to start nurturing play. Noe's behavior was getting better, and Dad was confused about why we needed to complete this phase of treatment. He was concerned about the need to find childcare for Noe's siblings. I told Mom and Dad that I wanted to have the whole family come to my office for a few sessions of filial play therapy. I described what this phase entailed and how they could contribute to Noe's progress by learning some of the skills I was using with him. I then used CPRT to teach Dad and Mom the basics of CCPT, and after they did four successful play sessions at home, it was time for them to bring the whole family to a session. Noe was excited for his siblings to see my office and to share with them what he had been doing for the past few months.

While the children were waiting in the lobby, I brought the parents to my office to talk about the plan for the session. I started, "Today, we are going to play the game of Sorry! I'm going to write down some of my observations throughout the session. Dad, I want you and the two-year-old to be on a team, while Mom and the four-year-old are another team. I'm going to ask the six-year-old twins to be on another team, while Noe is by himself. I have rigged the game by taking out a few cards so it will go a little bit faster than usual. Each time the deck runs out and I need to shuffle the deck, I will turn the board so that each person's color is different. They will continue to play as the new color for the rest of the round."

"Are you sure you want to do that?" smiled Dad.

"Yeah, I know that Noe has made quite a bit of progress, but with his siblings he is still a little aggressive. I'm afraid this won't go well," warned Mom.

"I'm sure it's a bit scary," I smiled back. "I've played this game this way with many families. It will be fun, either for the kids, for you, or for me."

When we brought the children in, they were buzzing with excitement. They saw the game board and practically jumped in their seats to choose a color. Noe introduced me to his siblings and explained to them that this was something different from what he usually does in my office. I divided them into the predetermined teams, with Noe being the only child without a team. Noe made sure to sit next to red, his favorite color. I gave them all the instructions on how to play the game (see the *Twist on the Game of Sorry!* handout at the end of this chapter) and told them that when the deck of cards needed to be reshuffled for the first time, I would initiate a special rule. I didn't tell them what the rule was, only when it would come. I instructed the team with the youngest player to go first and sat back and watched.

As the game progressed, Noe (red), the twins (green), and Dad's team (blue) had a pawn out of "start." Noe had just drawn the last card, which was a Sorry! card. This card allowed him to boot one of the other team's pawns back to start, and his pawn would take its place. Unfortunately for Noe, he chose to kick the green team (the twins) back to start. I paused the game so I could shuffle the cards and place them back in the draw pile. I then exclaimed, "Okay, now I'm going to institute the new rule for this game! The board will now make one turn to the left. Everyone that was blue is now red, those who were red are now green, green team is now yellow, and yellow team is now blue."

Noe looked at me in shock. I could tell he felt a little betrayed and troubled by the turn of events. He would constantly tell me how jealous he was of the twins (the green team) and how eager he was to see them get "justice." Now, after he had knocked them back to start, he was facing their consequence. Everyone else either cheered, jeered, or laughed at the turn of events. We continued to play the game until the board had turned four times (enough for everyone to play each color at least once).

During the second rotation, one of the twins swore under his breath. Dad turned slightly toward that sibling but didn't say anything. Mom also didn't do anything. Later, that same sibling drew a Sorry! card, which he decided to play on Noe. Noe grunted and expressed frustration with a downturned face. At this, both of his parents jumped up and scolded him, "Noe, stop acting up, it's only a game."

Several instances of this type of "double standard" took place throughout the rest of the game.

When I turned the board for the last time, I asked the following question: "If we were to stop the game right now, who would have won the game?"

Everyone looked at the board and examined who had the most pawns out on the board and in their homes. The team that Mom was on was clearly the winner, with the most pawns in home and on the game board, and none stuck in start.

At this, everyone pointed at Mom and said in unison, "Mom's team."

"Okay, just keep that in mind for a second. Now tell me who would have lost the game?" I countered.

Again, they all looked at the game board and pointed at Dad's team. Smiling, they said, "Dad's team!"

"Okay, so Mom is yellow, and Dad is blue. I'm curious, who played yellow?" I asked.

Everyone raised their hands.

I also asked, "So, then who played blue?"

Again, everyone raised their hands.

Then I said, slower and more deliberately, "What do you think that means?"

Noe, having been in therapy with me the longest and understanding where I was going, pointed out, "It means we all won. And we all lost."

I looked at him and invited, "Tell me more about that?"

"Well, we all played yellow, and yellow won the game. That means we each helped yellow get home, even if we tried to battle against yellow sometimes. They still won."

"Interesting. What about blue?" I questioned.

"Everyone was ganging up on Dad and did everything they could to get his pieces back to start. He was blue last, and we all focused on him, instead of yellow. But by doing that, we hurt ourselves because we took out all our progress we made when we were blue."

Smiling, I said, "Thank you, Noe. You are correct. Now, think about what happens at home. Do you guys sometimes pick on each other?"

The three oldest nodded their heads yes.

Looking at them, I asked, "And who does that help or hurt?"

One of the twins said, "I guess by picking on each other, we are hurting ourselves."

"And when we help each other, we are also helping ourselves!" Noe exclaimed.

"Wow, you guys really thought that through. Thank you. Thank you for coming to play with me today. Mom and Dad, I would like you to think about this game throughout the week, and we'll meet next time to discuss some of my observations."

I either debrief with parents immediately after the Sorry! game, or I schedule a follow-up session if their children are ready to leave. With Noe's parents, I scheduled a follow-up session for one week later, and when they came into my office, they seemed more confident in the work they were doing at home.

I asked what had changed, and Dad replied, "After our session, we talked a lot about the analogy of helping or hurting each other by how we interact. I think that is what you have been trying to teach us all along, but we just couldn't see it."

Mom added, "Dad recognized that how he has been interacting with Noe is not helpful. He took it upon himself to point out to the kids when they were helping each other or hurting each other."

Dad explained, "Yeah, I realized that by yelling at Noe all the time, I am contributing to how he treats his siblings. I saw that he treats them just like I treat him. It nearly broke me when I realized that."

Curious to know more, I asked, "So what have you been doing to change that?"

A little sheepishly, he replied, "We are doing more of the family meetings you told us about to help organize our expectations of the kids, and we are now using encouragement with Noe more often. I like it more than praise. With praise I felt like I was not being myself. But giving him encouragement in the way you taught us really seems to make both of us feel good."

Mom added, "I'm continuing to do the play sessions with Noe, and I've started with one of the other kids as well. Noe seems to be taking a little bit more responsibility at home and seems to take some pride in that as well."

I shared my feedback, which was similar to what they had already noticed: They had been treating Noe differently from the other kids and holding him to standards that weren't age appropriate. They agreed with my observations and committed to continuing their changes.

It is surprising to me that, many times, parents will pick up on the same systemic observations I do and will initiate changes on their own. Once they see these patterns and processes during the game, they feel obligated to start change.

Key Takeaway

The key takeaway from the nurturing play phase is to reinforce the shift of therapy from being therapist led to parent led. Having greater ability to see the full hues of color in their child, the parents begin to feel empowered to advocate for and assist their child. Conversely, the child starts to feel the warmth and involvement of the parents and family, allowing them to see brighter hues of color in their parents as well. These reciprocating dynamics can continue to build, further fortifying against the return of the coercion cycle.

THERAPIST HANDOUT

Twist on the Game of Sorry!

The following guidelines will help you facilitate this modified version of Sorry! during the nurturing play phase of treatment.

Game Preparation:

Classic Game (Pre-2013 Editions)	Winning Moves Editions (Post-2013 Editions)
• Remove the following cards: 3, 5, and 8. • Assign seating to draw out problematic family dynamics. • Shuffle cards. • Begin play.	• Remove the following cards: 1, 5, and 8. • Assign seating to prioritize family dynamics. • Shuffle cards. • Begin play.

Game Rules:

Classic Game (Pre-2013 Editions)	Winning Moves Editions (Post-2013 Editions)
• 1 or 2 gets you out of start. • CANNOT slide on your own color. • You MUST bump other players according to rules. • When cards run out, shuffle and turn the board.	• Any card gets you out of start (except 4). • ONLY slide on your own color. • You MUST bump other players according to rules. • When cards run out, shuffle and turn the board.

Game Debrief:
- After everyone has played one round on each color (typically 30 to 35 minutes), end the game to debrief (typically takes 10 to 15 minutes).
- Ask who won the game. Try to get a response from everyone, along with their reasoning for their response.
- Ask who lost the game and why they think that person lost the game.
- Discuss the systemic dynamics that you observed, including the fact that all players won and all lost, since all played each color.
- Describe what you saw in the game play, especially between players. Discuss how these dynamics play out in real life in the family.
- Meet with parents alone (on the same night or at the next session) to:
    - Discuss how the game play would be different if done at home.
    - Discuss strategies and interventions that could be used at home to increase cooperation and decrease conflict.
    - Encourage parents to use this game/session as a point of reference when addressing family conflict.

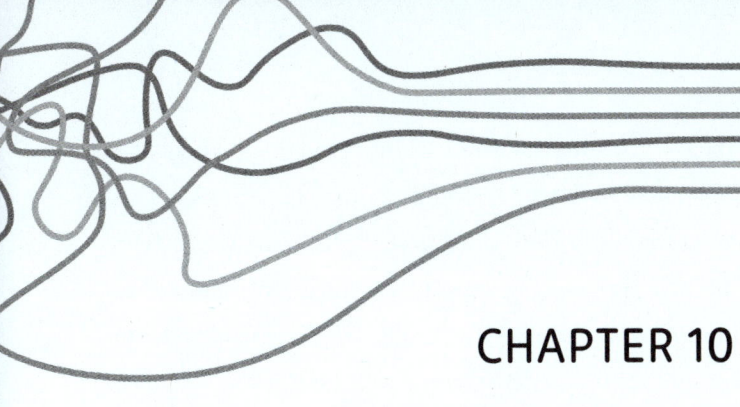

CHAPTER 10

Troubleshooting and Maintenance

As you've learned thus far, a typical course of ISPT treatment includes therapy once per week, especially when working in the bio-emotion regulation and individual play phases. When the child is demonstrating sustained emotion regulation and the parents are regularly holding one-on-one play sessions with the child, it is time to shift into the successful communication phase. During this phase, I typically meet with the child one week and the parents the next week. This rotation ensures that I'm seeing one constellation of the family system every week. We are building up the realization that the parents are to be the final change agents in the child's life.

After the family is holding regular family meetings and primarily relying on the use of effective commands, I enter the organized play and nurturing play phases. Their appointments might occur on an every-other-week basis during these phases. This again refocuses the time and energy on the parents intervening and building the relationship of trust with their child. Throughout the treatment, I assess the parents' commitment level to applying the skills and techniques taught in therapy, with the nurturing play phase culminating in the full transfer of responsibility to the parents. Once parents have the tools to intervene with their children through filial play therapy, all that remains is maintaining the progress gained.

Unfortunately, treatment doesn't occur quite so smoothly all the way through for most families. As treatment progresses throughout the BISON phases, issues may crop up that require different troubleshooting steps or interventions. For example, you might find parents are used to using triangulation and child behavior problems to avoid their marital concerns, which would require in-depth couples therapy before progressing into successful communication or later phases. Or you may run into situations where the child is progressing at home but not at school, which would require collaboration and connection with school officials to ensure skills from the different phases are used in the school environment as well. While troubleshooting and maintenance can fluctuate in and out of the other phases as other challenges arise, the idea is to always reinforce the parents as the change agents and ensure second-order systemic transformation.

Common Troubleshooting During BISON Phases

Sometimes, you might identify issues in earlier phases that require a bit of an adjustment in the approach, such as lack of school involvement, parental triangulation, trauma, underlying medical concerns, and more. Since ISPT is a systems-informed approach, you need to be prepared to either recognize and address these common issues or identify them and have referral resources available to address them. If you need to refer someone to additional services, you should remain in collaboration and communication with these outside providers. This continued collaboration will ensure treatment is not undermined or slowed. In the following section, I discuss some of these most common issues that require troubleshooting through the ISPT approach.

Lack of School Involvement

An essential aspect of ISPT is involvement with school systems, as children with DBDs are often ostracized by their peers and lack prosocial skills because of this history of ostracism. Although this problem typically involves peers, it can quickly perpetuate with teachers and other adult staff members as well, who may develop a negative attribution view of the child and only see them as troublemakers. Since many children with DBDs also experience other comorbid concerns (e.g., ADHD, autism, sensory processing disorder), you need to be diligent and available to work with school systems to advocate for appropriate accommodations. This might involve attending IEP or 504 meetings with parents to provide specific suggestions for the school. It may require maintaining weekly or biweekly communication between you and the school to address issues as they come up in the school. It can also look like offering to teach school staff the different skills taught to the child and family during the individual play and successful communication phases.

If teachers and school systems are not involved in the treatment process, especially during the individual play and successful communication phases, changes may occur at home but not at school. Some schools or teachers may be resistant to collaboration, which will require you to use your therapeutic joining skills to resolve any concerns that may arise. Be sure to empathize first and acknowledge the struggle these schools are experiencing with your client. Recognize that school staff are doing the best they can with what they have. Emphasize that you want to have them on your team and that you are not trying to enter their system to tell them what to do. You are merely sharing different tools that you have found effective for your client. You may also use the research spotlights in the appendix to help schools and teachers understand the value of the BISON phase interventions.

Triangulation from Parental Relationship Problems

When triangulation is the primary driving force behind the coercion cycle—and the parents need to address their own relational concerns—troubleshooting may mean transitioning into couples therapy for the parents. If the parents are having relationship distress themselves, they will find it difficult to be a united front when implementing any of the BISON phases. A parent who can't regulate themselves within their romantic relationship will have difficulty learning to do so within the parent-child relationship. Additionally, if they are unable or unwilling to date their partner, they will find it difficult to spend one-on-one time with a child whom they deem a problem. When parents have difficulties communicating with each other, they will struggle to implement any of the successful communication interventions.

If you are uncomfortable with or untrained in conducting effective couples therapy, it will be ideal for you to find someone you trust to complete that intervention. If the couples therapy is outsourced, it is imperative that you have regular contact with the provider since these parents are used to triangulating their child's problems to avoid their relationship distress. It is common for parents with this struggle to try to get parent training from the couples therapist to avoid dealing with their relationship concerns. Sometimes, parents will ask to pause regular therapy with the child during this time, which may be appropriate if the child is responding well at home and their behavior problems have been reduced, and it is clear that additional progress won't be made unless the marriage concerns are addressed.

Individual Parental Mental Health Concerns

Other times, one or both parents may be experiencing their own mental health concerns (e.g., depression, anxiety, bipolar disorder) that contribute to the negative systemic processes that have developed in the family. For example, a parent with obsessive compulsive disorder (OCD) who suffers from orderliness obsessions may unwittingly use the coercion cycle to manage their anxiety around their obsession and compulsions. This parent may compulsively organize different aspects of the house and require the child to place their shoes, backpack, and coat in a certain place by the front door. Due to the level of compulsivity (and anxiety) that comes from this obsession, if the child leaves their items by the couch or back door, the parent may at first request that the child correct this "misdeed." However, if the child continues to make this mistake, the parent will escalate their response to more intense and harsher communication. The child may experience this as criticism of who they are as a person.

As this criticism increases and this cycle strengthens, the child will become more resistant and defiant to the requests, increasing the escalation of the parent in their approach. Over time, the use of harsh and swift discipline with a child who creates a developmentally appropriate mess will lead to greater instances of resistance from the child and ruptured attachment bonds. Even though the parent is dealing with a serious concern (OCD), the child only feels criticized and demeaned for (what to them is) an inconsequential expression of play.

Understandably, it would not likely be possible to successfully implement many of the BISON phases without first addressing the underlying OCD concern. When the parent and the family fully understand the concerns that this parent is experiencing, it is easier to work together to find appropriate ways to accomplish this treatment. Therefore, always be prepared to assess for and be aware of any potential for parental mental health concerns—and then treat the concerns accordingly or refer out.

Trauma

When any member of the family system has experienced trauma, it decreases the family's ability to remain present and regulated throughout treatment. This is especially true if one or both parents, the identified patient, or the identified patient's siblings have trauma histories, whether they have been treated or not. If you identify trauma in a caregiver, you may need to conduct additional individual sessions with them if you are trained and comfortable doing so; otherwise, you will need to refer them to individual therapy with another provider.

If you identify trauma in the child—or trauma in the family that has resulted from the child's DBD—you may need to slow down the transitions between phases and spend more time on the bio-emotion regulation and individual play phases specifically. These first two phases essentially address trauma head-on and may need to be extended until the trauma is appropriately navigated. Additionally, these phases are helpful at reducing the biological reactivity that the child and other members of the family experience from trauma and allow extra time for healing from trauma and repairing or building attachment.

Medical Concerns

Some children experience DBDs as a result of an underlying medical or biological condition. While this is not an exhaustive list, here are some of the more common examples:

- **PANS/PANDAS:** Pediatric autoimmune neuropsychiatric disorder associated with streptococcus (PANDAS) involves the sudden onset of different neuropsychiatric behaviors (e.g., OCD, anxiety, irritability) after a recent streptococcal infection. The anxiety and irritability may contribute to DBDs in a child who seemed to be developing typically and hadn't previously experienced disruptive behavior.

- **Sleep apnea:** This involves the obstruction of the breathing pathways during sleep, often due to enlarged tonsils or other structural issues in the nose and throat. When sleep apnea occurs in young children, they experience prolonged sleep deprivation, which leads to ADHD symptoms along with DBDs.

- **Traumatic brain injury:** Individuals who suffer from a traumatic brain injury (TBI) may experience changes in mood, personality, and temperament. However, when the TBI is centralized in the frontal lobe, there is an increased chance of DBD development.

- **Environmental toxins (lead, heavy metals):** Prolonged exposure to lead or other heavy metals can impair brain functioning and lead to the development of DBDs.

- **Lyme disease:** Lyme disease is an infection that occurs when someone is bitten by a deer tick infected with the bacteria responsible for the disease. Left untreated, individuals experience several neurological conditions and changes, including increased irritability, mood swings, and disruptive behaviors.

- **Hormone deficiencies:** Some children may experience thyroid disease and blood sugar fluctuations resulting from untreated diabetes. Since thyroid and glycemic fluctuations play a large role in mood, fatigue, and aggressiveness, children with these conditions can be viewed as having DBDs.

- **Autoimmune disorders:** Several autoimmune disorders can contribute to increased irritability and mood shifts in children, such as juvenile arthritis, thyroid disorders, or type 1 diabetes. When children are experiencing these disorders, they may use the coercion cycle and other systemic dynamics as a way of coping with their disorder. For instance, I had a client who suffered from juvenile arthritis who found that when he would exhibit irritability (a natural consequence of arthritic pain), his parents would allow him to skip school and not do chores. It got so bad that this client was referred to therapy by his rheumatologist because he was more than capable of attending school and doing household chores, but he had blown up so much at his parents that they were effectively no longer parenting.

- **Celiac disease:** Children with undiagnosed or poorly managed gluten sensitivities or celiac disease may experience irritability, struggle with attention difficulties, and develop disruptive behaviors.

- **Genetic disorders (MTHFR gene mutations):** While not directly connected to disruptive behaviors, some genetic disorders like the MTHFR gene mutation can create nutritional and hormonal deficiencies that lead to anxiety, attention issues, or irritability and poor behavioral control.

Since so many of these biological or medical conditions could be masked by disruptive behaviors, you should be attentive to these possibilities during the assessment process and throughout treatment. Should you suspect any of these concerns, coordinate care with a medical professional to identify an appropriate treatment plan. You can support the parents and the child through this process by utilizing any BISON phase that seems appropriate to the family system.

Divorce or Remarriage

If the parents are already divorced, or they experience a divorce or remarriage during treatment, it is important that you give extra attention to each BISON phase. When divorced parents continue to have conflict within their co-parenting relationship, this often results in increased disruptive behaviors among their children. This is one version of triangulation that requires co-parenting coaching or counseling to address. Due to the specialized nature of this task, you should only attempt this if you have the training. You can find qualified providers who are trained to do this on the Association of Family and Conciliation Courts website (https://www.afccnet.org).

Should parents get divorced or remarried while treatment is occurring, recognize that these transitions can be extremely difficult for children. This may result in behavioral backsliding and require revisiting any of the appropriate BISON phases. Pay attention to how the coercion cycle may reappear and which relational system changes reoccur, as this will help in deciding which of the phases to repeat.

Entering Graduation and Maintenance

Once a family has successfully completed all the necessary phases, and additional concerns have been resolved through troubleshooting, it is time to discuss graduation and maintenance. I generally start by tracking the family's progress, both formally and informally, and when I see a consistent pattern of success and progress (e.g., the child is no longer engaging in deliberate acts of defiance, parents are continuing to use the skills introduced, parents understand how regulation works), I recommend to them that we transition to an appointment once per month.

After four monthly appointments with little or no backtracking, we schedule a follow-up to happen in six months. This allows the family to feel safe in moving off my regular schedule and know that they can always call if something erupts unpredictably. In addition, many families have had to wait on an extensive waiting list prior to beginning therapy with me, and after spending quite a bit of time with me throughout treatment, they are generally reluctant to end therapy for fear that recidivism will occur. This slower titration helps ease these concerns. Once they are on a biannual appointment rotation (every six months), I am better able to intervene faster and more effectively due to already having a relationship and historical background of the situation.

Generally, I recommend keeping families on a biannual appointment rotation. By the time therapy has been terminated, I have gotten to know several members of the family and can easily intervene if anything pops up with anyone. This continues to provide a level of comfort and security for these families who have often been dismissed by others.

Key Takeaway

The key takeaway for troubleshooting and maintenance is that as you interact with and gain an understanding of the family system and other relevant systems, you are in the perfect position to address situations that may undermine progress. These can involve referring parents to individual therapy or couples therapy, as well as addressing school behavioral issues and training or collaborating with school staff. When you are aware of these concerns and have a plan to tackle them, they do little to hinder the treatment process. On the other hand, when these concerns are not addressed, the systemic cycles continue to worsen, leading treatment progress to significantly stall or families to drop out altogether.

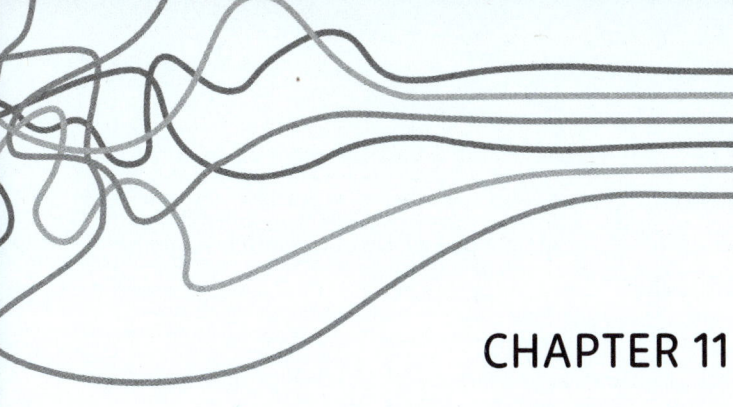

CHAPTER 11

Putting It All Together

In the epigraph of her book *Making Contact*, Virginia Satir (1976) wrote, "I believe the greatest gift I can conceive of having from anyone is to be seen by them, heard by them, to be understood and touched by them. The greatest gift I can give is to see, hear, understand and to touch another person." When I first read this quote, I was captivated by the reality that this has been the only thing my clients with disruptive behaviors have been asking for. Many times, they ask for it in ways that can be harmful or in ways that seem counterproductive. Every story in this book has had a component of the individual (or family) begging to be seen for who they are. When individuals are finally seen, acknowledged, and honored, there is a steep decline in disruptive behaviors. In this chapter, I will share a few stories from people in my own life that reiterate this concept in hopes they will be recognized for what they are: calls for help and acknowledgment. The next time you see a family or child struggling with disruptive behaviors, I hope you will recognize that seeing these people as *people* will give you the power to change their lives for the better.

My Brother Marcus

Throughout my childhood, I often babysat my younger siblings. I am the oldest of four boys. Marcus is the third child in my family and was the youngest child in my family for seven years. He was only three and a half years younger than me, but I recall feeling like the gap was much bigger when I was young. As a toddler, Marcus struggled with speech, and I remember myself and our other brother interpreting his words for our parents because if they didn't understand him quickly, he would tend to explode and cause massive disruption in our home. Even though he eventually grew out of his speech impediment, his anger continued to be a big problem. He was easily triggered, especially by anyone who seemed to be an authority over him, whether it was me when I was babysitting, my parents, or teachers. One time, he punched a hole in the wall because he didn't do his chore correctly. Another time, he called my mother a "bitch" when she told him he needed to clean the dishes better. He would often get into verbal altercations with his teachers at school, which led to massive explosions both at school and at home.

As I look back on my interactions with Marcus, I recognize the same patterns I am now trained to help families eliminate. I think some of my experiences with Marcus have helped me identify and see these interactions more quickly in other families. The coercion cycle was very clearly entrenched in my family and between Marcus and our parents.

Another important example of Marcus's explosive anger occurred in his kindergarten class. However, the stage had been set for him well before he even joined this class, as in the preceding years, I had been assigned this same teacher. As a natural people pleaser and anxious person, I was always trying to follow the rules. My first recollection of having issues with peers was in kindergarten. Within a few days of starting kindergarten, I remember hearing another child use a curse word. I immediately went up to the teacher and tattled, which quickly endeared me to the teacher but isolated me from my peers. My reputation began to circulate among the teachers. I was helpful and wanted to learn all I could.

At the end of my third-grade year, my teacher mentioned that she would be teaching kindergarten the following year and had found out my younger brother Marcus would be in her class. She told my mother, "I'm so excited to teach another Whitehead. Michael is such a good kid; I can't wait to meet his brother." I remember my mom and me looking at each other, trying to decide whether we should warn the teacher. I can't remember whether my mom prepped that teacher, but I do remember what happened the following fall.

After one of the first few days of the school year, I went to the place where I was supposed to meet Marcus to walk him home, but he wasn't there. I went to his classroom, where my old teacher, looking shell-shocked, informed me that Marcus had been sent home earlier that day. I asked her why, and she told me she couldn't tell me and that I would have to talk to my parents. As I walked home, I was afraid something had happened to him. What else could cause a kindergartner to be sent home? When I got home, my mother informed me that as Marcus was headed to sharpen his pencil in class, one of his friends jumped up and started using the sharpener. Any other child might have been annoyed or frustrated but would have waited in line until they were finished. Marcus, on the other hand, started arguing with his classmate because "he was taking too long" and Marcus *needed* to sharpen his pencil *immediately*.

Our family recollection is that Marcus waited impatiently for his friend to finish, after which Marcus proceeded to sharpen his own pencil. On his way back to his desk, Marcus forcefully jabbed the newly sharpened pencil into the other child's back! The pencil lodged into that kid's skin, blood was drawn, and Marcus was ejected from the classroom. He was allowed to return to school after about a week, but only after he had been instructed that he could not use the pencil sharpener; he would have to ask the teacher to sharpen his pencils from that point forward. Nowadays, it is likely this would have led to litigation, expulsion, therapy, and myriad other repercussions. As far as we can recall, the only "punishment" enforced was a few days' suspension.

Unfortunately, this seemed to be exactly what Marcus wanted. He was able to get out of school a few days at a time by throwing chairs, hitting classmates, or verbally assaulting the teacher and recess staff. A few weeks later during an assembly, Marcus tied another child's shoelaces together. When that child stood up and tried walking back to class, he fell over. The teacher got frustrated with Marcus and told him he was going to go to the principal's office, so he called her a "bitch." While at the principal's office, he called her a "fucking bitch." Marcus was expelled from school for the rest of the year.

Our family has thousands of "Marcus stories" dealing with his school or home behavior. When he was in fourth grade, Marcus had been out playing with other neighborhood kids, and I was in the house with my other brothers. All of a sudden, Marcus burst through the door, begging us for help. He said that a mob of kids was threatening to beat him up. Myself, my other brothers, and a few of our other friends headed down the street to find out what was going on. The other group of kids saw Marcus with us and headed our way. I asked them why they were bullying my younger brother. They replied that he was "egging them on" and wouldn't stop cursing or calling them names. When I turned around to confront Marcus, he had bolted toward home, realizing that now he had to contend with two big groups of kids. This type of behavior, purposefully pushing buttons and creating commotion among everyone around them, is typical of children with DBDs. They are seeking acknowledgment in whatever way they can find it.

I wish Marcus's story ended with outcomes similar to that of many of my clients. Unfortunately, I believe his struggle to be seen, heard, acknowledged, and felt was too often overlooked, even by myself. After completing my master's program in marriage and family therapy, and exactly one month after I had moved to Michigan to begin my doctoral program in a similar mental health program, Marcus took his own life. My last interactions with him were more of the same: him pushing buttons, creating commotion, and in my view, desperately trying to be seen. He left behind his life partner and their child. I only include the end of his story because I think it portrays very clearly what can happen if children like my brother, those with disruptive behaviors, are only seen for their behavior and not for who they really are.

My Daughter Abigail

When I train other therapists about how to work with kids and families with disruptive behaviors, I use my own children as examples. They provide some of the best examples I couldn't make up if I wanted to. My wife and I have four children, three boys and one daughter, Abigail. Each one of my children has taught me many lessons that I incorporate in my trainings and therapy, but Abby (as we call her) is a special case. When Abby was four years old, the school district encouraged all families to have their children prescreened for school readiness. During this time, many schools were transitioning to full-day kindergarten classes. They wanted to make sure that when children started these classes, they had the ability to remain in class for the full day.

We took Abby in for her prescreening, and they encouraged us to have her do some additional tests to determine any potential deficits. After these tests, the school urged us to enroll her in the "behavioral preschool" program, as they had noticed some behaviors that were likely to create problems in kindergarten if left unaddressed. Abby has a summer birthday, so we had anticipated that she may not have been socially ready for school. She really loved to play, but my wife and I had noticed that she struggled with following through with our commands to clean up or complete a task that did not interest her. Therefore, we decided that it would be a good idea to enroll her in this preschool program. After all, it couldn't hurt for her to have more social interactions and get some extra preparation for kindergarten.

Abby *loved* preschool. She really enjoyed the opportunity to socialize and make new friends. She was a social butterfly and did not give her mother or me any trouble about going to school. Her adjustment to school seemed to be going well—that is, until our first parent-teacher conference. I remember this conference well because for some reason my wife was unable to attend, and she wanted me to record the conference in case I forgot to tell her something.

The teacher started off by praising our little girl and explaining how much fun it was to have Abby in her class. She showed me some of her schoolwork and addressed some things we as parents could do to strengthen Abby's educational experience. Then, the teacher took a deep breath (she knew what I did professionally, so I think she was gearing up for me to react negatively to her feedback) and said, "I don't really know how to say this, so I'll just say it. Abigail has got to be one of the most defiant children I have ever worked with." She paused for a moment, expecting me to say something. I just raised my eyebrow, smiled a little, and said, "Really? Abby?"

She quickly reaffirmed how "lovely" my daughter was and then described what she meant: "Abby is *actively* defiant. She *purposefully* defies authority."

This was a bit surprising for me to hear. I could understand how she would call Abby defiant—I saw it and dealt with it at home—but being actively, purposefully defiant? I wasn't sure I understood what she meant.

She could tell I was a bit confused, so she shared the following story: "The other day, we needed to get ready to go to circle time. It was right at the beginning of the day, and Abby was playing with something on the floor. I told the whole class that it was circle time, and most of the class gradually put their toys away and started moving toward the circle. That is, all except Abby and a few kids near her. The other kids kept looking between myself and Abby as if to try to figure out who they should follow. I called Abby's name a few times, and she didn't budge. At first, I thought she might have some hearing loss; we had seen similar behaviors from her before and attributed it to her not hearing us. Finally, I said, 'Abby did you hear me say it was circle time?' She instantly responded with, 'Yes, I heard you, I just don't want to listen to you.'"

By this time, the teacher had a small smile on her face, and my mouth was wide open. I was surprised, worried, and shocked about what this teacher was sharing about my daughter. I had recollections of my brother Marcus and his behaviors. I had flashes of clients I had worked with who were just as defiant in middle and high school. Seeing that she had my full attention, she then shared the following with me: "Abby is a natural leader. She could be a bully, but she protects other kids from bullies. She befriends new kids instantly, and everyone wants to be her friend. This is both good and bad because she can get the kids to listen to her over the teacher. I think it would be a great idea to have her take preschool for one more year to help her get more used to authority figures in school. I'm just worried that other teachers wouldn't take this behavior as comedically as I do, and I wouldn't want her fire extinguished from her."

I can't express how grateful both my wife and I are for this teacher. She *saw* my daughter. She didn't see a bad kid. She saw Abigail. She knew the potential she had as a leader and a champion for the underdog. We did decide to hold Abby back one year to help her catch up socially with her peers. This turned out to be a massive blessing for Abby and many other kids around her. She is now one of the oldest in her class and still gives people a run for their money, but in a good way. Just this last year, her grade-school teacher presented her with an end-of-year note that read, "Abby, you bring such a fun, positive energy wherever you go! I've loved having you in my class. I also love your determination. When you set your mind to something, it gets done. That is such an awesome trait! Love, *Your Teacher*."

My daughter's story is still in progress. She still has lots of life to live, but the foundation laid for her by her teachers and by my wife and me using the skills and techniques found within this book should prepare her for success. She is still a *little* defiant toward her mother and me. She still expresses her stubborn streak from time to time. However, most of the time this stubbornness or defiance is used in a way to help others who are underprivileged or can't speak up for themselves. I couldn't ask for anything more than for her to use her natural-born temperament to help others.

Case Example: *Adam*

The following example is much like the others I have presented throughout this book except it shows the process from intake to graduation and through all the BISON phases. This example should help you see how each phase can fluctuate and support the others, all while attending to a variety of systemic concerns.

Assessment (Three Sessions)

Raelynn, a single mother, had Adam on my waiting list for almost 14 months. Raelynn contacted my office after trying several other providers with concerns for her son, who was defiant, explosive, and violent. He had been hospitalized twice, each time for two months, due to his violent outbursts toward Raelynn. She would call my office monthly for an update on Adam's place on the waiting list. Upon graduating another client from therapy, I noticed the notes from her last call seemed a bit more desperate than previous ones. I called her and told her that I had an opening with a very narrow window, but I wanted to try to get Adam into that time slot. She told me to schedule it, and she would rearrange her work schedule to be at the appointment.

Due to Adam's violent behavior and previous hospitalization, I asked to meet with both Raelynn and Adam during the intake. When I approached the lobby of my office, I noticed a teen between the ages of 10 and 13 sitting in the chair farthest from an adult female. I assumed this was Raelynn and Adam and could already tell the intake was going to be rough.

As I approached the adult, I asked, "Are you Raelynn?" She submissively nodded her head. "And is this Adam?" I continued, looking toward the teen boy. Again, she nodded her head and waited for me to say something else.

Continuing to look at Adam, I invited, "Adam, good to meet you. Would you like to join us?" Barely looking up, he shrugged his shoulders, then pushed himself up from the chair. They both followed me into my office.

I went through the intake process as described in chapter 4 and learned quite a bit about Adam and his mom. Raelynn reported that Adam, age 12, would lie all the time, steal things from her room, and act out violently toward her when she tried to set limits. Adam hated school, didn't have any friends there, and just wanted to play video games all the time. He expressed sorrow about his violence toward his mom and was concerned that she was going to drop him off at another hospital and never pick him up. He hated the hospital programs and did not much care for therapy either. My assessment with Adam only lasted three sessions, as I quickly learned that the coercion cycle was deeply entrenched in his dynamic with his mother and that neither of them could regulate themselves effectively. Raelynn was seeing Adam in only black-and-white terms. There was no color to his personality in her mind at all. Equally, Adam only saw his mom in black-and-white terms as someone who was dedicated to his misery.

Bio-Emotion Regulation Phase (15 Sessions)

The bio-emotion regulation phase took 15 sessions for Adam. The first three sessions focused on recognizing his HRV rate and teaching him different HeartMath tools to use at home. After three HeartMath-focused sessions, he slightly increased his HRV. It was around this time that he opened up more to me and discussed his hobby of skateboarding. He loved to try new tricks on his skateboard, so juggling and balance interested him more than the HeartMath tools. By the seventh session, he started to talk more about his relationship with his mother. He mentioned that she seemed mad all the time and there was nothing he could do to make her happy. He felt guilty about his anger and behaviors because, as her only son, he thought it was his responsibility to make her happy.

For sessions 8–15, I alternated working with him and Raelynn every other week. As with Adam, I introduced the HeartMath device and explained HRV to her. When I initially connected her to the device, her HRV was rock bottom, and her heart rate was well over 100 bpm. We worked on addressing her stressors with Adam and exploring how they impacted her employment and social life. Even though alternating sessions every other week between Raelynn and Adam slowed the treatment process down, increasing both her and Adam's HRV helped us transition to the next phase.

By the time we were ready to move into the individual play phase, Raelynn's HRV was around 50, and Adam's was around 45. Both were consistently completing the homework I assigned to them (e.g., heart-focused breathing, juggling, line walking), and both had started to notice differences in each other's personalities. Adam was starting to see that his mom wasn't only trying to punish him and that she also had other things she liked to do. Similarly, Raelynn was realizing that Adam could control his emotional outbursts and wasn't defective.

Individual Play Phase (Four Sessions)

To transition to the individual play phase, I invited Raelynn to start one-on-one interactions with Adam at home on a weekly basis. One-on-one time with Adam looked a bit different from how I described it in chapter 6 since Adam was a teenager. I generally want the child to decide what they do, but since Adam was a teenager, he didn't want to spend time with his mom. I had to prescribe that Raelynn watch Adam skateboard (using the same basic principles from chapter 6) and play video games with him once per week, for about 45 to 60 minutes. Having a more favorable view of Adam, she was only slightly reluctant to try. My work with Adam changed as well. Instead of focusing on HeartMath, biofeedback, and skill building, we talked about his interests and the things he worried about. He told me about his school and the people he considered his friends. He ranted about different teachers and how frustrated he was about always getting in trouble at school.

Since Raelynn and Adam were each better at regulating, I had transitioned to only meeting with Adam every other week and checking in with Raelynn at the end of those sessions. Unfortunately, after the fourth session of this phase, Adam was kicked out of his middle school.

Troubleshooting (Three Months)

Even though I had informed Adam's middle school of my treatment approach and offered to work closely with them regarding Adam, they did not reciprocate. About two months had passed after I had initially contacted his school when I received a frantic email from Raelynn detailing why Adam had been kicked out. I scheduled an emergency session to meet with both Raelynn and Adam.

"Tell me again what happened. I'm not sure I understood," I questioned.

Rolling his eyes, smiling smugly, and slouching in his seat, Adam said, "I was in the hallway talking to my friends when the vice principal walked by. I looked over at him and did this—." Sitting up slightly, Adam stuck his nose in the air and mimicked a snob. "Then I turned around and started looking in my locker. Suddenly, the vice principal was standing right next to me, breathing down my neck and asking what I said."

Concerned, I asked, "Did you say anything?"

Shaking his head, Adam assured me, "NO. I just looked at him, and he was right next to me. I told him I didn't say anything, and he took my arm and led me to the office."

Raelynn jumped in. "That's probably when they called me. The principal was all up in arms that Adam had threatened the vice principal and said the school could no longer tolerate Adam's blatant disrespect of authority."

Nodding, I said, "Okay. So now you can't return to school?"

With a big smile on his face, Adam responded, "NOPE! I get to stay home for the rest of the year!"

Raelynn was less enthusiastic about this. "He can't even return to this school next year. He has to enroll at the other middle school."

This is a great example of how the coercion cycle changes how people view and respond to the child. We were just beginning to address Adam's nonresponsiveness to positive social stimuli when his school kicked him out for giving the vice principal a "look." The school's reaction to Adam's behavior reflects the punishment acceleration phase of the coercion cycle in that they were quick to dole out major consequences for a seemingly minor infraction. This threatened to reignite the emotion dysregulation from the first step of the coercion cycle, but both Raelynn and I were determined to keep that change further at bay.

Not having to deal with school for a few months and not having drastic increases in concerns, Raelynn decided to pause therapy until the summer ended and Adam started at a new school. We had a four-month break in sessions before we restarted the individual play phase.

Once we did start up again, I contacted the new school's principal in anticipation of Adam's reputation preceding him. To my surprise, they were also unwilling to meet with me about Adam or his needs. I scheduled a session with Adam and informed his mom about my attempt to connect with the school. I cautioned them that we needed to work with the school as closely as possible to ensure Adam's success, so Raelynn met with the principal and convinced him to meet with me. During my meeting with the principal, I explained the coercion cycle and the state of Adam's treatment, and I invited him to collaborate with me for Adam's benefit. He agreed.

However, three weeks into the new school year, I received a call from the principal: "Dr. Whitehead, I'm sorry, but we have to suspend Adam for the next few days. His blatant disrespect toward and disregard for authority cannot be tolerated."

"What happened?" I asked hesitantly.

"He took control of a teacher's AV system in the middle of a lesson, which created confusion, frustration, and disruption of the learning environment," the principal reported.

"Okay, that's fair," I replied. "Have you talked with him about his behavior and what you expect of him?"

"There's no talking to kids like this. He's just a bad egg, and we unfortunately got stuck with him," the principal lamented.

"Is it okay if we touch base again after I meet with Adam and his mother this week?" I asked.

"Sure, but don't get your hopes up that he's going to change. I know these types of kids. They just aren't worth the time of day."

After meeting with Adam and Raelynn to discuss the incident leading to his suspension, and recognizing this as another sign of Adam's coercion cycle, I proposed a radical intervention.

"Adam, it *seems* like you like getting in trouble. But I know you are someone who just likes to have fun. What do you think will need to happen so you can stop getting suspended?" I asked.

Laughing at me, Adam replied, "What if I like getting suspended?"

Turning toward Raelynn, I smiled and said, "See what I'm talking about? I think Adam is just trying to be home with you."

Looking shocked, Adam blurted, "That's not what I said. I just don't like school."

Smiling, I joked, "But every time you get in trouble with school, you have to spend extra time with your mom. Now that you guys are getting along better, it seems like you are working extra hard to get to be with her."

Raelynn joined me in the joking and said, "I think you might be right, Dr. Whitehead. Adam has been doing a lot better with me, and now we seem to only have problems with school. Maybe I should just go to school with him."

Adam retorted, "You wouldn't dare."

I looked at them both and said, "I actually think that is a brilliant idea!" Looking straight at Raelynn, I asked, "Could you really arrange for that?"

Looking even more panicked, Adam exclaimed, "Wait, what? You're not seriously considering this?"

After further discussion, we decided Raelynn would reach out to the principal to arrange for her to attend one full school day with Adam each week. I would also call the school to see whether they would let me meet with the principal and Adam once a month. Raelynn successfully connected with the principal and got permission to sit with Adam during the classes where his behavior was the worst. The principal also agreed to let me meet with him and Adam once a month during the lunch period.

Raelynn's presence and Adam's time with the principal were more about them seeing and being with Adam than they were about discipline or correction. In fact, I explicitly instructed Raelynn and the principal that she was not to actively interact with Adam during class but to just sit next to him and observe him. If he misbehaved, the teacher would correct him, and Raelynn would just observe. In this way, Raelynn sitting with Adam during his classes and my meeting with Adam and his principal became extensions of the individual play phase. During my weekly lunch meetings with Adam and the principal, the principal began to see Adam with more color. He was opening to Adam's sense of humor, his hobbies, and his plans for the future. This extension of the individual play phase lasted for three months. When the principal started to advocate for Adam during staff meetings and Raelynn no longer needed to attend classes with Adam, we moved on to the next phase.

Successful Communication Phase (Five Sessions)

I interwove the successful communication phase between the previous phase and the troubleshooting sessions. During the weeks I met with Adam's principal, I met with his mother weekly to teach her successful communication interventions. Still seeing Adam with darkened hues, Raelynn had a difficult time implementing effective commands and family meetings. She believed that as a child, Adam needed to comply instantly and shouldn't have any say in how the family functioned. Thankfully, Raelynn had seen that my other interventions were starting to make a difference for Adam and was willing to try the new ones. It took Raelynn two full sessions of role-playing effective commands before she was confident trying them at home. Not surprisingly, Adam responded well to her efforts.

In my last meeting with the principal, he asked me about these interventions. "Dr. Whitehead, before you leave, I want to ask you about something Adam's mom told me."

"Sure, what's your question?" I replied.

"I was talking about how well Adam has responded to me and to her, but he is still struggling with other teachers. I like him a lot now, but many of his teachers still don't. They just think he is a delinquent and get upset when he doesn't listen to them. She mentioned something you were having her try at home called effective commands. Can you tell me more about that?"

Thinking about how best to help Adam, I suggested, "How about we schedule a meeting with all of Adam's teachers, and I'll walk you and them through that process. What do you think?"

"That'd be amazing. Let's do it," he responded.

It took another three weeks before I could arrange a meeting with everyone who needed to be there, but the time finally came. I taught Adam's teachers and the principal about effective commands, family (or in this case, class) meetings, and adolescent development. The process of using effective commands for teachers is the same as for parents, which sometimes draws greater resistance from teachers or school staff due to the belief that they can't wait for the 15 seconds. In explaining effective commands, I compared the 15 seconds to the actual time that is lost when typically engaging in a battle of wills with a student. Most teachers (and parents) quickly realize that the time to institute effective commands is far less than the approach they are already using. I role-played with some of the teachers and explained how to address noncompliance.

I completed two more such training sessions with the principal and teachers about a month apart. By this time, Adam was attending therapy once every other week, and things were starting to get better for him at school as well. Raelynn started dating someone, which unbalanced the equilibrium Adam and Raelynn had found during the past few phases of treatment. We readdressed the first three phases with Raelynn's new partner, which leveled things out for a time. This allowed us to move into the organized play phase.

Organized Play Phase (Three Sessions)

When geared toward adolescents, this phase is less about play and more about skill building through activities (as discussed in chapter 8). Adam was gaining ground at school, starting to connect with Raelynn's new partner, and feeling more confident in himself as a person. Unfortunately, he still had angry outbursts every once in a while that would scare Raelynn and create a slight resurgence of distance between them.

During the second session of organized play, Adam was really struggling with the advanced origami. He was generally good at maintaining his cool throughout this practice, but for some reason, he couldn't during this session.

"Fuck it all!" Adam yelled.

"This aggravates you that you can't get these papers to fold correctly," I empathized.

"Damn it, Michael, I'm not in the mood! Why the hell am I still here? I shouldn't have to do this shit anymore," Adam growled.

"I'm sorry, Adam. You're still learning to maintain your cool. Outbursts like this can't happen at school anymore," I replied.

Clearly incensed that I would bring up his past, he looked at me, stood up, and ran out of my office. Confused, I followed him outside as he paced back and forth in front of my office building.

"Get away from me. I just want to be alone," Adam warned.

"Gotcha. I just need to see you, to make sure you are safe," I explained.

Still angry, he said, "You dumbass, I don't need to be babysat. Just go back and sit in your office."

"Adam, you know that I can't leave you alone. I'll just sit over here," I replied, ignoring the name-calling and explaining my actions.

Adam started kicking a light pole outside the office while repeating all the curse words he could remember.

"Adam, I know you want to kick that light pole, and I can see that you are angry for some reason, but remember the property is not for breaking. If you need to break something, let's go back to my office, and I'll get something for you to break," I instructed.

Confused by my calm demeanor, Adam looked at me, turned, and stormed into my office.

As I closed my door, Adam was back on the couch, head in his hands, breathing heavily, and said, "Just admit it, you hate me."

"You think I hate you?" I asked.

"Yes. I just called you all sorts of names, ripped your paper, kicked the light pole, and now you are going to punish me."

Again, confused about what had happened, I replied, "Adam, it seems like you are really struggling with a lot of emotions. It's okay to be angry, it's okay to have bad days. Did you want to break something?"

With that final reassurance, Adam started weeping. This caught me so off guard because I thought he had hurt himself somehow by kicking the light pole. "Are you okay? Did you get hurt outside?" I asked.

Struggling to answer me through his tears, he said, "No one has ever just sat with me when I was angry. This is about the time I get punished for something. Are you sure you don't hate me?"

Now understanding what was happening, I replied, "It feels different in here when I don't react. Sometimes you do things to test the waters to see how others are going to respond. This hasn't happened to you before, where someone just sat with you."

The rest of the session we just sat there casually chatting about his past experiences in therapy, at school, with his mom, and with his mom's partners. He became regulated quickly after he broke down in tears and was able to leave the session without additional safeguards put in place. His mom reported to me at the end of that session that he had been caught trying to steal something from a store, which led to a criminal case being opened against him. She was hoping he would have talked with me about it, but he didn't. They were scheduled to report to the juvenile justice office after this session.

With a better understanding of where his outburst had come from and after coordinating with the juvenile court to find out what Adam's consequences would be, I was prepared for a very different session the following week. The final session of this phase was focused on decompressing the legal troubles he was in and developing a path forward, which led to another stint of troubleshooting.

Troubleshooting (Six Sessions)

Thankfully, this was Adam's first real offense, and in his jurisdiction, they gave him diversion probation. This essentially meant that if he kept himself out of trouble for a specific period of time (six months for Adam) and wrote a statement to the store owner acknowledging his role in the attempted theft, all charges would be dropped. Next, we needed to work with his probation officer to coordinate care in Adam's best interest.

I invited his probation officer to two of our sessions, and we focused those sessions on helping him see Adam in full color as well. In the first session, we explored many of the topics addressed in the previous phases, and I requested feedback about how his therapy could be altered to increase his probability of success with probation. Specifically for Adam, we readdressed the bio-emotion regulation phase with the probation officer, and in several individual sessions with Adam, to help the officer feel comfortable that Adam was better able to regulate himself. We also slightly altered the organized play interventions to include a cognitive behavioral therapy (CBT) worksheet that was required for Adam to successfully fulfill his probation. After completing a few sessions of CBT worksheets and HRV biofeedback, we invited the probation officer back and discussed the progress Adam had made during those six troubleshooting sessions.

Nurturing Play Phase (Seven Sessions)

After those sessions with the probation officer and Adam, we entered the last phase of treatment, nurturing play. Remember that the key takeaway for this phase is full transfer of care back to the parent. By the time we entered this phase, I had been meeting with Adam and his mother for nearly a year. Raelynn was using individual play regularly with Adam and was dedicated to using effective commands and family meetings. Adam was doing better at school, and many of his teachers were starting to get on board with seeing his real personality.

During this phase, all our sessions were family sessions with both Raelynn and Adam present. I gave Adam many opportunities to express his frustrations about her parenting, her job, and her dating practices. Even though these conversations were hard for her, she was able to respond emphatically and compassionately. Adam started to teach his mom how to skateboard, and he was learning how to cook. Her new partner was introducing him to fishing and hunting, and they were developing a bond with each other. Surprisingly, Adam's language didn't change toward me in my office. He always felt comfortable speaking to me like a peer. However, he did adjust his language with his mother, her partner, and his teachers.

Graduation and Maintenance (Two Years)

As the school year was closing, and Adam's probation was about to end, it was the perfect opportunity to enter graduation and maintenance. However, Raelynn and Adam's principal were a bit wary of moving in this direction. They thought any reduction in my meeting with Adam would increase his disruptive behaviors. I assured them both that if anything came up, we could easily resume any previous phase. I met Adam and Raelynn every six months for two years. The last time I met with Adam, he had been enrolled in all honors classes in high school and was no longer known as the "problem child."

Key Takeaway

Whether a child is like Marcus, Abigail, or any number of the client portrayals I described throughout this book, I believe the core of what these children want and need is to be seen, heard, understood, and felt by a caring adult in their life. Each of these kids is like Wild Thing from chapter 1. Wild Thing needed leadership, love, care, and compassion. He, like other buffaloes, needed structure and direction to channel his immense power and majesty. Likewise, if these kids are not given direction, structure, compassion, and love, they may end up fulfilling the unfortunate projection that many have of them: that they are without hope and criminally driven.

Interactions with hundreds of parents have taught me that teachers, providers, and family members don't expect much from these kids. They errantly believe that these kids would be better having the "devil beat out of them," either literally or figuratively. Bootcamp-style residential treatment centers are full of kids who sometimes only comply because their "fire is extinguished"—often by force or unhealthy coercion. Parents, teachers, and providers are struggling to know how to help these kids. I hope the interventions outlined in this book will give more providers insight into how to see, hear, understand, and touch these wonderful human beings. ■

APPENDIX

Exploring the Impact of Child-Centered Play Therapy for Children Exhibiting Behavioral Problems: A Meta-Analysis*

Implications for counselors:

"Interestingly, results examining externalizing behaviors compared to an active treatment resulted in the highest effect size obtained, demonstrating CCPT [child-centered play therapy] may be moderately more effective than the alternative treatment."

The diagnostic criteria this definition may match:

- *Oppositional defiant disorder*
- *Childhood onset of conduct disorder*
- *Attention-deficit/hyperactivity disorder*
- *Autism spectrum disorders*

Reason for the study:

"The purpose of this study is to evaluate the effectiveness of play therapy on mitigating behavioral problems among children referred for treatment due to disruptive behaviors . . . to conduct a meta-analysis exploring the impact for CCPT on children's disruptive behaviors."

Methods:

- Meta-analysis: An examination of data from a number of independent studies of the same subject used to understand the overall conclusions regarding results from that research.

- Study qualities were determined based on agreed-upon standards. Of the 23 studies examined, 10 were of higher quality (7+ on an 11-point scale, 11 being highest quality).

---

* Parker, M. M., Hunnicutt Hollenbaugh, K. M., & Kelly, C. T. (2021). Exploring the impact of child-centered play therapy for children exhibiting behavioral problems: A meta-analysis. *International Journal of Play Therapy, 30*(4), 259–271. https://doi.org/10.1037/pla0000128

Results:

	"Diagnosis"	Overall Effect Size (p)
CCPT vs. No Treatment	Externalizing Behaviors	–0.34 (.00)
CCPT vs. Alternative Treatment	Externalizing Behaviors	–0.56 (.00)
CCPT vs. No Treatment	Overall Problem Behaviors	–0.48 (.00)
CCPT vs. No Treatment	Aggressive Behaviors	–0.26 (.10)

This study used + and - to indicate CCPT vs. "Other." In this study, when effect sizes are negative, they indicate a positive change from CCPT.

Conclusion:

- CCPT is an effective treatment for externalizing problem behaviors in children.
- There is a moderate effect size (0.56 or about 70% better) when comparing CCPT to alternative child therapy treatments (e.g., cognitive behavioral therapy, parent training).

Effects of Child-Centered Play Therapy for Students with Highly Disruptive Behavior in High-Poverty Schools*

Highly disruptive behavior was defined as:
"causing significant and persistent interference with one's own and peers' learning and instruction, through frequent aggression toward peers or teacher and/or noisiness and frequent refusal or failure to follow directions."

The diagnostic criteria this definition may match:

- *Oppositional defiant disorder*
- *Childhood onset of conduct disorder*
- *Attention-deficit/hyperactivity disorder*

Reason for the study:
"CCPT [child-centered play therapy] was provided . . . for students who were not showing a decrease in highly disruptive behavior in spite of multiple other intervention facets, including social work resource assistance, parent programs, teacher support, alternative disciplinary programs, extensive mentoring, and school counselor services."

Treatment:

- Thirty-minute CCPT sessions twice weekly. The sessions were a full 30 minutes, not including travel time from the classroom to the therapy room.
- Play therapy areas ranged from a section of an empty classroom, a section of a short hallway, and some administrative offices, and some providers had to change locations throughout the study.

Participants:

- 52.4% kindergarten to second grade
- 47.6% third grade to fifth grade
- 76.9% male
- 52.3% Caucasian
- 38.5% African American
- 7.7% Hispanic

---

* Cochran, J. L., & Cochran, N. H. (2017). Effects of child-centered play therapy for students with highly-disruptive behavior in high-poverty schools. *International Journal of Play Therapy, 26*(2), 59–72. https://doi.org/10.1037/pla0000052

Providers:

- Many were graduate students with one semester of CCPT instruction.

Results:

- Teacher reports found that students significantly improved from a clinical rating to a normal rating during the nine-week treatment as evidenced by a:
    - 47% reduction in disciplinary referrals
    - 61% reduction in suspensions
    - 40% reduction in absences

Conclusion:

- Most school administrators doubted that the students treated in this study would ever change and were surprised with the results.
- The approach to limit setting in CCPT encourages students to become self-motivated in limit setting, translating to greater control and attention during school hours.

For more information about play therapy or CCPT, see https://www.a4pt.org.

Emotion Coaching—A Strategy for Promoting Behavioural Self-Regulation in Children/Young People in Schools: A Pilot Study*

Why emotion coaching should be used:
"This approach recognizes that socially competent children who are able to understand and regulate their emotions are better equipped to go on to achieve higher academic success than those who lack impulse control or have poor social skills."

The diagnostic criteria this definition may match:

- *Oppositional defiant disorder*
- *Childhood onset of conduct disorder*
- *Attention-deficit/hyperactivity disorder*

Reason for the study:
"Katz et al.'s (2012)** recent review of emotion coaching research calls for more studies that explore the role of emotion socialization agents other than parents, such as teachers and peers. Productive interactions between individuals are fundamental to effective educational practice, and teachers have identified that emotional management is integral to their work."

Methods:

- Senior and junior teaching staff, teaching assistants, school support staff, and some parents received training in emotion coaching.
- The majority of emotion coachers were teachers (80%).
- Students of trained teachers were followed for one year after the training took place.

---

* Rose, J., McGuire-Snieckus, R., & Gilbert, L. (2015). Emotion coaching—a strategy for promoting behavioural self-regulation in children/young people in schools: A pilot study. *The European Journal of Social & Behavioural Sciences, 13*(2), 130–157. https://doi.org/10.15405/ejsbs.159

** Katz, L. F., Maliken, A. C., & Stettler, N. M. (2012). Parental meta-emotion philosophy: A review of research and theoretical framework. *Child Development Perspectives, 6*(4), 417–422. https://doi.org/10.1111/j.1750-8606.2012.00244.x

Results:

- Student callouts (referrals) decreased by 26% with an effect size of 0.36.
- Student exclusions (suspensions) decreased by 30% with an effect size of 0.39.
- Student consequences (in class) decreased by 15% with an effect size of 0.45.

Conclusion:

- There was a significant reduction in disruptive behavior and a positive impact on behavioral regulation across the research settings.
- Results indicate that emotion coaching can be used successfully alongside, or as a supplement to, the existing behaviorist model focusing on behavior modification.
- Teacher warmth and empathy were strongly associated with positive social and educational outcomes.

The Efficacy of Play Therapy with Children: A Meta-Analytic Review of Treatment Outcomes*

Implications for counselors:

"The obvious implication of this research is that play therapy demonstrates itself to be an effective intervention for children's problems, one that is uniquely responsive to children's developmental needs. Of significant note, play therapy has a large effect on children's behavior, social adjustment, and personality."

The diagnostic criteria this definition may match:

- *Behavioral concerns*
- *Social adjustment*
- *Sense of self*
- *Family relationship concerns*
- *Developmental concerns*
- *Personality*
- *Fear/anxiety concerns*

Reason for the study:

"Today, play therapy is widely used among clinicians to treat a wide range of emotional and behavioral problems . . . [yet] play therapy has not received widespread acceptance from the scientific community and has often been criticized for a lack of sound empirical evidence to support its use."

Methods:

- Meta-analysis: An examination of data from a number of independent studies of the same subject used to understand the overall conclusions regarding results from that research.

- This meta-analysis included 93 studies, with a total of 3,248 child participants. The studies that were included in the analysis were chosen for their experimental designs. Random assignment to treatment groups was present in 70% of the studies examined.

---

* Bratton, S. C., Ray, D., Rhine, T., & Jones, L. (2005). The efficacy of play therapy with children: A meta-analytic review of treatment outcomes. *Professional Psychology: Research and Practice, 36*(4), 376–390. https://doi.org/10.1037/0735-7028.36.4.376

Results:

	Overall Effect Size (p)
Play Therapy vs. Control Group	0.89 (.05)
Play Therapy vs. Alternative Treatment (traditional child therapy)	0.79 (.05)
Registered Play Therapist (RPT) Provider	0.72 (.05)
Parent trained by RPT Provider	1.15 (.05)

Conclusion:

- "After play therapy, the average treated child was functioning at 0.80 standard deviations better than children not treated."
- When play therapy is conducted by a trained RPT, parents are involved from the beginning, and the treatment is approximately 35 sessions or more, the impact and effectiveness of play therapy is long-lasting and significant.

Maternal Criticism and Children's Neural Responses to Reward and Loss*

Reason for the study:

Research evidence suggests that parental criticism is linked to depression, anxiety, oppositional defiant disorder, and other internalized and externalized behavioral concerns in children and adolescents. Parental criticism is usually defined as expressing hostility toward a child's character rather than describing specific behaviors that need to be changed. No study has identified how criticism increases negative outcomes for children, but one possibility is that children who experience criticism are less likely to respond to typical reward programs.

Methods:

- Children (ages 7–11) and their biological mothers were included.
- Children with developmental or learning disabilities were excluded.
- Children were presented with a task designed to activate the reward centers of the brain.
- Mothers were asked to describe their child for five minutes uninterrupted. This task has been shown to measure expressed criticism toward children.
- During the "reward" task, children received an electroencephalogram (EEG) to identify activation of the reward and loss systems in the brain.

Results:

- All children, regardless of maternal criticism, had higher activation in the reward system than the loss system (indicating children respond better to rewards than punishments).
- Children whose mothers scored "high" on the measure of criticism had less activation in both the reward system and the loss system (indicating that children who experience maternal criticism have a harder time responding to both rewards and punishments).
- When parental and child anxiety and depression were controlled for, the results were the same (indicating that it is expression of criticism, not mental health, that is impacting the reward and loss systems).

---

* James, K. M., Foster, C. E., Tsypes, A., Owens, M., & Gibb, B. E. (2021). Maternal criticism and children's neural responses to reward and loss. *Journal of Experimental Child Psychology, 211*, Article 105226. https://doi.org/10.1016/j.jecp.2021.105226

Conclusion:

- While not fully generalizable, the findings do indicate that children with critical parents experience a blunted response to both rewards and punishments.
- Results also indicate that children with critical parents may not be learning from experiences typically prescribed for behavior management (e.g., reward charts, punishments).
- While future research is needed, the results suggest that family therapy focused on increasing the positive relationship between parent and child, and particularly reducing parental expressions of criticism, may help increase the response that children have to rewards and punishments.

References

For your convenience, purchasers can download and print selected resources from this book at pesipubs.com/disruptive.

Achtergarde, S., Postert, C., Wessing, I., Romer, G., & Müller, J. M. (2015). Parenting and child mental health: Influences of parent personality, child temperament, and their interaction. *The Family Journal*, *23*(2), 167–179. https://doi.org/10.1177/1066480714564316

Allen, B. (2020). Child-parent relationship therapy for externalizing problems: A meta-analysis and methodological critique. *Evidence-Based Practice in Child and Adolescent Mental Health*, *5*(4), 426–436. https://doi.org/10.1080/23794925.2020.1784054

American Academy of Child and Adolescent Psychiatry. (2024). *Frequently asked questions*. Oppositional Defiant Disorder Resource Center. https://www.aacap.org/AACAP/Families_and_Youth/Resource_Centers/Oppositional_Defiant_Disorder_Resource_Center/FAQ.aspx

American Psychiatric Association. (2022). *Diagnostic and statistical manual of mental disorders* (5th ed., text rev.). https://doi.org/10.1176/appi.books.9780890425787

American Psychological Association Presidential Task Force on Evidence-Based Practice. (2006). Evidence-based practice in psychology. *American Psychologist*, *61*(4), 271–285. https://doi.org/10.1037/0003-066X.61.4.271

Astill, R. G., Van der Heijden, K. B., Van Ijzendoorn, M. H., & Van Someren, E. J. W. (2012). Sleep, cognition, and behavioral problems in school-age children: A century of research meta-analyzed. *Psychological Bulletin*, *138*(6), 1109–1138. https://doi.org/10.1037/a0028204

Axline, V. (1981). *Play therapy*. Ballantine Books.

Bizzi, F., & Pace, C. S. (2020). Attachment representations in children with disruptive behavior disorders: A special focus on insecurity in middle childhood. *Clinical Child Psychology and Psychiatry*, *25*(4), 833–846. https://doi.org/10.1177/1359104520918637

Bowen, M. (1966). The use of family theory in clinical practice. *Comprehensive Psychiatry*, *7*(5), 345–374. https://doi.org/10.1016/S0010-440X(66)80065-2

Bratton, S. C., Ray, D., Rhine, T., & Jones, L. (2005). The efficacy of play therapy with children: A meta-analytic review of treatment outcomes. *Professional Psychology: Research and Practice*, *36*(4), 376–390. https://doi.org/10.1037/0735-7028.36.4.376

Bronfenbrenner, U. (1977). Toward an experimental ecology of human development. *American Psychologist*, *32*(7), 513–531. https://doi.org/10.1037/0003-066X.32.7.513

Buehler, C. (2020). Family processes and children's and adolescents' well-being. *Journal of Marriage and Family*, *82*(1), 145–174. https://doi.org/10.1111/jomf.12637

Burke, J. D., Butler, E. J., Shaughnessy, S., Karlovich, A. R., & Evans, S. C. (2024). Evidence-based assessment of *DSM-5* disruptive, impulse control, and conduct disorders. *Assessment*, *31*(1), 75–93. https://doi.org/10.1177/10731911231188739

Burke, J. D., Waldman, I., & Lahey, B. B. (2010). Predictive validity of childhood oppositional defiant disorder and conduct disorder: Implications for the *DSM-V*. *Journal of Abnormal Psychology*, *119*(4), 739–751. https://doi.org/10.1037/a0019708

Carr, A. (2014). The evidence base for family therapy and systemic interventions for child-focused problems. *Journal of Family Therapy, 36*(2), 107–157. https://doi.org/10.1111/1467-6427.12032

Carr, A. (2019). Family therapy and systemic interventions for child-focused problems: The current evidence base. *Journal of Family Therapy, 41*(2), 153–213. https://doi.org/10.1111/1467-6427.12226

Chess, S., & Thomas, A. (1977). Temperamental individuality from childhood to adolescence. *Journal of the American Academy of Child Psychiatry, 16*(2), 218–226. https://doi.org/10.1016/s0002-7138(09)60038-8

Chiu, H. T., Ip, I. N., Ching, F. N. Y., Wong, B. P.-H., Lui, W.-H., Tse, C.-S., & Wong, S. W. H. (2024). Resting heart rate variability and emotion dysregulation in adolescents with autism spectrum disorder. *Journal of Autism and Developmental Disorders, 54*(4), 1482–1493. https://doi.org/10.1007/s10803-022-05847-x

Christensen, C. M., Allworth, J., & Dillon, K. (2012). *How will you measure your life?* HarperBusiness.

Cochran, J. L., & Cochran, N. H. (2017). Effects of child-centered play therapy for students with highly-disruptive behavior in high-poverty schools. *International Journal of Play Therapy, 26*(2), 59–72. https://doi.org/10.1037/pla0000052

Cornett, N., & Bratton, S. C. (2014). Examining the impact of child parent relationship therapy (CPRT) on family functioning. *Journal of Marital and Family Therapy, 40*(3), 302–318. https://doi.org/10.1111/jmft.12014

Deater-Deckard, K., Hong, Y., Bertrand, C., & Folker, A. (2024). Cognition and emotion: Family member similarity and intergenerational transmission. In M. A. Bell (Ed.), *Child development at the intersection of emotion and cognition* (2nd ed., pp. 135–157). American Psychological Association.

DeKlyen, M. (1996). Disruptive behavior disorder and intergenerational attachment patterns: A comparison of clinic-referred and normally functioning preschoolers and their mothers. *Journal of Consulting and Clinical Psychology, 64*(2), 357–365. https://doi.org/10.1037/0022-006X.64.2.357

de Looff, P. C., Cornet, L. J. M., de Kogel, C. H., Fernández-Castilla, B., Embregts, P. J. C. M., Didden, R., & Nijman, H. L. I. (2022). Heart rate and skin conductance associations with physical aggression, psychopathy, antisocial personality disorder and conduct disorder: An updated meta-analysis. *Neuroscience & Biobehavioral Reviews, 132*, 553–582. https://doi.org/10.1016/j.neubiorev.2021.11.003

De Los Reyes, A., & Lee, S. S. (2017, June 1). *The high cost of childhood disruptive behavior disorders.* STAT. https://www.statnews.com/2017/06/01/disruptive-behavior-disorders-children

Dormal, V., Vermeulen, N., & Mejias, S. (2021). Is heart rate variability biofeedback useful in children and adolescents? A systematic review. *The Journal of Child Psychology and Psychiatry, 62*(12), 1379–1390. https://doi.org/10.1111/jcpp.13463

Ducharme, P., Kahn, J., Vaudreuil, C., Gusman, M., Waber, D., Ross, A., Rotenberg, A., Rober, A., Kimball, K., Peechatka, A. L., & Gonzalez-Heydrich, J. (2021). A "proof of concept" randomized controlled trial of a video game requiring emotional regulation to augment anger control training. *Frontiers in Psychiatry, 12*, Article 591906. https://doi.org/10.3389/fpsyt.2021.591906

Dunsmore, J. C., Booker, J. A., & Ollendick, T. H. (2013). Parental emotion coaching and child emotion regulation as protective factors for children with oppositional defiant disorder. *Social Development, 22*(3), 444–466. https://doi.org/10.1111/j.1467-9507.2011.00652.x

Dunsmore, J. C., Booker, J. A., Ollendick, T. H., & Greene, R. W. (2016). Emotion socialization in the context of risk and psychopathology: Maternal emotion coaching predicts better treatment outcomes for emotionally labile children with oppositional defiant disorder. *Social Development*, *25*(1), 8–26. https://doi.org/10.1111/sode.12109

Frick, P. J., & Kemp, E. C. (2021). Conduct disorders and empathy development. *Annual Review of Clinical Psychology*, *17*, 391–416. https://doi.org/10.1146/annurev-clinpsy-081219-105809

Fristad, M. A., Wolfson, H., Algorta, G. P., Youngstrom, E. A., Arnold, L. E., Birmaher, B., Horwitz, S., Axelson, D., Kowatch, R. A., Findling, R. L., & the LAMS Group. (2016). Disruptive mood dysregulation disorder and bipolar disorder not otherwise specified: Fraternal or identical twins? *Journal of Child and Adolescent Psychopharmacology*, *26*(2), 138–146. https://doi.org/10.1089/cap.2015.0062

Gottman, J. M. (2011). *The science of trust: Emotional attunement for couples*. W. W. Norton.

Gottman, J. M., & DeClaire, J. (1997). *Raising an emotionally intelligent child*. Simon & Schuster Paperbacks.

Greene, R. W., & Ablon, J. S. (2005). *Treating explosive kids: The collaborative problem-solving approach*. Guilford Press.

Guerney, B., Jr. (1964). Filial therapy: Description and rationale. *Journal of Consulting Psychology*, *28*(4), 304–310. https://doi.org/10.1037/h0041340

Hangül, Z. (2024). DMDD and bipolar disorder in children and adolescents. In S. Goldstein (Ed.), *Clinician guide to disruptive mood dysregulation disorder in children and adolescents* (pp. 125–132). Springer International Publishing.

Hawes, D. J., Gardner, F., Dadds, M. R., Frick, P. J., Kimonis, E. R., Burke, J. D., & Fairchild, G. (2023). Oppositional defiant disorder. *Nature Reviews Disease Primers*, *9*(1), 1–17. https://doi.org/10.1038/s41572-023-00441-6

Hazell, P. (2010). Review of attention-deficit/hyperactivity disorder comorbid with oppositional defiant disorder. *Australasian Psychiatry*, *18*(6), 556–559. https://doi.org/10.3109/10398562.2010.498049

Hicks, B., & Baggerly, J. (2017). The effectiveness of child parent relationship therapy in an online format. *International Journal of Play Therapy*, *26*(3), 138–150. https://doi.org/10.1037/pla0000033

Hudec, K. L., & Mikami, A. Y. (2018). Diagnostic issues for ODD/CD with ADHD comorbidity. In J. E. Lochman & W. Matthys (Eds.), *The Wiley handbook of disruptive and impulse-control disorders* (pp. 55–71). John Wiley & Sons.

Jacobvitz, D., Aviles, A. I., Aquino, G. A., Tian, Z., Zhang, S., & Hazen, N. (2022). Fathers' sensitivity in infancy and externalizing problems in middle childhood: The role of coparenting. *Frontiers in Psychology*, *13*, Article 805188. https://doi.org/10.3389/fpsyg.2022.805188

James, K. M., Foster, C. E., Tsypes, A., Owens, M., & Gibb, B. E. (2021). Maternal criticism and children's neural responses to reward and loss. *Journal of Experimental Child Psychology*, *211*, Article 105226. https://doi.org/10.1016/j.jecp.2021.105226

Karam, E. A., & Blow, A. J. (2023). *Bringing common factors to life in couple and family therapy*. Routledge.

Karnik, N. S., & Steiner, H. (2005). Disruptive behavior disorders. In W. M. Klykylo & J. L. Kay (Eds.), *Clinical child psychiatry* (2nd ed., pp. 191–202). John Wiley & Sons.

Katz, L. F., Maliken, A. C., & Stettler, N. M. (2012). Parental meta-emotion philosophy: A review of research and theoretical framework. *Child Development Perspectives*, *6*(4), 417–422. https://doi.org/10.1111/j.1750-8606.2012.00244.x

Kazdin, A. E. (2017). Addressing the treatment gap: A key challenge for extending evidence-based psychosocial interventions. *Behaviour Research and Therapy, 88*, 7–18. https://doi.org/10.1016/j.brat.2016.06.004

Lahey, B. B., Loeber, R., Burke, J. D., & Applegate, B. (2005). Predicting future antisocial personality disorder in males from a clinical assessment in childhood. *Journal of Consulting and Clinical Psychology, 73*(3), 389–399. https://doi.org/10.1037/0022-006X.73.3.389

Landreth, G. L., & Bratton, S. C. (2005). *Child parent relationship therapy (CPRT): A 10-session filial therapy model*. Taylor & Francis.

Lecavalier, L., McCracken, C. E., Aman, M. G., McDougle, C. J., McCracken, J. T., Tierney, E., Smith, T., Johnson, C., King, B., Handen, B., Swiezy, N. B., Arnold, L. E., Bearss, K., Vitiello, B., & Scahill, L. (2019). An exploration of concomitant psychiatric disorders in children with autism spectrum disorder. *Comprehensive Psychiatry, 88*, 57–64. https://doi.org/10.1016/j.comppsych.2018.10.012

Lee, R., & Coccaro, E. (2001). The neuropsychopharmacology of criminality and aggression. *The Canadian Journal of Psychiatry, 46*(1), 35–44. https://doi.org/10.1177/070674370104600106

Lewis, K. G. (1987). Systemic play therapy: Consultation to inner-city community mental health centers. *Journal of Independent Social Work, 1*(2), 33–43. https://doi.org/10.1300/J283v01n02_04

Lin, X., He, T., Heath, M., Chi, P., & Hinshaw, S. (2022). A systematic review of multiple family factors associated with oppositional defiant disorder. *International Journal of Environmental Research and Public Health, 19*(17), Article 10866. https://doi.org/10.3390/ijerph191710866

Lin, Y.-W., & Bratton, S. C. (2015). A meta-analytic review of child-centered play therapy approaches. *Journal of Counseling & Development, 93*(1), 45–58. https://doi.org/10.1002/j.1556-6676.2015.00180.x

López-Morales, H., del-Valle, M. V., López, M. C., Andrés, M. L., García, M. J., Canet-Juric, L., & Urquijo, S. (2023). Maternal anxiety, exposure to the COVID-19 pandemic and socioemotional development of offspring. *Journal of Applied Developmental Psychology, 86*, Article 101517. https://doi.org/10.1016/j.appdev.2023.101517

Mannweiler, M., Schuermann, H., Peechatka, A., & Kahn, J. (2023). Biofeedback-based videogames: Fostering emotion regulation at a diverse community summer camp. *Games for Health Journal, 12*(5), 350–357. https://doi.org/10.1089/g4h.2023.0013

Matheson, A. S., & Shriver, M. D. (2005). Training teachers to give effective commands: Effects on student compliance and academic behaviors. *School Psychology Review, 34*(2), 202–219. https://doi.org/10.1080/02796015.2005.12086283

McCart, M. R., Priester, P. E., Davies, W. H., & Azen, R. (2006). Differential effectiveness of behavioral parent-training and cognitive-behavioral therapy for antisocial youth: A meta-analysis. *Journal of Abnormal Child Psychology, 34*(4), 525–541. https://doi.org/10.1007/s10802-006-9031-1

Metcalf, L. (2023). *Marriage and family therapy: A practice-oriented approach* (3rd ed.). Springer Publishing.

Minuchin, S., Reiter, M. D., & Borda, C. (2021). *The craft of family therapy: Challenging certainties*. Routledge.

Murphy, S. E., Boyd-Soisson, E., Jacobvitz, D. B., & Hazen, N. L. (2017). Dyadic and triadic family interactions as simultaneous predictors of children's externalizing behaviors. *Family Relations: Interdisciplinary Journal of Applied Family Studies, 66*(2), 346–359. https://doi.org/10.1111/fare.12225

Nevo, I., & Slonim-Nevo, V. (2011). The myth of evidence-based practice: Towards evidence-informed practice. *The British Journal of Social Work, 41*(6), 1176–1197. https://doi.org/10.1093/bjsw/bcq149

Nock, M. K., Kazdin, A. E., Hiripi, E., & Kessler, R. C. (2007). Lifetime prevalence, correlates, and persistence of oppositional defiant disorder: Results from the National Comorbidity Survey Replication. *The Journal of Child Psychology and Psychiatry, 48*(7), 703–713. https://doi.org/10.1111/j.1469-7610.2007.01733.x

Opiola, K. K., & Bratton, S. C. (2018). The efficacy of child parent relationship therapy for adoptive families: A replication study. *Journal of Counseling & Development, 96*(2), 155–166. https://doi.org/10.1002/jcad.12189

Parker, M. M., Hunnicutt Hollenbaugh, K. M., & Kelly, C. T. (2021). Exploring the impact of child-centered play therapy for children exhibiting behavioral problems: A meta-analysis. *International Journal of Play Therapy, 30*(4), 259–271. https://doi.org/10.1037/pla0000128

Patterson, G. R. (2016). Coercion theory: The study of change. In T. J. Dishion & J. J. Snyder (Eds.), *The Oxford handbook of coercive relationship dynamics* (pp. 7–23). Oxford University Press.

Patterson, G. R., Dishion, T. J., & Bank, L. (1984). Family interaction: A process model of deviancy training. *Aggressive Behavior, 10*(3), 253–267. https://doi.org/10.1002/1098-2337(1984)10:3<253::AID-AB2480100309>3.0.CO;2-2

Patterson, G. R., & Forgatch, M. S. (2010). Expanding the coercion model. In E. Befring, I. Frones, & M. A. Sorlie (Eds.), *Young and vulnerable: New perspectives and approaches* (pp. 168–179). Gyldendal Akademisk.

Perry, B. D. (2017). *The boy who was raised as a dog*. Basic Books.

Perry, N. B., Calkins, S. D., Dollar, J. M., Keane, S. P., & Shanahan, L. (2018). Self-regulation as a predictor of patterns of change in externalizing behaviors from infancy to adolescence. *Development and Psychopathology, 30*(2), 497–510. https://doi.org/10.1017/S0954579417000992

Pishdadian, S., Asgharinekah, S. M., & Ziaee, S. S. (2024). A COVID-19 study: Child-parent relationship therapy for children's behavioral problems. *Journal of Fundamentals of Mental Health, 26*(5), 309–315. https://doi.org/10.22038/JFMH.2024.77201.3109

Porges, S. W. (2011). *The polyvagal theory: Neurophysiological foundations of emotions, attachment, communication, and self-regulation*. W. W. Norton.

Ray, D. C. (2015). *A therapist's guide to child development: The extraordinarily normal years*. Routledge.

Rezaeianzadeh, Z., & Yazdanfar, F. (2024). Effectiveness of TheraPlay and filial therapy on aggression in preschool boys. *Current Psychology, 43*(19), 17602–17613. https://doi.org/10.1007/s12144-024-05743-w

Ritzi, R. M., Ray, D. C., & Schumann, B. R. (2017). Intensive short-term child-centered play therapy and externalizing behaviors in children. *International Journal of Play Therapy, 26*(1), 33–46. https://doi.org/10.1037/pla0000035

Rose, J., McGuire-Snieckus, R., & Gilbert, L. (2015). Emotion coaching—a strategy for promoting behavioural self-regulation in children/young people in schools: A pilot study. *The European Journal of Social & Behavioural Sciences,, 13*(2), 130–157. https://doi.org/10.15405/ejsbs.159

Rowe, R., Costello, E. J., Angold, A., Copeland, W. E., & Maughan, B. (2010). Developmental pathways in oppositional defiant disorder and conduct disorder. *Journal of Abnormal Psychology, 119*(4), 726–738. https://doi.org/10.1037/a0020798

Salisbury, T. (2013). The relationship between oppositional defiant disorder, conduct disorder, antisocial personality disorder and psychopathy: A proposed trajectory. *Western Undergraduate Psychology Journal, 1*(1), Article 2.

Salter, K., Beamish, W., & Davies, M. (2016). The effects of child-centered play therapy (CCPT) on the social and emotional growth of young Australian children with autism. *International Journal of Play Therapy, 25*(2), 78–90. https://doi.org/10.1037/pla0000012

Satir, V. (1976). *Making contact*. Celestial Arts.

Schoorl, J., Van Rijn, S., De Wied, M., Van Goozen, S. H. M., & Swaab, H. (2016). Variability in emotional/behavioral problems in boys with oppositional defiant disorder or conduct disorder: The role of arousal. *European Child & Adolescent Psychiatry, 25*(8), 821–830. https://doi.org/10.1007/s00787-015-0790-5

Schroeder, M. O. (2016, February 4). *Is your child becoming a psychopath?* U.S. News & World Report. https://health.usnews.com/health-news/health-wellness/articles/2016-02-04/is-your-child-becoming-a-psychopath

Scott, K. M., Lim, C. C. W., Hwang, I., Adamowski, T., Al-Hamzawi, A., Bromet, E., Bunting, B., Ferrand, M. P., Florescu, S., Gureje, O., Hinkov, H., Hu, C., Karam, E., Lee, S., Posada-Villa, J., Stein, D., Tachimori, H., Viana, M. C., Xavier, M., & Kessler, R. C. (2016). The cross-national epidemiology of *DSM-IV* intermittent explosive disorder. *Psychological Medicine, 46*(15), 3161–3172. https://doi.org/10.1017/S0033291716001859

Shafi, R. M. A., Bieber, E. D., Shekunov, J., Croarkin, P. E., & Romanowicz, M. (2019). Evidence based dyadic therapies for 0- to 5-year-old children with emotional and behavioral difficulties. *Frontiers in Psychiatry, 10*, Article 677. https://doi.org/10.3389/fpsyt.2019.00677

Sheidow, A. J., McCart, M. R., & Drazdowski, T. K. (2022). Family-based treatments for disruptive behavior problems in children and adolescents: An updated review of rigorous studies (2014–April 2020). *Journal of Marital and Family Therapy, 48*(1), 56–82. https://doi.org/10.1111/jmft.12567

Siegel, D. J. (2011). *The neurobiology of "we."* Sounds True.

Sikora, D. M., Johnson, K., Clemons, T., & Katz, T. (2012). The relationship between sleep problems and daytime behavior in children of different ages with autism spectrum disorders. *Pediatrics, 130*(Supplement 2), S83–S90. https://doi.org/10.1542/peds.2012-0900F

Smith, J. D., Dishion, T. J., Shaw, D. S., Wilson, M. N., Winter, C. C., & Patterson, G. R. (2014). Coercive family process and early-onset conduct problems from age 2 to school entry. *Development and Psychopathology, 26*(4 pt. 1), 917–932. https://doi.org/10.1017/S0954579414000169

Sori, C. F., Hecker, L., & Bachenberg, M. E. (Eds.). (2015). *The therapist's notebook for children and adolescents: Homework, handouts, and activities for use in psychotherapy* (2nd ed.). Routledge.

Sparks, G. M., Axelson, D. A., Yu, H., Ha, W., Ballester, J., Diler, R. S., Goldstein, B., Goldstein, T., Hickey, M. B., Ladouceur, C. D., Monk, K., Sakolsky, D., & Birmaher, B. (2014). Disruptive mood dysregulation disorder and chronic irritability in youth at familial risk for bipolar disorder. *Journal of the American Academy of Child & Adolescent Psychiatry, 53*(4), 408–416. https://doi.org/10.1016/j.jaac.2013.12.026

Stutey, D. M., Dunn, M., Shelnut, J., & Ryan, J. B. (2017). Impact of Adlerian play therapy on externalizing behaviors of at-risk preschoolers. *International Journal of Play Therapy, 26*(4), 196–206. https://doi.org/10.1037/pla0000055

Walker, M. (2018). *Why we sleep: Unlocking the power of sleep and dreams*. Penguin Books.

Wampler, R. S. (2020). *The handbook of systemic family therapy*. Wiley-Blackwell.

Wampler, R. S., & Whitehead, M. R. (2020). Disordered behavior and behavior disorders. In K. Wampler (Ed.), *Systemic family therapy with children and adolescents* (Vol. 2). John Wiley & Sons.

Wampold, B. E. (2001). *The great psychotherapy debate: Models, methods, and findings.* Erlbaum.

Weinberg, M. K., & Tronick, E. Z. (1996). Infant affective reactions to the resumption of maternal interaction after the still-face. *Child Development, 67*(3), 905–914. https://doi.org/10.1111/j.1467-8624.1996.tb01772.x

Weiss, B., Catron, T., Harris, V., & Phung, T. M. (1999). The effectiveness of traditional child psychotherapy. *Journal of Consulting and Clinical Psychology, 67*(1), 82–94. https://doi.org/10.1037/0022-006X.67.1.82

Weisz, J. R., Kuppens, S., Ng, M. Y., Eckshtain, D., Ugueto, A. M., Vaughn-Coaxum, R., Jensen-Doss, A., Hawley, K. M., Krumholz Marchette, L. S., Chu, B. C., Weersing, V. R., & Fordwood, S. R. (2017). What five decades of research tells us about the effects of youth psychological therapy: A multilevel meta-analysis and implications for science and practice. *American Psychologist, 72*(2), 79–117. https://doi.org/10.1037/a0040360

Wilson, B. J., Berg, J. L., Zurawski, M. E., & King, K. A. (2013). Autism and externalizing behaviors: Buffering effects of parental emotion coaching. *Research in Autism Spectrum Disorders, 7*(6), 767–776. https://doi.org/10.1016/j.rasd.2013.02.005

Woodard, T. J., Ume, U., & Davis, R. (2019). An introduction to oppositional defiant disorder and conduct disorder. *U.S. Pharmacist, 44*(11), 29–32.

Acknowledgments

Growing up, my least favorite subject in school was English language arts. I wasn't the fastest reader, and I really didn't like grammar lessons. I wasn't the worst in my classes, I just didn't like the idea of having to write things out or "waste" time reading. My high school guidance counselors recommended that I not pursue a career that required a lot of reading or writing. Despite this, I found my passion and calling in helping families in a profession that requires a ton of reading and writing.

In that light, I must first acknowledge the many divine interventions that led to my acceptance and completion of the Marriage and Family Therapy master's program at Brigham Young University. Dr. Roy Bean, you recognized my areas of strength and provided detailed feedback encouraging my continued growth. Without your mentorship, guidance, and consistent encouragement, the work that this book is based on would not have been possible. Your continuous push for me to pursue a doctorate degree in marriage and family therapy, and always believing in my potential, gave me the confidence I needed to continue my education and training.

I would also like to recognize the connections and mentors I made at Michigan State University, especially Drs. Richard and Karen Wampler, Dr. Ruben Parra-Cardona, and Dr. Adrian Blow. Each of you drove me harder than I could have ever imagined. I learned important lessons about myself, my profession, and my clients from my MSU mentors. Richard, you and Karen were both extremely compassionate and caring, while at the same time challenging and demanding. Sitting with each of you while we line edited reaccreditation documents or scrupulously reviewed my therapy tapes gave me a front-row seat in discovering the strengths about myself that you could see but I couldn't. Ruben, having the privilege to work closely with you on your research program, and to learn firsthand from your kindness and love for humanity, proved to me what it means to be a servant-leader. Adrian, you continued to advocate for me to develop unique interventions using the common factors model and insisted that I continue urging for the inclusion of children in family therapy interventions. This push inspired me to keep trying, failing, working, and succeeding.

I must also extend deep gratitude to Drs. Gerald Patterson and Marion Forgatch, whose groundbreaking work on coercion theory and GenerationPMTO fundamentally shaped my clinical foundation. Their research did more than illuminate the mechanisms of parent-child interaction patterns—it offered a clear, compassionate road map for interrupting cycles of negative behavior and fostering resilience in families. Reading Patterson's empirical clarity and Forgatch's applied brilliance gave me language for what I had long sensed in clinical work but couldn't yet articulate. Their commitment to rigorous science combined with a heart for real-world families inspired me to believe that research could truly transform practice. The echoes of their work are woven through my approach to systemic play therapy, and I hope this book carries forward their legacy of innovation, discipline, and hope.

I am indebted to Drs. Scott Grewe and Peter Stewart for giving me the opportunity of a lifetime when I joined their clinic in Washington state. I grew, developed, and matured as a therapist while working at Sageview Youth Psychology, and my Sageview family will always be close to my heart. Your trust and willingness to allow me to operate and function the way I was trained showed me that my interventions worked and that I could rely on the common factors and integrative approach found herein.

I express my deep gratitude for the publishing team at PESI and my private editors for helping this book become a reality. Roseanne Cheng has been extremely helpful at guiding me through this process. You recognized the potential for a book before I was even contemplating the outline. Your gentle encouragement and answers to my consistent questions have been invaluable in bringing this book to life. When I committed to accomplishing this task, I knew I couldn't do it alone. I turned to Sarah Belliston, who helped edit my dissertation, and Meghan Scoresby, with whom I served on the board for the Children's Museum of the Magic Valley. These two worked with me on the first rounds of edits. Your quick returns of chapter drafts and many suggestions for the structure, composition, and style helped me fine-tune the essence of the interventions and client examples. The suggestions and edits proposed by the PESI developmental editor, Jenessa Jackson, really expanded on the original draft and suggestions by Sarah and Meghan. I am profoundly appreciative of all your contributions to this process.

Finally, I must acknowledge you, the reader. Your passion for helping children and families likely led you to this book. I hope you will find it as helpful for you as you read it as I have found it in writing it. I originally did not think another therapy book was needed, but after completing the final manuscript, I found myself aching for the chance to give a copy of it to therapists who find themselves wanting more guidance and direction on how to help these marvelously challenging families. Thank you for investing your time in finding a way to help your clients. ■

About the Author

Dr. Michael Whitehead, PhD, LMFT, RPT-S™, is a licensed marriage and family therapist, registered play therapist supervisor, and esteemed educator with a passion for strengthening families and empowering individuals. With a career spanning clinical practice, academia, and professional leadership, Dr. Whitehead brings a wealth of expertise in systemic family therapy, child development, and evidence-based interventions for behavioral disorders.

He earned his PhD in human development and family studies with a specialization in couple and family therapy from Michigan State University, his MS in marriage and family therapy from Brigham Young University, and his BS in marriage, family, and human development from Brigham Young University.

Currently in full-time clinical practice at Aspen Grove Family Therapy in Twin Falls, Idaho, Dr. Whitehead specializes in working with families navigating high-conflict dynamics, childhood behavioral challenges, and family reunification processes. His integrative approach emphasizes play therapy, parent training, and systemic interventions to foster resilience and healing.

Beyond his clinical work, Dr. Whitehead is a dedicated educator, serving as a part-time professor in marriage and family therapy programs. He has authored and coauthored book chapters and research articles on treating disruptive behavior disorders and play therapy, and is a sought-after speaker at local, national, and international conferences. He holds the Certificate in Leadership from the American Association for Marriage and Family Therapy and has served in various professional board roles, advocating for the advancement of family therapy and play therapy practices.

When he's not teaching, writing, or working with families, Dr. Whitehead enjoys spending time outdoors with his family—camping, hiking, skiing, and exploring new places.